CAPITAL PUNISHMENT
IN THE PENTATEUCH

CAPITAL PUNISHMENT IN THE PENTATEUCH

Why the Bible Prescribes Ritual Killing

Simon Skidmore

LONDON • NEW YORK • OXFORD • NEW DELHI • SYDNEY

T&T CLARK
Bloomsbury Publishing Plc
50 Bedford Square, London, WC1B 3DP, UK
1385 Broadway, New York, NY 10018, USA
29 Earlsfort Terrace, Dublin 2, Ireland

BLOOMSBURY, T&T CLARK and the T&T Clark logo
are trademarks of Bloomsbury Publishing Plc

First published in Great Britain 2023
Paperback edition published 2024

Copyright © Simon Skidmore, 2023, 2024

Simon Skidmore has asserted his right under the Copyright, Designs and Patents Act, 1988,
to be identified as Author of this work.
For legal purposes the Acknowledgements on p. vii constitute an extension of this copyright
page.

Cover design: Charlotte James
Cover image: *Stoning of the blasphemer* (Leviticus, Chapter 24) © ZU_09/Getty Images

All rights reserved. No part of this publication may be reproduced or transmitted in any form or by
any means, electronic or mechanical, including photocopying, recording, or any information storage
or retrieval system, without prior permission in writing from the publishers.

Bloomsbury Publishing Plc does not have any control over, or responsibility for, any third-party
websites referred to or in this book. All internet addresses given in this book were correct at the
time of going to press. The author and publisher regret any inconvenience caused if addresses have
changed or sites have ceased to exist, but can accept no responsibility for any such changes.

A catalogue record for this book is available from the British Library.
Library of Congress Control Number: 2022020587

ISBN:	HB:	978-0-5677-0719-2
	PB:	978-0-5677-0723-9
	ePDF:	978-0-5677-0720-8
	eBook:	978-0-5677-0722-2

Typeset by Trans.form.ed SAS

To find out more about our authors and books visit www.bloomsbury.com
and sign up for our newsletters.

Contents

Acknowledgements	vii
Chapter 1	
INTRODUCTION	1
1. The Conundrum of Capital Punishment in the Pentateuch	1
2. Previous Interpretations of Biblical Capital Punishment	2
3. Book Summary	7
Chapter 2	
IMAGO DEI AND HUMAN IMMOLATION	10
1. Imago Dei *as Divine Parentage*	13
2. Rivalry and Genesis 9:6	23
3. Conclusion	34
Chapter 3	
METHOD	35
1. The Primary Text	35
2. Reading Method	37
3. Mimetic Theory and the Scapegoat Mechanism	42
4. Human Immolation and the Scapegoat Mechanism	50
5. Criticisms of Girard and How the Current Study Addresses these Concerns	53
6. Conclusion	59
Chapter 4	
THE BLASPHEMER OF LEVITICUS 24:10-23	60
1. The Blasphemer Prose (Leviticus 24:10-14, 23)	61
2. The Casuistic Legal Formula (Leviticus 24:15-16)	67
3. *Lex Talionis* (Leviticus 24:17-22)	76
4. Conclusion	78
Chapter 5	
THE SABBATH-GATHERER OF NUMBERS 15:32-36	80
1. The Sabbath	80
2. Human Immolation and Sabbath Desecration in Exodus 31:12-17	83

3. The Sabbath-gatherer of Numbers 15:32-36	89
4. Girard's Four Stereotypes	94
5. Conclusion	97

Chapter 6
HOMICIDE IN THE PENTATEUCH

	98
1. The First Homicide	99
2. Interpreting כִּפֶּר	102
3. Numbers 35:30-34	109
4. The Dualistic Nature of Bloodshed	115
5. Homicide in Deuteronomy and Exodus	116
6. Conclusion	120

Chapter 7
THE MANAGEMENT OF MIMETIC RIVALRY IN LEVITICUS 18 AND 20

	122
1. Leviticus 18:24-30	123
2. Leviticus 20	127
3. Conclusion	153

Chapter 8
SEXUAL OFFENCES AND MIMETIC RIVALRY IN DEUTERONOMY 22:13-29

	154
1. Deuteronomy 22:13-21	154
2. Deuteronomy 22:22-29	161
3. Conclusion	168

Chapter 9
THE REBELLIOUS SON OF DEUTERONOMY 21:18-21

	169
1. Interpreting Deuteronomy 21:18-21	170
2. Mimesis in Deuteronomy 21:18-21	178
3. Conclusion	181

Chapter 10
CONCLUDING COMMENTS

	182
1. Key Findings	182
2. Theoretical Implications	186
3. Suggestions for Future Research	194
4. Closing Remarks	196

Bibliography	197
Index of References	211
Index of Authors	218

ACKNOWLEDGEMENTS

I would like to thank my doctoral advisors, Drs Tom Aechtner, Leigh Trevaskis and AJ Culp, for their valuable insight and guidance.

Also, many thanks to my family, Hayley, Elijah, Jayda and Anastasia, whose patience and love made this book possible.

Chapter 1

INTRODUCTION

1. *The Conundrum of Capital Punishment in the Pentateuch*

The presence of capital punishment within the Pentateuch has presented a difficult challenge for the Jewish and Christian faith traditions, which both place a high value upon human life. For example, the Jewish Rabbinic tradition has grappled with how to uphold the valuable nature of human life, while remaining faithful to the Torah's command to execute capital offenders.[1] This struggle is reflected in the *Mishnah*, which argues that capital punishment should be carried out very rarely, because when excessively enforced it leads to increased bloodshed:

> A court that has put a person to death once in a seven-year period is called 'a hanging court' [literally, a destructive court]. Rabbi Elazar ben Azariah says, 'Even once in seventy years'. Rabbi Tarfon and Rabbi Akiva say, 'Were we members of the court, no person would ever be put to death'. Rabban Simeon ben Gamliel retorted, 'If so, they would increase those who shed blood in Israel'.[2]

The anxiety over killing another human has also been echoed in the Christian tradition. Traditionally, Christian thought assigns a high value to human life because all humans are believed to bear the image of God.[3] This belief impacts practical Christian ethics in various ways. For example, some have argued that euthanasia is immoral because killing

---

1. The term 'Torah' in this study refers to the practical laws observed within the Pentateuch. The first five books of the Hebrew Bible, which are called the 'Torah' with the Jewish tradition, will be referred to as 'the Pentateuch'.
2. *Mishnah Makot* 1:10.
3. Peter J. Harland, *The Value of Human Life: A Study of the Story of the Flood (Genesis 6–9)* (Leiden: Brill, 1996), 204; Gordon J. Wenham, *Genesis 1–15*, WBC 1 (Waco: Word, 1987), 194; Kenneth A. Mathews, *Genesis 1–11: 26*, NAC (Nashville:

another human desecrates the divine image.⁴ Some have also argued that pregnancy terminations are immoral because human foetuses in utero also bear the divine image.⁵ At first glance, biblical laws such as 'you shall not kill' (Exod. 20:13) appear to echo this sentiment. Yet, the killing of humans who commit capital offences is also described and prescribed in various texts throughout the Pentateuch. Among these texts, the Pentateuch narrates two cases of divinely approved capital punishment (Lev. 24:10-23; Num. 15:32-36), and prescribes the death penalty for various crimes including homicide, sexual misconduct, idolatry, blasphemy, and desecrating the Sabbath.⁶ By prescribing the execution of these offenders the Pentateuch appears to violate the Jewish and Christian belief that all human life, without exception, is valuable.

2. Previous Interpretations of Biblical Capital Punishment

In this section, I briefly review and critique the major approaches adopted by Hebrew Bible scholars to explain capital punishment within the Pentateuch. Yet, as I shall argue, none of these approaches is sufficient to explain all biblical cases of capital punishment. Having discussed the limitations of each of these approaches, I suggest that mimetic theory may provide a more fruitful approach to capital punishment within the Pentateuch. Mimetic theory was developed by the French literary critic Réne Girard to illuminate certain social mechanisms, which may lead to the execution of a communal scapegoat. Through his study of various novels, myths, and stories, Girard discerned a particular pattern. According to Girard, humans imitate one another, as they attempt to establish their own personal identities. This imitation brings people into conflict with each other, as they begin to strive and compete for the same desired objects.⁷ If this imitation and conflict spreads throughout an entire community, the survival of the community may be threatened by excessive violence, as everyone engages in rivalry with everyone else.⁸ Fortunately, in this situation the same wide-

---

Broadman & Holman, 1996), 405; Eugene F. Roop, *Genesis*, Believers Church Bible Commentary (Scottdale: Herald, 1987), 321–3.

4. John S. Feinberg and Paul D. Feinberg, *Ethics for a Brave New World: Updated and Expanded* (Eugene: Crossway, 2010), 114; James P. Eckman, *Biblical Ethics* (Eugene: Crossway, 2004), 32–6.

5. Mathews, *Genesis 1–11: 26*, 405–6.

6. Exod. 31:12-17; Lev. 18:24-30; 20:1-5; 24:16; Num. 35:30-34.

7. Réne Girard, *Violence and the Sacred*, trans. Patrick Gregory (Baltimore: Johns Hopkins University Press, 1977), 145–6.

8. Ibid., 52–5.

spread imitation, which originally generated the conflict, may also resolve it. The community's continued imitation of each other unites the community against an arbitrary scapegoat, who they select and blame for the conflict. The community then resolve the conflict, and restore peace and order, by either executing the scapegoat or expelling them from the community.[9] As I shall attempt to demonstrate over the course of the present study, this process successfully accounts for the Pentateuch's prescription and description of communal execution for various offences.

Peter J. Harland has argued that the Pentateuch prescribes the execution of all murderers because homicide constitutes a direct act of defiance against YHWH:

> [M]urder confronts God, and is a revolt against him. The story [viz. the flood narrative of Gen. 6–9] singles out murder from all the sins of the Decalogue as being particularly wicked, emphasizing that God will exercise the ultimate sanction in this matter. This is not just a command for Israel, but is binding on all peoples wherever they may be, in a world where the murder of one's fellow is a choice which faces man.[10]

Harland argues that the flood narrative 'singles out' murder as a particularly heinous crime, for which the death penalty must be enforced across all times and cultures. While this interpretation may justify the execution of murderers, it cannot explain why the Pentateuch prescribes the death penalty for other offences, such as Sabbath desecration or blasphemy (Exod. 31:12-17; Lev. 24:10-23). Furthermore, this approach ignores the impurity and natural-disaster imagery which other Pentateuchal texts associate with homicide (e.g. Num. 35:30-34). For this reason, the current study leaves this explanation of biblical capital punishment behind.

Others have attempted to explain capital punishment in cases of murder by asserting that homicide, according to the Pentateuch, upsets the 'natural balance' of the earth's blood reservoir. According to this reading, the only way to restore the earth's blood reservoir is to execute the murderer.[11] This interpretation takes seriously the Pentateuch's claim that homicide negatively affects the natural order. It also grapples with how this order is restored through the execution of murderers (Num. 35:30-34). There are,

---

9. René Girard, *The Scapegoat*, trans. Yvonne Freccero (Baltimore: Johns Hopkins University Press, 1989), 12–17.

10. Harland, *The Value of Human Life*, 162–3.

11. Baruch A. Levine, *Numbers 21–36: A New Translation with Introduction and Commentary* (New York: Doubleday, 2000), 561–2; Jacob Milgrom, *Numbers: The JPS Torah Commentary* (Philadelphia: Jewish Publication Society, 1990), 509.

however, a few difficulties with this interpretation. For example, while passages such as Num. 35:30-34 employ purity language to communicate the damage inflicted upon the natural order by homicide, no reference to an ecological blood-balance is mentioned. Moreover, this theory cannot explain the rationale behind the Pentateuchal prescription of capital punishment for crimes other than homicide, such as sexual misconduct, idolatry, blasphemy, and desecrating the Sabbath.[12] The present study presents an alternative approach to capital punishment within the Pentateuch, which explains the execution of these offenders, while accounting for the impurity and natural-disaster imagery associated with capital offences (e.g. Lev. 18:24-30; Num. 35:30-34).

Jonathan Klawans and Tikvah Frymer-Kensky both claim that capital offences, such as murder, idolatry, and certain sexual offenses, generate a powerful impurity which endangers the entire community. According to Klawans and Frymer-Kensky, this impurity and the danger associated with it necessitates the execution of capital offenders.[13] Yet, this approach has its difficulties. First, while the Pentateuch describes some capital offences as generating impurity (e.g. Lev. 18:24-30; 20:1-21; Num. 35:30-34), other offences, such as blasphemy and Sabbath desecration, are never explicitly associated with impurity (Exod. 31:12-17; Lev. 24:10-23). This observation suggests a poor correlation between impurity and capital offences within the Pentateuch.[14] Second, the association of certain offences with impurity is not consistent throughout the Pentateuch. For example, homicide is not ubiquitously associated with impurity. Although Num. 35:30-34 associates bloodshed with impurity, Deut. 19:11-13 discusses homicide in terms of bloodguilt. Both of these texts prescribe the execution of murderers, but justify this consequence through different

12. Exod. 31:12-17; Lev. 18:24-30; 20:1-5; 24:16.
13. Tikvah Frymer-Kensky, 'Pollution, Purification, and Purgation in Biblical Israel', in *The Word of the Lord Shall Go Forth: Essays in Honor of David Noel Freedman in Celebration of His Sixtieth Birthday*, ed. Carol L. Meyers (Winona Lake: Eisenbrauns, 1983), 407–8; Jonathan Klawans, *Impurity and Sin in Ancient Judaism* (Oxford: Oxford University Press, 2000), 58.
14. This is not to say that embodied emotions, such as disgust and contempt, play no role in the development of ancient Israel's capital legislation and conceptions of purity. Kazen's work on the correlation between disgust and impurity in the Hebrew Bible suggests that ancient Israelite purity conceptions, and by extension capital legislation, were somehow influenced by disgust. However, Klawan's and Frymer-Kensky's claim that purity concerns explain *all* capital offences, even those which are never explicitly associated with impurity, cannot be sustained. At best, it could be said that *some* Pentateuchal texts attempt to justify human immolation for *certain* offences (e.g. Lev. 20:1-21) through a rhetoric of impurity and danger.

aetiologies. The lack of a consistent explanation of capital punishment, even across texts which address the same offence, renders the search for a single unified aetiology for capital punishment within the Pentateuch untenable. In light of this realization, the current study seeks an alternative interpretation of capital punishment, one which goes beyond the various aetiologies offered within certain texts.

David P. Wright argues that capital punishment is prescribed within the Pentateuch for those offences which are 'most detrimental to society'.

> They arise out of sinful conditions, many of which threaten the foundation of the group, often in a very direct...way: for example, children are killed in idolatrous sacrifice, and marriage and family patterns are upset by illicit sexual relations. On the other end of the spectrum are impurities that are much less dangerous and not prohibited. Their threat to the social order are minimal and negligible.[15]

One major strength of Wright's schema is its ability to explain why minor breaches of Torah, such as the consumption of impure meat, are tolerated, while more severe breaches attract the death penalty. However, this approach does not consider the violent, natural-disaster imagery associated with some capital offences within the Pentateuch.[16] Furthermore, Wright does not explain how capital offenses which appear to be victimless crimes, such as blasphemy and Sabbath desecration, can threaten the established social order (cf. Lev. 24:10-23; Num. 15:32-36). For these reasons, the present study accepts Wright's assertion that capital offences threaten the social order, yet employs an alternative approach to consider the conundrum of how seemingly victimless, capital crimes might threaten the community.

J. J. Finkelstein attempts to shed some light on the conundrum of capital punishment within the Pentateuch by arguing that capital offences attack the community's 'most cherished values to the degree that the commission of the offence places the community itself in jeopardy'.[17] For Finkelstein, the observance of core communal values is critical to

---

15. David P. Wright, 'The Spectrum of Priestly Impurity', in *Priesthood and Cult in Ancient Israel* (Sheffield: Sheffield Academic Press, 1991), 171.

16. As Raymond Schwager notes, in their examination of the Hebrew Bible, many scholars neglect themes, such as 'jealousy, anger, violence, vengeance, mob action, and projections, all of which recur constantly'. Raymund Schwager, *Must There Be Scapegoats? Violence and Redemption in the Bible* (Leominster: Gracewing, 1987), 45.

17. Jacob J. Finkelstein, 'The Ox That Gored', *Transactions of the American Philosophical Society* 71, no. 2 (1981): 27.

maintaining the social order. In this way, seemingly victimless, capital crimes, such as blasphemy and Sabbath desecration, may threaten the community's integrity. However, this observation alone is insufficient to illuminate the phenomenon of capital punishment within the Pentateuch, because it does not explain the move from recognizing capital offenders as a threat, to the institution of capital punishment. This lack of explanatory power reflects a gap in the current literature on capital punishment within the Pentateuch. None of the approaches surveyed above adequately explain all the biblical prescriptions and descriptions of capital punishment. The present study addresses this gap by applying mimetic theory to a synchronic reading of the key Pentateuchal texts concerned with capital punishment. In so doing, the current work attempts to read capital punishment texts within their immediate literary context and in conversation with other texts throughout the Pentateuch. For this reason, the synchronic approach is less tentative than other common methods, which either attempt to read the text within a debatable historical context or as part of a hypothetical source document. Furthermore, a synchronic approach is essential to grappling with the role played by capital punishment within the received Pentateuchal tradition. By combining this approach with mimetic theory, the present study draws valuable insights concerning the Pentateuch's description and prescription of capital punishment.

Some scholars have applied mimetic theory to argue that the modern practice of capital punishment, as it is carried out in Northern America, represents a form of human sacrifice.[18] Along these lines, James McBride has applied mimetic theory to argue that capital punishment functions as a form of ritual bloodletting:

> Putting the condemned to death – even if they be factually innocent – is therefore a surrogate for the bloodletting that would otherwise ensue if the state did not substitute its own ritual of government-sponsored executions for the extra-legal spiral of citizen violence… The death penalty is justified not as a legal recourse to punish the individual but rather as a social mechanism to vent the violence which would otherwise destroy the social order.[19]

---

18. Roberta M. Harding, 'Capital Punishment as Human Sacrifice: A Societal Ritual as Depicted in George Eliot's Adam Bede', *Buffalo Law Review* 48 (2000): 175–297; Brian K. Smith, 'Capital Punishment and Human Sacrifice', *Journal of the American Academy of Religion* 68, no. 1 (2000): 3–25; Scott Cowdell, *René Girard and Secular Modernity: Christ, Culture, and Crisis* (Indiana: University of Notre Dame Press, 2013), 140–1.

19. James McBride, 'Capital Punishment as the Unconstitutional Establishment of Religion: A Girardian Reading of the Death Penalty', *Journal of Church and State* 37, no. 2 (1995): 269.

This research presents a method which may be fruitfully employed to address the current gap in the literature concerning biblical capital punishment. The present study addresses this gap by applying mimetic theory to produce a fresh reading of capital punishment within the Pentateuch. This reading views biblical capital punishment as a social mechanism, which provides a controlled release of violence, and draws the community together, at the expense of capital offenders. Through the death of the capital offender, peace and order is restored within the community. When viewed from this perspective, the term 'capital punishment' is somewhat problematic, because it assumes a punitive justice approach to the communal killing of human perpetrators, and fails to grasp the ritual significance of these executions. The term 'human immolation', however, stresses the ritual nature of these acts, while avoiding punitive overtones. For this reason, throughout the remainder of the current project, the term 'human immolation' will be used to refer to the ritual killing of a human, who has been found guilty of a capital crime, within the Pentateuch. The term 'capital punishment' will be used solely to refer to the modern practice of executing offenders found guilty of capital crimes.

3. *Book Summary*

In Chapter 2 I address the apparent tension between the practice of capital punishment and the concept of *imago dei*, viz. the idea that humans are created in the image of God. These two concepts are juxtaposed in Gen. 9:6, a passage in which Gerhard von Rad perceives a 'strange tension' between 'the inviolable holiness of human life' and human immolation in cases of homicide.[20] However, this apparent tension can be resolved by reading the Pentateuchal human immolation texts within their wider context of the struggle between the faithful Israelite community and their rivals (cf. Gen. 3:15). This rivalry is traced throughout the Pentateuch through the enemy brothers of Genesis, Israel's conflict with Egypt and other nations, and the rivalry between the faithful Israelite community, who observe YHWH's commands, and capital offenders who do not.

I argue that according to the Pentateuch, the faithful Israelite community are considered children of YHWH, whose lives are rendered precious because they bear the divine image by observing YHWH's commands. Conversely, those who disobey these commands do not reflect the divine image. In this way, *imago dei* functions as a group identifier which

---

20. Gerhard von Rad, *Genesis: A Commentary*, trans. John H. Marks (Louisville: Westminster John Knox, 1972), 132–3.

attributes value to the lives of its bearers (cf. Gen. 9:6). These image-bearers are called to execute capital offenders to support core communal values and, in so doing, maintain the community's identity as the children of YHWH. This reading of human immolation paves the way for Chapter 3, which explains how mimetic theory will be applied to examine a narrative reading of major Pentateuchal texts concerned with human immolation in the following chapters. Through this examination, I argue that human immolation facilitates the Israelite community to reflect the divine image by eliminating those whose disobedience jeopardizes this divinely sanctioned vocation.

Chapters 4 and 5 both examine narratives which describe the execution of capital offenders. Chapter 4 discusses the execution of the Blasphemer in Lev. 24:10-23, and the Sabbath Gatherer's stoning is the focus of Chapter 5. In both these texts, the capital offenders are associated with Israel's foreign rival, Egypt. Through the application of mimetic theory I argue that the offenders in these texts are executed because they are perceived as dangerous foreign influences who threaten the community's identity. These malefactors threaten the community's core values by serving as potential models for others within the community to imitate. In a time of crisis, the community then vents their violence by stoning these offenders, which generates a type of catharsis, as peace and order are restored to the community. The mode of execution employed in these texts, communal stoning, is particularly significant because this ritual requires the community's active participation. As each person physically vents their violent urges by pelting stones, the community stands united against the offender.

Chapters 6 through to 9 present fresh readings of major texts which prescribe the execution of capital offenders throughout the Pentateuch. The command to execute murderers in Num. 35:30-34 and Deut. 19:11-13 is discussed in Chapter 6, with reference to Asylum Cities and the prevention of blood feuds. Although these texts employ different terminology and concepts, they both assert that murderers threaten the Israelite community and must, therefore, be executed to maintain peace and order. Chapter 7 focuses on Leviticus 18 and 20, which claim that practices, such as Molech worship and sexual misconduct, defile the Land and may cause Israel's expulsion from the Land (Lev. 18:25, 28). Deuteronomy 22:13-28, which discusses the management of various sexual offences, is discussed in Chapter 8. While some of these offences may be resolved through pecuniary compensation and marriage without the possibility of divorce, reconciliation for other offences can only be achieved through execution. I examine the execution of capital offenders throughout Chapters 6 to 8, and argue that each of these executions functions to restore peace and order to the community.

Chapter 9 considers the final human immolation text examined in this book: the case of the Rebellious Son in Deut. 21:18-21. This text is particularly interesting because no specific crime is mentioned, other than the offender's refusal to listen to his parents' instruction. At first glance, the ambiguity surrounding the son's offence seems problematic, because it allows almost any parent to stone their child for any act of disobedience. But when viewed from a mimetic perspective, this ambiguity highlights the Rebellious Son's role as the community's arbitrarily selected scapegoat. The offender is portrayed as a monstrous threat to the community, because he contradicts the Deuteronomistic ideal as he spurns his parents' instruction (e.g. Deut. 6:1-3). Furthermore, the Rebellious Son's behaviour echoes that of Israel's rebellious wilderness generation (cf. Deut. 1:26-46). Just as the unfaithful wilderness generation died and failed to inherit the Land of Canaan, so the Rebellious Son dies before receiving his share of the Land. Moreover, the Rebellious Son's refusal to respect communal norms identifies him as a threat to the faithful Israelite community (cf. Deut. 28:15-68). In response to this threat, the community vent their violence upon the Rebellious Son as he is stoned by 'all the men of the city' (Deut. 21:21). The peace and order achieved through this process is described as a purgation of evil from the community. The texts examined in Chapters 6 to 9 assert that capital offences place the community in danger, and that this danger can only be alleviated through the execution of the offender.

Chapter 10 concludes this study by summarizing chief findings, and discussing the theoretical implications of these findings. I suggest that the Pentateuch prescribes human immolation as a means of restoring peace and order within the community. In so doing, this study presents a robust and novel explanation of human immolation within the Pentateuch. I also assess the most common pro-capital punishment arguments, which are built upon Pentateuchal texts and their associated theological constructs, in light of this study's findings. In closing, I also suggest some more potential applications for the method employed in the present study.

Chapter 2

IMAGO DEI AND HUMAN IMMOLATION

As noted in the previous chapter, the high value which the Jewish and Christian traditions attach to human life, on account of their belief that all humans bear the divine image, seems inconsistent with the practice of human immolation. Yet, Gen. 9:6 attempts to justify the execution of murderers by asserting that האדם bears the divine image:

Whoever sheds the blood of man,	שֹׁפֵךְ דַּם הָאָדָם
by man shall his blood be shed,	בָּאָדָם דָּמוֹ יִשָּׁפֵךְ
for God made man in his own image.	כִּי בְּצֶלֶם אֱלֹהִים עָשָׂה אֶת־הָאָדָם:

This text has been cited by many to support the execution of murderers.[1] For example, Kenneth Mathews writes that the justification for 'penal execution is the value of the victim, the "image of God"'.[2] The question remains, however, if Gen. 9:6 assumes that all humans bear the divine image, without exception, then does the execution of murderers also represent an attack upon the divine image? According to Nahum Sarna,

> Murder is the supreme and capital crime because the dignity, sanctity, and inviolability of human life all derive from the fact that every human being bears the stamp of the divine Maker. The murderer may be put to death because his unspeakable act effaces the divine image in his victim and within himself as well, so that his own life forfeits its claim to inviolability.[3]

Sarna addresses the question posed above by insisting that those who commit murder no longer bear the divine image, and for this reason

---

1. Nahum Sarna, *Genesis*, JPS Torah Commentary (Philadelphia: Jewish Publication Society, 1989), 62; Harland, *The Value of Human Life*, 204; Wenham, *Genesis*, 194; Mathews, *Genesis 1–11: 26*, 404–5; Roop, *Genesis*, 321–3.
2. Mathews, *Genesis 1–11: 26*, 405.
3. Sarna, *Genesis*, 62.

murderers may be executed. If his assertion is correct, then *imago dei* is not an attribute shared by all humanity, but rather a boundary marker, which separates murderers from the rest of their community. The idea of *imago dei* as a boundary marker, which determines the sanctity of one's life, is also reflected in one of the original footnotes to *Yebamoth* 61a in the Babylonian Talmud:

> only an Israelite who, as a worshipper of the true God, can be said to have been like Adam created in the image of God. (Cf. Gen. I, 27 and V, I, where the Heb. text has in each case Adam for 'man'). Idol worshippers having marred the Divine image forfeit all claim to this appellation.[4]

Applying similar reasoning to Sarna, this comment argues that idol worshippers may be executed, because they no longer bear the divine image. A similar approach may prove helpful for reading Gen. 9:6 in conversation with other texts, which either prescribe or describe human immolation. The Pentateuch assumes that there are circumstances in which other humans must be killed, including the Canaanite conquest and cases involving capital crimes.[5] Furthermore, passages such as Genesis 6–9 portray YHWH killing great numbers of people, while preserving the lives of a few who are deemed righteous and 'find favour' in his eyes (Gen. 6:8). Those who reflect the divine image might be expected to act in a similar manner. It is, therefore, fitting that some texts within the Pentateuch call faithful Israel to imitate YHWH by killing certain people under particular circumstances.[6] Any reading of the final form Pentateuch must embrace the challenge of interpreting *imago dei* in a way that allows for human immolation under certain circumstances.[7]

---

4. Quoting an explanatory note added as a footnote (n. 3) to the text of *Yebamoth*. See also *b. B. Mez.* 114b and footnotes to *Ker.* 6b. Translation cited from Carol A. Valentine, 'Soncino Babylonian Talmud: Translated into English with Notes, Glossary and Indices under the Editorship of Rabbi Dr. I. Epstein', http://www.come-and-hear.com/yebamoth/yebamoth_61.html#61a, accessed 12 October 2018.

5. For example, while the Pentateuch prescribes the negotiation of peace with conquered enemies, it also commands the wholesale slaughter of the Canaanites (e.g. Deut. 20:1-18). The different treatment of people groups in this passage is difficult to reconcile with the idea that all human lives are considered precious because they bear the divine image.

6. Human immolation is prescribed within the Pentateuch in passages such as Lev. 20:1-16; 24:10-23; Num. 15:32-36; 35:30-34; Deut. 21:18-21; and 22:20-25.

7. Conversely, a diachronic reading of Pentateuch can explain the inconsistency between the high value attributed to human life in some passages and other texts, which appear to undervalue human life, by attributing these divergent viewpoints to

The current chapter approaches this challenge by arguing that the Pentateuch assumes that only the faithful Israelite community bear the divine image. As a type of identity marker, *imago dei* therefore distinguishes the faithful Israelite community from other people. When this interpretation of *imago dei* is brought to Gen. 9:6, it seems that this text prohibits only the killing of faithful Israelites. This reading of *imago dei* in Gen. 9:6 fits better with the Pentateuch's instruction to kill certain people under certain circumstances than the traditional Jewish and Christian approaches, which assume that all human life is inviolable because everyone bears the divine image. By demonstrating that the Pentateuch portrays the faithful Israelite community as the sole bearers of the divine image, this chapter argues that, according to the Pentateuch, it is the faithful Israelite community who are blessed and whose lives are considered truly valuable.

This thesis is argued over two sections. The first section argues that *imago dei* conveys the concept of divine parentage, which implies a similarity in character and a submissive relationship to YHWH, and a shared vocation between the faithful Israelite community and YHWH. In contrast to this ideal, some Israelites do not display YHWH's character, as they obstinately refuse to participate in their divinely granted vocation. This group is not considered children of YHWH and do not, therefore, reflect the divine image. Moreover, these people threaten faithful Israel's ability to reflect the divine image and, for this reason, must be immolated. This concept is central to understanding the dynamic of human immolation within the Pentateuch, which prescribes the execution of those who actively threaten the wellbeing of the faithful, Israelite community.

The second half of the current chapter applies this interpretation of *imago dei* to Gen. 9:6. Genesis 9:6 makes a good starting point for the present study because it represents the first prescription of human immolation within the Pentateuch, and is often quoted to support the modern practice of capital punishment.[8] The current chapter employs a fresh interpretation of *imago dei* to construct a contextual and coherent reading of Gen. 9:6. To this end, Gen. 9:6 is read within the context of the rivalry between the faithful Israel and those who direct their hostility towards them in the early chapters of Genesis. This exercise will lay the foundation for the present study's application of mimetic theory to human immolation within the Pentateuch in subsequent chapters.

different sources. This approach, however, does not respect the Pentateuch as a document that deserves to be read synchronically in its own right.

8. Sarna, *Genesis*, 193–4; Harland, *The Value of Human Life*, 204; Wenham, *Genesis*, 194; Mathews, *Genesis 1–11: 26*, 405; Roop, *Genesis*, 321–3.

1. Imago Dei *as Divine Parentage*

1.1. *Three Views of* Imago Dei

Although a full review of the literature on the image of God goes well beyond the scope of the current project, this section briefly surveys the most common interpretations of *imago dei*. Most interpretations of this concept focus upon Gen. 1:26-28. For ease of discussion, I shall group these interpretations into three general categories: the substantive view, the relational view, and the functional view.[9] More recently, however, Carly Crouch has convincingly argued that *imago dei* conveys the idea of divine parentage.[10] As I argue below, reading *imago dei* as a declaration of divine parentage ties the substantive, relational, and functional perspectives together in a way that also pays careful attention to the employment of the image of God within the biblical narrative. I shall adopt and build upon Crouch's interpretation of *imago dei*, as this concept is applied to a synchronic reading of the Pentateuch throughout the remainder of this chapter. In so doing, the current study leaves behind the question of how *imago dei* may have been originally understood by its priestly authors within in their historical context, to read this enigmatic concept in conversation with the rest of the Pentateuch. In light of Israel's unique status as YHWH's children throughout the Pentateuch (e.g. Exod. 4:22-23), I argue that *imago dei* describes Israel's unique vocation of reflecting the divine image and, in this way, functions as a group identifier.

1.1.1. *The Substantiative View of* Imago Dei

The substantiative view focuses on the lexical meaning of 'image' (צלם), interpreting *imago dei* as a quality or characteristic shared between God and humanity.[11] The characteristics shared between God and humanity, which have been suggested as the substance of the *imago dei*, range

---

9. I have borrowed this threefold paradigm for discussing the concept of *imago dei* from Millard J. Erickson, *Christian Theology*, 2nd edn (Grand Rapids: Baker Academic, 1998), 520.

10. Carly L. Crouch, 'Genesis 1:26-27 as a Statement of Humanity's Divine Parentage', *Journal of Theological Studies* 61, no. 1 (2010): 1–15.

11. Erickson, *Christian Theology*, 520–3. In addition to these three interpretations, others have developed a so-called dynamic view of *imago dei*, which draws upon the work of Irenaeus, in dialogue with palaeoanthropology. J Wentzel Van Huyssteen, *Alone in the World? Human Uniqueness in Science and Theology* (Grand Rapids: Eerdmans, 2009); Johan Smedt and Helen Cruz, 'The Imago Dei as a Work in Progress: A Perspective from Paleoanthropology', *Zygon* 49, no. 1 (2014): 135–56. As an inter-disciplinary theological construct a review and appraisal of the dynamic view of *imago dei* goes beyond the scope of this chapter. This chapter concentrates

from physical appearance to rationality.[12] Some of the Rabbinic Jewish writings on *imago dei* fall into this category, because they interpret the divine image as a luminous quality possessed by the first persons, but which was subsequently lost.[13] The Western Christian tradition also took a substantive approach to *imago dei* as it interpreted the image as humanity's unique ability to reason, up until the time of Aquinas.[14] The major weakness of the substantiative view is its inability to define the image beyond an arbitrary, static characteristic, such as luminescence or reason, which is shared between YHWH and humanity.[15] As argued below, *imago dei* does indeed communicate a characteristic that is shared between YHWH and the faithful Israelite community. However, interpretation must be informed by the text itself, rather than philosophical speculation.

1.1.2. *The Relational View of* Imago Dei

The relational view of *imago dei* was made popular by Karl Barth and focuses on humanity's creation in the image of God as 'male and female' in Gen. 1:27. For Barth, humanity as 'male and female' live in 'differentiation and relationship, and therefore in natural fellowship with God'.[16]

---

on the afore mentioned interpretations of *imago dei*, which have been developed in close conversation with the Hebrew Bible itself.

12. In a similar vein, Philo writes, 'and the invisible divine reason, perceptible only by intellect, he calls the image of God' (*On the Creation* 31); translation cited from *The Works of Philo*, trans. Charles D. Yonge [Peabody: Hendrickson, 1993], 6). Another interpretation is that of Ludwig Kohler, who argues that *imago dei* refers to humanity's upright posture. See Ludwig Köhler, *Old Testament Theology*, trans. A. Stewart Todd (Philadelphia: Westminster, 1957), 147. John of Damascus takes another approach, which involves treating the terms 'image' and 'likeness' separately, by arguing that the creation of humanity 'after his image' refers to the human mind and free will, while 'after his likeness' refers to virtuous conduct (*An Exact Exposition of the Orthodox Faith* II.12).

13. Shai Cherry, *Torah through Time: Understanding Bible Commentary from the Rabbinic Period to Modern Times* (Philadelphia: Jewish Publication Society, 2010), 45.

14. Van Huyssteen, *Alone in the World?*, 126. See also Rambam, *Guide for the Perplexed* 1:1, cited in Cherry, *Torah through Time*, 46. In contrast, the Eastern Church holds to the doctrine of theosis, in which one is said to reflect the divine image in increasing measure as they become more like Jesus both ethically and ontologically. Stanley J. Grenz, *The Social God and the Relational Self: A Trinitarian Theology of the Imago Dei* (Philadelphia: Westminster John Knox, 2001).

15. Van Huyssteen, *Alone in the World?*, 133–4.

16. Karl Barth, *Church Dogmatics: Volume III. The Doctrine of Creation: Part One*, trans. Harold Knight, A. Hart Edwards, and Oscar Bussey (Edinburgh: T. & T. Clark, 1958), 185.

According to this interpretation, humanity bears the divine image as they live 'in genuine confrontation with God'.[17] Claus Westermann develops Barth's concept of *imago dei* as humanity's relationship with God:

> What God has decided to create must stand in relation to him. The creation of man in God's image is directed to something happening between God and man. The Creator created a creature that corresponds to him, to whom he can speak, and who can hear him. It must be noted that man in the Creation narrative is a collective. Creation in the image of God is not concerned with an individual, but with mankind, the species, man. The meaning is that mankind is created so that something can happen between God and man. Mankind is created to stand before God.[18]

However, Phyllis Bird argues against this view by claiming that the 'male and female' nature of האדם does not describe humanity's relationship with their creator, but rather anticipates the divine mandate of procreation and proliferation in v. 28.[19] Contra Barth and Westermann, Bird writes:

> The two parallel cola contain two essential and distinct statements about the nature of humanity: *adam* is created *like* (i.e., resembling) God, but as creature, and hence male and female. The parallelism of the two cola is progressive, not synonymous. The second statement adds to the first; it does not explicate it.[20]

According to Bird, the description of האדם as 'male and female' describes humanity's ability to procreate, and fulfil the divine mandate of v. 28. Despite this criticism, the concept of *imago dei* communicates a relationship between YHWH and those who bear the divine image, albeit one slightly different from that proposed by Barth and Westermann. But, before discussing this relationship, one more interpretation of *imago dei* must be considered.

1.1.3. *The Functional View of* Imago Dei
The functional view of *imago dei* focuses upon the link between the divine image and humanity's dominion over the rest of creation expressed

---

17. Ibid., 184.
18. Claus Westermann, *Creation* (Philadelphia: Fortress, 1974), 56.
19. Phyllis A Bird, '"Male and Female He Created Them": Gen 1:27b in the Context of the Priestly Account of Creation', *Harvard Theological Review* 74, no. 2 (1981): 146–50.
20. Ibid., 149–50.

in vv. 26 and 28.[21] Norman Snaith represents this view, asserting that the concept of *imago dei* 'refers only to man's dominion of the world and everything that is in it. It says nothing about the nature of God, but everything concerning the function of man.'[22] The functional view correctly identifies the link between *imago dei* and humanity's vocation in relation to the land and animals in Genesis 1. Another representative of the functional view, J. Richard Middleton, painstakingly trawls through a catalogue of ancient Near Eastern texts to reach the following conclusion:

> It is my judgment that the description of ancient Near Eastern kings as the image of a god, when understood as an integral component of Egyptian and/or Mesopotamian royal ideology, provides the most plausible set of parallels for interpreting the *imago Dei* in Genesis 1. If such texts – or the ideology behind them – influenced the biblical *imago Dei*, this suggests that humanity is dignified with a status and role vis-à-vis the nonhuman creation that is analogous to the status and role of kings in the ancient Near East vis-à-vis their subjects. Genesis 1…thus constitutes a genuine democratization of ancient Near Eastern royal ideology. As *imago Dei*, then, humanity in Genesis 1 is called to be the representative and intermediary of God's power and blessing on earth.[23]

Middleton correctly sees the doctrine of *imago dei* as a protest against the oppressive ideology of ancient Near Eastern kingship. As argued below, however, this protest does not extend the divine image to all humanity, but only to a select group, specifically, the children of YHWH, the faithful Israelite community.

1.2. Imago dei *as Divine Parentage*

After examining the same ancient Near Eastern literature as Middleton, Crouch argues that *imago dei* references humanity's divine parentage. Crouch concludes that just as Adam 'fathered a son in his own likeness,

---

21. In the ancient Near East rulers would place images of themselves throughout their territory to signify their dominion. David J. A. Clines, 'The Image of God in Man', *Tyndale Bulletin* 19 (1968): 80–5; J. Richard Middleton, *The Liberating Image: The* Imago Dei *in Genesis 1* (Ada: Brazos, 2005), 104–8.

22. Norman Snaith, 'The Image of God', *The Expository Times* 86, no. 1 (1974): 24–4. Cf. W. Randall Garr, *In His Own Image and Likeness: Humanity, Divinity, and Monotheism* (Leiden: Brill, 2003); Clines, 'The Image of God in Man'; Walter Brueggemann, *Genesis,* Interpretation: A Bible Commentary for Teaching and Preaching (Louisville: John Knox, 1982), 33; Gerhard von Rad, *Old Testament Theology, 1,* trans. D. M. G. Stalker (New York: Harper & Row, 1962), 146–7.

23. Middleton, *The Liberating Image*, 121.

after his image' (Gen. 5:3), so the concept of *imago dei* in Gen. 1:27, of which 5:3 is a definite echo, describes divine parentage.[24] The correlation between *imago dei* and divine parentage is also noted in Simon Simango's article, 'The Law and the Image of God':

> In summary, the theme of the image of God is developed and seen in the narrative and legal sections of the law. Creation language depicts the Israelites as God's new creation and this implies that they are in the image of God. However, this is not a reality for most Israelites but symbolic of the need for a substantive (or moral) change (i.e. regeneration). General statements in the law suggest that defining God-likeness (morally) is one of the purposes of the law. The Israelites are portrayed as God's children. This implies they are in the image of God, since sonship implies image.[25]

Although in other sources, such as J, E and D, Israel is called God's 'son' (e.g. Exod. 4:22-23; Deut. 14:1), this language is not found in the Priestly source. The Priestly source, however, as Crouch and Simango suggest, communicates the idea of divine parentage through the language of *imago dei*. If the concept of *imago dei* in Gen. 1:26-28 is interpreted through *imago adam* in Gen. 5:1-3, then the recipient of the divine image is האדם, the individual, who passes the divine image onto the people of Israel through the line of his son, Seth. Genesis 5 traces this line, which reflects the divine image, through to Noah and his sons in a linear fashion by recording details such as the name and the age at which the image-bearer died.[26] Other siblings are, however, glossed over with the recognition that image-bearers also had 'other sons and daughters'. In light of the link between sonship and image in 5:1-3, this chapter interprets Genesis 5 as

---

24. Crouch, 'Genesis 1:26-27'. The shared structure and terminology between these two texts confirms an intertextual relationship. For more on the role of these features in determining intertextual echoes, see Richard B. Hayes, *Echoes of Scripture in the Letters of Paul* (New Haven: Yale University Press, 1989), 29–32; Cynthia Edenburg, 'How (Not) to Murder a King: Variations on a Theme in 1 Sam 24; 26', *Scandinavian Journal of the Old Testament* 12, no. 1 (1998): 72–3.

25. Simon Simango, 'The Law and the Image of God', *Old Testament Exegesis* 26, no. 2 (2013): 468.

26. Alexander notes that the linear genealogies within Genesis serve to 'ensure the main line of descent is clearly established'. See T. Desmond Alexander, *From Paradise to the Promised Land: An Introduction to the Pentateuch* (Grand Rapids: Baker Academic, 2012), 102. Moreover, as Harland writes, Noah 'fulfilled the responsibilities of the imago Dei blamelessly… He is an ideal who shows the way for all to follow.' Harland, *The Value of Human Life*, 62.

tracing the passage of the divine image through Adam to Noah. Following this paradigm, I argue that the use of *imago dei* within the Pentateuch (Gen. 1:26-27; 5:1-3; 9:6) describes the divine parentage of Seth's faithful lineage.

1.3. *Divine Parentage within the Pentateuch*
If, as Crouch has argued, *imago dei* references the concept of divine parentage (cf. Gen. 5:1-3), then an appreciation of parentage and lineage within the Hebrew Bible is central to the interpretation of the divine image. The Hebrew Bible commonly employs the term, בן, to describe descendants. Furthermore, this term is used in Gen. 5:1-3 to describe the passage of the divine image from Adam through to Seth. For these reasons, an understanding of בן and its usage is necessary for interpreting how this term illuminates the concept of *imago dei*. In what follows, I briefly outline some of the ways בן is employed within the Hebrew Bible, and how this information should inform the approach to *imago dei* described above.

The understanding of *imago dei* as divine parentage illuminates the substantive approach to the divine image. The term, בן, within the Hebrew Bible often ascribes a particular quality or characteristic of a person.[27] As Crouch has demonstrated, the creation of Adam in the divine image communicates his divine parentage. When Adam bears his בן, Seth, in his own image and likeness, Adam passes on his god-like character to Seth (Gen. 5:1-3). Furthermore, the conduct of sons within the Genesis narrative often resembles that of their fathers. For example, Isaac's behaviour very closely parallels that of his father, Abraham, who 'pretends that his wife is his sister (26:1-11; cf. 12:10-20; 20:1-18), is involved in a dispute...over the ownership of certain wells (26:17-25; cf. 21:22-34), and enters into a covenant with Abimelech (26:26-31; cf. 21:22-34)'.[28] When viewed from a substantive perspective, YHWH's children resemble him, just as sons mirror the characteristics of their earthly fathers.

The concept of *imago dei* as divine parentage also defines the relational aspect of the divine image. The term בן can be used to denote the servile partner in a political relationship, such as Samuel's submission to Eli (1 Sam. 3:6), Ben-Hadad's submission to Elisha (2 Kgs 8:9), and Ahaz's

27. בן can refer to a person valor (לבן־חיל; 1 Sam. 18:17; 2 Sam. 2:7); wickedness (בני־עולה; 2 Sam. 3:34; Hos. 10:9); foreignness (בן־נכר; Gen. 17:12; Exod. 12:43); affliction (בני־עני; Prov. 31:5); poverty (בני אביון; Ps. 72:4); and royal qualities (בני המלך; Judg. 8:18; 2 Sam. 9:11).

28. Alexander, *From Paradise to the Promised Land*, 108.

submission to Tiglath-pileser (16:7). Thus, divine parentage also conveys a relationship of submission and servitude to YHWH (cf. Exod. 4:23). This characteristic of the faithful Israelite community is demonstrated in the lives of those such as Enoch, who 'walked with God' (Gen. 5:24), and Noah, who is characterized as 'righteous' and 'complete', and 'walked with God' (Gen. 6:9). Furthermore, the special relationship between YHWH and the faithful Israelite community, from Adam through to Jacob, is demonstrated as YHWH preserves this lineage despite threats posed by their enemies, drought, and barrenness.[29] When viewed as divine parentage, *imago dei* communicates the parent–child relationship between YHWH and Israel.

Finally, the understanding of *imago dei* as divine parentage also sharpens the functional approach to the divine image. Within the Hebrew Bible, בן is also used to attribute people to a specific vocation or guild.[30] Therefore, from a functional perspective, the children of YHWH engage in the same vocation as YHWH. The unique command to 'subdue' (כבש) the land and 'exercise dominion' (רדה) over its creatures in Gen. 1:28 further specifies the uniquely divine vocation of the faithful Israelite community. Although the call to כבש and רדה has received its fair share of criticism, these terms should be interpreted as describing the continuation of YHWH's creative work.[31] The creation of humanity in the צלם and דמות of YHWH mirrors the practice of ancient monarchs who set up images to represent themselves throughout their kingdom.[32] Furthermore, the term רדה is often used within the Hebrew Bible to describe YHWH's sovereignty over the world (e.g. Pss. 72:8-11; 110:2).

---

29. Ibid., 107.

30. For example, בן־הרקחים ('perfumers'; Neh. 3:8); בני הכהנים ('priests'; Ezra 10:18); בני הנביאים ('prophets'; 1 Kgs 20:35).

31. In his article in *Science* magazine, Lynn White Jr. blames destructive ecological attitudes on the Judeo-Christian demythologization of nature. White rather cynically comments on Genesis 1 and 2: 'Finally, God had created Adam and, as an afterthought, Eve to keep man from being lonely. Man named all the animals, thus establishing his dominance over them. God planned all of this explicitly for man's benefit and rule: no item in the physical creation had any purpose save to serve man's purposes. And, although man's body is made of clay, he is not simply part of nature: he is made in God's image.' Lynn White, 'The Historical Roots of Our Ecological Crisis', *Science* (1967): 1205. For a rebuttal of White's article, see James Barr, 'Man and Nature – the Ecological Controversy and the Old Testament', *Bulletin of the John Rylands Library of the University of Manchester* 55 (1972): 9–32.

32. Hans Walter Wolff, *Anthropology of the Old Testament*, trans. Margaret Kohl (Philadelphia: Fortress, 1974), 160–1.

Thus, Genesis 1:1–2:3 portrays the faithful Israelite community as 'YHWH's plenipotentiary', who are created in the divine image, to רדה over the world.[33] The implication is that the faithful Israelite community, as children of YHWH who are created in his צלם and דמות, represent God by continuing his creative work of liberating creation from futility and inviting it into fecundity.[34]

The term כבש is often used within the Hebrew Bible to describe successful military conquest (e.g. 2 Sam. 8:11; 2 Chron. 28:10), and Josh. 18:1 records the fulfilment of the prototypical command to כבש the land in Gen. 1:28.[35] כבש, however, entails more than just the iconoclastic activity of wiping out an enemy along with all remnants of their cult. In Josh. 18:1, the כבש of the land is only complete once the Tabernacle is erected. This detail suggests that the כבש of the land describes both the destruction of one's enemies, along with all remnants of their religion, and the proper establishment and maintenance of the Israelite cult (cf. Deut. 12). As Jon Levenson notes:

> the creative ordering of the world has become something that humanity can not only witness and celebrate, but something in which it can also take part. Among the many messages of Genesis 1:1–2:3 is this: it is through the cult that we are enabled to cope with evil, for it is the cult that builds and maintains order, transforms chaos into creation, ennobles humanity, and realizes the kingship of God who has ordained the cult and commanded it to be guarded and practiced.[36]

In sum, the concept of *imago dei* communicates the divine parentage of the faithful Israelite community. The faithful Israelite community bears the divine image, as they reflect the character of YHWH, and they continue his creative work by keeping Torah and maintaining the cult. In this way, the faithful Israelite community brings blessing and fecundity to the world around them (cf. Gen. 1:28). According to the Pentateuch, Israel fulfils this vocation through Torah observance (Lev. 26:1-13;

---

33. Jon Levenson, *Creation and the Persistence of Evil* (Princeton: Princeton University Press, 1988), 113–14. Von Rad, *Old Testament Theology*, 1:146–7; Garr, *In His Own Image and Likeness*, 155–8.

34. Gina Hens-Piazza, 'A Theology of Ecology: God's Image and the Natural World', *Biblical Theology Bulletin* 13 (1982): 108–9.

35. Seth Postell, *Adam as Israel: Genesis 1–3 and the Introduction to the Torah and Tanakh* (Eugene: Pickwick, 2011), 102.

36. Levenson, *Creation and the Persistence of Evil*, 127.

Deut. 28:1-14).[37] Conversely, those Israelites who refuse to follow Torah threaten to bring a curse and a lack of fecundity (Lev. 26:14-39; Deut. 28:15-68). For this reason, the faithful Israelite image-bearers must continue YHWH's creative work by obeying the Torah's command to execute capital offenders.

Excursus: Imago dei *and Divine Sonship in the Jewish Tradition*

Some later texts within the Jewish tradition have also suggested that *imago dei* may communicate Israel's special status as YHWH's children, and that the value of one's life depends upon Torah observance. In what follows, I survey some of these texts, which resonate with the interpretation of *imago dei* presented above. For example, in *Mishnah Avot* Rabbi Akiva writes:

> Beloved is אדם, for he was created in the image of God...
> Beloved are the people of Israel, for they are called children of God...
> Beloved are the people of Israel, for a precious tool was given to them, with which the world was created. (3:14)

There has been some discussion as to whom Rabbi Akiva refers with the term, אדם. This term could be interpreted as synonymous with 'the people of Israel' in lines two and three. The thrice-used formula 'beloved is [or are]...for...' implies the same relationship exists between God and אדם as between God and 'Israel'. Such a reading would present Israel as the full expression of humanity who are entrusted with Torah, the vital tool for carrying on God's work of creation. As I shall argue throughout this book, faithful Israel incarnate the full expression of humanity by continuing YHWH's creative work through Torah observance. As faithful Israel imitate YHWH in this way, they reflect the divine image. This interpretation views the divine image as a marker of faithful Israel's unique identity and vocation over and against other peoples. Yet, this distinction appears to be one of behaviour rather than ethnicity. If the nations adopt Torah, they too may become children of YHWH as they express their humanity more fully. In this way, Torah functions as the key, which unlocks humanity's potential to reflect the divine image.

---

37. Although it may be argued that key figures of the Pentatcuch, such as Abraham and Noah, did not yet have access to Torah, these figures are, nonetheless, presented as paradigms of faithfulness. Moreover, later Jewish tradition claims that Abraham fulfilled the complete Torah (*Yoma* 28b) and that YHWH commanded Isaac to keep his commands, statutes, and laws in order to receive the blessing promised to Abraham (*Gen. Rab.* 26:5). *Genesis Rabbah* also claims that Jacob studied Torah (95:3). Even though, according to the Penateuch, Torah was given through Moses, later Jewish tradition still casts the Patriarchs as exemplars of Torah obedience.

An alternative interpretation, presented by Yair Lorerbaum, reads the three lines as a 'textual flow' from humanity to Israel's role in creation.[38] Lorerbaum claims that:

> all men – are created in God's image... Israel are called 'children' because they were designed to be the more perfect, fuller images of their Father in Heaven... Israel's uniqueness [however] has no relation to matters of essence or of race; rather, it is based upon action, acts, and lifestyle. Sanctity is not an inborn, innate quality, but is acquired through action – the performance of commandments.[39]

Although seeking to uphold the doctrine of humanity being universally created in the image of God, Lorerbaum stresses the particularity of Israel, and their unique position as divine children. As Lorerbaum correctly notes, the children of Israel represent 'more perfect, fuller images of their Father'. This comment certainly fits the Pentateuchal pattern discussed above in which the faithful Israelite community, who observe Torah, are considered the divine image-bearing children of YHWH. While Lorerbaum's attempt to treat *imago dei* and divine parentage as separate concepts overlooks the link between these two ideas (cf. Gen. 5:1-3), his assertion that through Torah Israel reflects a 'more perfect, fuller image' of YHWH finds much support in the Pentateuch.[40]

Lorerbaum is also correct in his assertion that human life is not inviolable in and of itself, but rather that the inviolability of one's life 'is acquired through action – the performance of commandments'. As argued below, any inviolability, which the Pentateuch attaches to human life, is dependent upon humanity's reflection of the divine image. The idea that Torah observance makes one's life precious is also reflected in the twelfth-century writings of Maimonides:

> If one slays a single Israelite, he transgresses a negative commandment, for Scripture says, 'Thou shalt not murder' (Exod. 21:13). If one murders wilfully in the presence of witnesses, he is put to death by the sword... Whether one kills an Israelite or a Canaanite slave, he must be put to death on his account, or – if he slays inadvertently – he must go into exile. If an Israelite kills a resident alien, he does not suffer capital punishment at the

---

38. Jair Lorerbaum, *In God's Image: Myth, Theology and Law in Classical Judaism* (Cambridge: Cambridge University Press, 2015), 282.

39. Ibid., 283–4.

40. In a similar vein, the early Christian writer, Irenaeus, also separates humanity into the dualistic categories of those who are righteous, bearing the divine image, and those who are unrighteous and do not bear the divine image. According to Irenaeus, the Christian Church is 'furnished...with salvation; so that what we had lost in Adam – namely, to be according to the image and likeness of God – that we might recover in Christ Jesus' (*Against Heresies* III.18.1); translation cited in *The Ante-Nicene Fathers, Volume 1: The Apostolic Fathers-Justin Martyr-Irenaeus* [Grand Rapids: Eerdmans, 1956], 446).

hand of the court, because Scripture says, 'and if a man come presumptuously upon his neighbour' (Exod. 21:12). Needless to say, one is not put to death if he kills a heathen. Whether one kills another's slave or his own, he must be put to death on the slave's account, seeing that a slave has taken upon himself the yoke of the commandments and is added to God's people. (*Torts* 1:1; 2:10-11)[41]

According to Maimonides, submission to YHWH's commandments makes one part of the Israelite community and, in so doing, makes one's life valuable. Even the life of a Canaanite slave is considered valuable on account of his or her submission to YHWH's commandments, which renders this person part of the faithful community. Killing a community member, whether foreign or native, slave or free, attracts the death penalty. However, killing those outside the community is not a capital offense because the lives of these people are not considered precious. For Maimonides, then, submission to Torah is what makes one's life valuable. As this excursus has shown, some voices within Judaism have postulated that the reflection of *imago dei* relies upon Torah observance which identifies one as part of faithful Israel and, in turn, determines the value of his or her life. These voices resonate with the interpretation of *imago dei* presented in the preceding section.

2. *Rivalry and Genesis 9:6*

2.1. *Rivalry between the Elect and the Anti-elect*

Reading *imago dei* as a unique attribute of the faithful Israelite community allows a fresh interpretation of Gen. 9:6. This section explores the context of Gen. 9:6 by briefly surveying the rivalry between Seth's lineage, who bear the divine image, and Cain's lineage who do not in the early chapters of Genesis. Genesis 9:6, which states that anyone who kills a divine image-bearer must also be killed, is then examined within this context. If, as this chapter has argued, only the faithful children of YHWH reflect the divine image, then Gen. 9:6 addresses the person who kills someone belonging to this specific group of people. This text cannot, therefore, be applied to cases in which someone outside the faithful Israelite community is killed. In this reading, although a high value is attributed to the lives of those who reflect the divine image, the life of the person who kills a divine image-bearer is not considered precious.

The rivalry between faithful Israel and its rivals manifests itself in the early chapters of Genesis as the conflict between Seth's faithful lineage and their rivals. The line of Seth from Adam through to Noah, who reflect the divine image through faithful obedience to YHWH, are

---

41. Translation cited from Michael Walzer et al., *The Jewish Political Tradition: Membership*, vol. 2 (New Haven: Yale University Press, 2006), 502.

engaged in continual rivalry with those who actively oppose them.[42] This rivalry extends back to Gen. 3:15, which foretells a struggle between Eve's offspring (זרע) and the offspring (זרע) of the serpent.[43] Throughout Genesis this struggle can be traced through the conflict between the enemy brothers, Cain and Abel, Isaac and Ishmael, Jacob and Esau; and Joseph and his brothers.[44] Once Israel multiplies and becomes a nation in its own right (Exod. 1:1-7), this rivalry is played out on a national level as Israel struggles with Egypt throughout the Exodus and the Canaanites in preparation for the Canaanite conquest. This rivalry has been noted and described by Joel Kaminsky.

In his book, *Yet I Loved Jacob*, Kaminsky argues that the Hebrew Bible splits humanity into three divisions: YHWH's elect, represented by the people of Israel; the anti-elect, represented by those nations who

---

42. The shrewdness of the serpent 'lies at the antipode of biblical wisdom, whose premise is "the fear of the Lord," and which finds its source in the Torah, the divine commandment... [The shrewdness of the serpent] is immediately anti-commandment, anti-Torah.' Andre LaCocque, *The Trial of Innocence: Adam, Eve, and the Yahwist* (Eugene: Wipf & Stock, 2006), 153.

43. Parts of the Rabbinic tradition also associate Cain and his offspring with the serpent of Gen. 3. For example, *Pirkei d'Rabbi Eliezer* 21 states that 'the serpent came into her [Eve] and she became pregnant with Cain, as it says, "And the human knew his wife Eve." What did he know? That she was already pregnant.' cited in Cherry, *Torah through Time*, 79. James E. Smith interprets Gen. 3:15 as describing the struggle between the righteous offspring of the woman and the unrighteous offspring of the serpent, which James refers to as 'the Devil': 'The seed of woman would embrace all those who share the woman's enmity toward the Devil, i.e., righteous mankind. The seed of the Devil would include all who yield to the Evil One without so much as a skirmish, i.e., wicked mankind.' James E. Smith, *Old Testament Survey Series: The Pentateuch* (Joplin: College Press, 2006), 72. Seth D. Postell is more specific, arguing that the offspring of the serpent in Gen. 3:15 refers to the Canaanites on account of the cursing of Canaan in 9:25 and the characterization of the Gibeonites' conduct as cunning (ערמה) in Josh. 9:4. While Postell is correct to note that the author(s) of Gen. 9:25 and Josh. 9:4 wish to demonize the Canaanites by casting them as the offspring of the serpent, there is little justification for limiting the despised 'offspring of the serpent' to the Canaanites by excluding other nationalities. Postell, *Adam as Israel*, 104–7. Mathews offers a more satisfactory interpretation of Gen. 3:15, arguing that the offspring of Eve refers to the offspring of Abraham, and therefore Israel, who are in constant conflict with the offspring of the serpent, which includes Cain, the Egyptians, and the Canaanites. Mathews, *Genesis 1–11: 26*, 245–7.

44. For more on the rivalry between brothers in Genesis, see Chapter 2, 'Enemy Brothers', in James G. Williams, *The Bible, Violence, and the Sacred: Liberation from the Myth of Sanctioned Violence* (Eugene: Wipf & Stock, 2007).

must be exterminated because they are 'so evil or dangerous', such as the Canaanites and Amalekites; and the non-elect, made up of foreigners with whom Israel share a cooperative and mutually beneficial relationship.[45] While Kaminsky's categories are very helpful, I would, however, note that they differ at various points within the Pentateuchal narrative. For example, while the Egypt is portrayed as a non-elect people in the latter chapters of Genesis, on account of Pharaoh's favourable treatment of Joseph and his family (Gen. 42–50), from Exodus 1 through to Num. 21:20 the Egyptians are presented as Israel's primary rival and must, therefore, be considered part of the anti-elect group. However, Egypt could be considered a non-elect people when their rivalry with Israel dissipates, and Israel focuses its rivalry upon the Moabites, Amorites, Midianites, and Canaanites, from Num. 21:21 through Deuteronomy 34.[46] Therefore, whether a foreign people group is treated as an anti-elect or non-elect group depends upon their relationship to the faithful Israel at that point in the Pentateuchal narrative.[47]

---

45. Joel S. Kaminsky, *Yet I Loved Jacob: Reclaiming the Biblical Concept of Election* (Nashville: Abingdon, 2007), 111.

46. Although Kaminsky hesitates to include Egypt as part of his anti-elect group on account of Deut. 23:8-9 (Eng. 23:7-8), which forbids anyone from abhorring an Egyptian (ibid., 123), I argue that Egypt as a nation should be considered part of Kaminsky's anti-elect category, at least from Exod. 1 to Num. 21:20, because of their rivalry with Israel throughout the Exodus, and the overwhelmingly negative portrayal of Egypt presented throughout most of the Pentateuch. I suggest that Deut. 23:8-9 envisages an Egyptian sojourning within Israel, who does not actively oppose Torah and, for this reason, may be considered part of the non-elect category, despite his or her nationality. In this way, Deut. 23:8-9 inverts the Exodus paradigm of Israel sojourning in Egypt, and challenges Israel to treat individual Egyptians with the respect and dignity that Israel, themselves, would have liked to receive during their stay in Egypt. This kind of altruism is made possible because at this stage of the narrative Egypt is considered a non-elect people because they are no longer engaged in rivalry with Israel. For an exploration of the negative portrayal of Egypt within the Pentateuch, see Franz V. Greifenhagen, *Egypt on the Pentateuch's Ideological Map: Constructing Biblical Israel's Identity* (London: Sheffield Academic Press, 2003).

47. This dynamic is also noted in the portrayal of Midian throughout the Pentateuch. While the portrait of Moses' Midianite father-in-law, Jethro, suggests the Midianites are present as a non-elect people on account of their cooperation with faithful Israel throughout Exodus (Exod. 3:1; 4:18; 18:1-12), in Num. 31:3-54 the Midianites are treated as the anti-elect, because they seduced Israel to breach YHWH's commands (יהוה למסר־מעל), which brought a plague upon the people (vv. 14-17). The treatment of the Midianites in this text, especially Moses' command to

As Kaminsky notes, 'ethnicity does not exclusively determine who belongs to the anti-elect and must therefore be annihilated'.[48] This observation is central to the examination of human immolation throughout the present study. Just as foreign nations might be considered non-elect or anti-elect depending on their cooperation with the faithful Israelite community, so the categorization of individual native-born Israelites, as either elect or anti-elect, depends upon the individual's obedience to Torah. Because those who disobey the commands of Torah threaten the faithful Israelite community's reflection of the divine image, these individuals may be categorized as anti-elect. For example, Noah's grandson, Canaan, as part of Noah's family, the select group of humanity who have been rescued from the cataclysm and charged with populating the post-cataclysmic world (Gen. 9:1, 7), may be considered anti-elect on account of his father's improper behaviour (vv. 21-27). Similarly, native-born Israelites who disobey Torah jeopardize faithful Israel's reflection of the divine image and must, therefore, be immolated as the community's anti-elect rivals. This concept explains why a member of the Israelite community who commits a capital offence must be immolated. Although the next chapter develops a method, which employs mimetic theory to analyse

---

'kill every male among the little ones, and kill every woman who has known man by lying with him, but all the young girls who have not known man by lying with him keep alive for yourselves' is reminiscent of Deuteronomy's prescribed treatment of Israel's anti-elect rivals in Deut. 20:12-18. The treatment of the Midianites in Num. 31:3-54 fits somewhere between the two procedures presented within Deut. 20:12-18, which address warfare against hostile nations who do not inhabit the land allotted to Israel, and nations which do inhabit this land. Israel are commanded to kill all of the males within the former group, while keeping 'the women and the little ones, the livestock, and everything else in the city' as plunder (Deut. 20:14). 'But in the cities of these peoples that YHWH your God is giving you for an inheritance, you shall save alive nothing that breathes, but you shall devote them to complete destruction, the Hittites and the Amorites, the Canaanites and the Perizzites, the Hivites and the Jebusites, as YHWH your God has commanded, that they may not teach you to do according to all their abominable practices that they have done for their gods, and so you sin against YHWH your God' (vv. 16-18). Note that the reason offered for the wholesale destruction of the second group is the protection of Israel's faithful obedience of YHWH. This reason mirrors the justification offered for Midian's destruction in Num. 35:14-16, which fits somewhere between the treatment of the two Canaanite groups prescribed in Deut. 20:12-18. For this reason, I would argue that while Num. 31:3-54 presents Midian as an anti-elect rival to Israel, earlier portraits of Midian in Exodus present this people group as part of the no-elect category.

48. Kaminsky, *Yet I Loved Jacob*, 113.

the interactions between faithful Israel and their rivals, in what follows I employ Kaminsky's insights to develop a fresh interpretation of *imago dei* that is then applied to the command to execute murderers in Gen. 9:6.

2.2. *Human Immolation and* Imago Dei

In this section I argue that the Pentateuch prescribes the immolation of capital offenders because their opposition to Torah observance threatens the faithful Israelite community's ability to reflect the divine image. For example, the man who desecrates the Sabbath by picking up sticks (Num. 15:32-36) violates a central aspect of Torah. This man fails to reflect the divine image, on account of his actions, and encourages others to do likewise. In contrast, although non-elect foreigners do not reflect the divine image themselves, neither do they hinder Israel's observance of Torah. The non-elect live peacefully and cooperatively with elect Israel.[49] For this reason, non-elect foreigners play no role in the rivalry between Eve's offspring and the offspring of the serpent (Gen. 3:15). This rivalry, which plays out between faithful Israel and the anti-elect, is spawned out of Israel's dedication to reflect the divine image through Torah observance and the unique threat which the anti-elect pose to this goal, through particular actions including, murder, idolatry, and certain sexual offenses.

As Finkelstein has noted, all capital offences within the Pentateuch attack the community's 'most cherished values to the degree that the commission of the offence places the community itself in jeopardy'.[50] In this book, I argue that these offences attract the death penalty because they pose a serious challenge to the core identity of the community as YHWH's image-bearing children. In contrast, minor impurities, such as the impurity associated with menstruation and childbirth, are a common, necessary part of the human existence. While these impurities may be viewed as less than ideal, they are still tolerated because they are inevitable.[51] Similarly, the consumption of impure meat does not constitute an attack upon the community's core identity because it is not a unique

---

49. Ibid., 121–2.
50. Finkelstein, 'The Ox That Gored', 27.
51. I suspect these tolerated impurities represent the community's efforts to grapple with the areas of life which they find particularly disgusting, and how the disgusting nature of these impurities effects their relationship with YHWH. For a discussion on the correlation between disgust and impurity in the Hebrew Bible, see Thomas Kazen, 'Dirt and Disgust: Body and Morality in Biblical Purity Laws', in *Perspectives on Purity and Purification in the Bible*, ed. Baruch J. Schwartz, et al. (New York: T&T Clark, 2008).

Israelite custom.⁵² Only those offences which directly threaten the Israelite community's ability to faithfully reflect the divine image through Torah observance, such as murder, sexual immorality, and Sabbath desecration, attract the death penalty.

2.3. *The Rivalry Surrounding Genesis 9:6*

In what follows, I argue that the faithful Israelite community's calling to reflect the divine image is threatened by their rivals, the serpent's offspring (cf. Gen. 3:15). After tracing this struggle through the early chapters of Genesis, I shall present a reading of Gen. 9:6 that accounts for the rivalry surrounding it. This rivalry, which is first described in Gen. 3:15, is realized when Cain murders his brother, Abel (Gen. 4:25). Abel's lineage continues, however, when Eve bears another son named Seth, and states that 'God has appointed for me another offspring (זרע) in Abel's place'.⁵³ As Mathews notes, the juxtaposition of Seth's genealogy (5:1-32) with that of Cain (Gen. 4:17-22) 'contributes to the unfolding motif of…rivalry between an unrighteous offspring and a righteous lineage'.⁵⁴ The contrast between these two lineages is emphasized in Gen. 6:5-9, which distinguishes Noah from the rest of his evil and corrupt generation, describing him as 'righteous' (צדיק) and 'complete' (תמים). This distinction is further emphasized as Noah finds favour with YHWH and is subsequently saved from the cataclysm. In contrast with Noah, the rest of humanity, who have destroyed (שחת) the earth and filled it with violence, are killed. The flood narrative of Genesis 6–9 separates humanity into two groups: faithful Noah and his family, whose lives are regarded as precious, and the wicked others, whose lives are not.⁵⁵ In this way, Genesis 6–9 draws a stark distinction between YHWH's faithful children and their rivals, who threaten YHWH's creation.

In the flood narrative, YHWH protects his faithful children by killing their rivals, along with everything else that breathes. YHWH then blesses Noah and his sons, and charges them to 'be fruitful, multiply, and fill

---

52. For a study of Israelite food laws and their relationship to those observed by other ancient Near Eastern people groups, see Walter Houston, *Purity and Monotheism: Clean and Unclean Animals in Biblical Law* (Sheffield: JSOT, 1993).

53. The link between Gen. 3:15 and 4:25 is noted by Mathews, who argues that Gen. 4:7 portrays חטאת as a predatory animal, such as a serpent or a demon waiting for a door of opportunity to be opened, which 'may well correspond to the "seed" of the serpent in 3:15, which will do battle with the "seed" of the woman'. Mathews, *Genesis 1–11: 26*, 270-1.

54. Ibid., 296.

55. Harland, *The Value of Human Life*, 69.

the land' (Gen. 9:1). This verse repeats the commission first given to the divine-image-bearing humanity of Gen. 1:26-28 and, in doing so, calls Noah and his sons to faithfully continue YHWH's creative work by reflecting the divine image (cf. 9:6).[56] The hope is that with faithful Israel's rivals now vanquished, Noah and his sons can repopulate the land without contaminating it with murderous violence and, in this way, fulfil their vocation as divine image-bearers. However, hope soon dissipates. Although the divine image appears to pass through Seth to Noah, Gen. 9:18-29 shows that the blessing uttered in 9:1 is dependent upon Noah and his sons faithfully reflecting the divine image.

The blessings and curses pronounced upon Noah's sons in Gen. 9:24-27 establish a hierarchy among the three brothers, Shem, Ham, and Japheth.[57] Canaan, the descendant of Ham, is cursed and designated as the lowliest servant (עבד עבדים) to his brothers because his father, Ham, saw the nakedness of Noah, his father (Gen. 9:22).[58] Although the exact nature of Ham's offence is unclear, uncovering the nakedness of one's father is regarded as a capital offence within the Pentateuch (Lev. 20:11). Ham's actions suggests that his son, Canaan, like his father lived a life of disobedience. Consequently, Canaan is cursed by his grandfather (v. 25), which reverses the divine blessing pronounced upon Ham in 9:1. This narrative pre-empts Israel's conquest of the Promised Land, by identifying

---

56. Noah's experience in Gen. 9 also mirrors that of Adam in Gen. 2–3. For example, Noah's drunken stupor in Gen. 9:21-24 mirrors Adam's divinely induced coma in Gen. 2:21-22. On both occasions the human awakes to discover something of significance has occurred. While Adam awakes to discover that YHWH has blessed him with an 'ideal counterpart', with whom he can be 'naked and unashamed', Noah awakes to find his son has brought shame and curse upon the entire family by uncovering his nakedness. Similarly, Ham and Canaan's role in Gen. 9:20-27 mirrors that of the serpent in Gen. 3. The serpent, uncovers the nakedness of Adam and Eve in Gen. 3, just as Ham does in Gen. 9:22. Moreover, like Adam, Noah also worked the soil. LaCocque, *The Trial of Innocence*, 134–6; Mathews, *Genesis 1–11: 26*, 388–9; Arthur W. Pink, *Gleanings in Genesis* (Chicago: Moody, 1922), 120; John Sailhamer, *The Pentateuch as Narrative: A Biblical-Theological Commentary* (Grand Rapids: Zondervan, 1992), 129–30.

57. Noah's three sons illustrate Kaminsky's three categories. Shem, who represents the elect, is blessed, while Canaan, as the anti-elect, is cursed. Meanwhile, the non-elect Japheth dwells peacefully in the tents of Shem. Kaminsky, *Yet I Loved Jacob*, 29.

58. Canaan's status as a 'servant of servants' to his brother asserts the inferior socio-political status of his eponymous descendants, the Canaanites. Ephraim A. Speiser, *Genesis: Introduction, Translation, and Notes* (New York: Doubleday, 1965), 61.

Canaan, and therefore his descendants who inhabit the Land of Canaan, as Israel's cursed, anti-elect rivals who must be exterminated. In contrast, Canaan's brothers avoid seeing their father's nakedness, and effectively undo their brother's actions, by walking backwards into their father's tent, and covering him with a garment (Gen. 9:23). Noah's words, 'blessed be the God of Shem', identify him as the one through whom the new creation will be blessed.

Genesis 10 confirms Noah's words, as it outlines the people groups who descend from each of his sons. From Japheth come various people groups, none of which fight against Israel throughout the Pentateuch (10:2-6). This observation identifies Japheth's descendants as the non-elect, who work co-operatively with Israel, just as the ancestor co-operated with Shem to cover over Noah's nakedness. The descendants of Ham clearly fit into the anti-elect category, as many of these people groups engage in fierce rivalries with the people of Israel, including Egypt, Babylon, and the Canaanites (vv. 6-19). Genesis 10:10-32 presents another linear genealogy, tracing the passage of *imago dei* from Shem through to Abraham, Israel's revered ancestor, who is also promised blessing. When read synchronically with the surrounding narratives, these genealogies suggest that the divine image has been passed from Adam through to Abraham. Like their ancestor, Abraham, Israel must continue YHWH's creative work by reflecting the divine image, even though they will face opposition from anti-elect foreigners.

In sum, the divine image is passed from Adam to Noah in a linear fashion through Seth. However, the divine image and the blessing associated with it (Gen. 1:26-28) is dependent upon the image-bearer's faithfulness. Fortunately, in each generation, one descendant has reflected the divine image, and successfully passed it on to one of their sons. As this chapter has argued, by observing Torah, faithful Israel reflect the divine image, which is passed on to them through Seth. Throughout the Pentateuch faithful Israel struggle against their rivals to fulfil their vocation of imitating YHWH through Torah observance.

2.4. *Analysis of Genesis 9:6*

In the midst of this struggle, Gen. 9:6 prescribes the execution of anyone who kills a member of the divine-image-bearing humanity. I shall now examine Gen. 9:6, which reads as follows:

Whoever sheds the blood of a man,	שֹׁפֵךְ דַּם הָאָדָם
by a man shall his blood be shed,	בָּאָדָם דָּמוֹ יִשָּׁפֵךְ
for God made man in his own image.	כִּי בְּצֶלֶם אֱלֹהִים עָשָׂה אֶת־הָאָדָם:

Genesis 9:6 addresses the homicide of Noah and his sons, who represent the divine-image-bearing humanity (האדם) in this text. This reading is supported by the recurrent employment of the personal pronoun, אתם, and second person imperatives throughout 9:1-7. Significantly, the killer is not referred to with the hominoid epitaph, האדם, but with the participle form of שפך in Gen. 9:6. In this way, the participle, שפך, contrasts the killer with האדם, and describes him or her as dangerous. Genesis 9:6, therefore, addresses the killing of האדם, a child of YHWH who bears the divine image, at the hands of a dangerous 'other'. The rivalry between this other and האדם is further emphasized through the killer's immolation. The ב attached to האדם in the second line of Gen. 9:6 is instrumental and, therefore, asserts that the enigmatic other, who sheds the blood of האדם, must be immolated by האדם. Mathews argues that this immolation represents a necessary expression of divine wrath which trumps any concern for the life of the murderer:

> After establishing the inviolability of human life, how can the divine directive at the same time exact killing the criminal who also is the divine 'image'? Capital punishment is not interpreted as a threat to the value of human life but rather is society's expression of God's wrath upon anyone who would profane the sanctity of human life.[59]

According to Mathews, the execution of murderers is justified as a righteous visitation of divine wrath, in accordance with the principle of *lex talionis*.[60] But, this interpretation fails to grapple with the relationship between the divine image and its implications for the value of human life in Gen. 9:6. If the presence of the divine image in all people renders human life inviolable, as Mathews contends, then how can the murderer, who supposedly bears the divine image be justly executed? Would not this execution also 'profane the sanctity of human life'? Alternatively, if *imago dei* functions as a marker for faithful Israel, then the murderer in Gen. 9:6 must be executed because he or she has executed one of YHWH's children. In this reading, there is no moral quandary over killing the murderer because he or she does not reflect the divine image. The concept of *imago dei* in Gen. 9:6 does not, therefore, address the 'the sanctity of human life', as Mathews contends, but rather the precious nature of faithful Israel.

---

59. Mathews, *Genesis 1–11: 26*, 406.
60. Ibid., 404.

Like Mathews, George W. Coats interprets the divine image as an essential attribute of all humanity, but offers a creative solution to the apparent problem posed by Gen. 9:5-6. According to Coats, this text employs irony to condemn the practice of human immolation:

> vv. 5b-6 extend the prohibition against blood in meat to a prohibition of blood vengeance. V. 5b is a statement of capital punishment for murder. The executor is God, however, not the man's brother. V. 6 then builds on a parallel couplet to establish an irony. Literally, the couplet reads: 'The shedder (*šōpēk*) of the blood of man (*dam hā'ādām*), by man (*bā'ādām*) his blood will be shed (*dāmô yiššāpēk*)'. The one who sheds the blood of a man will have his blood shed by a man; that is blood vengeance. But the man who executes the killer becomes himself a shedder of blood, thus creating a tragic chain. The answer to the chain is to leave the life and death of each man to God (v. 5b). The motivation for this irony lies in the affirmation that God made the man in his own image (cf. 1:27), and as a consequence of the image his life belongs to God.[61]

However, Coats' interpretation of Gen. 9:6 is problematic for a number of reasons. First, Coats' interpretation contradicts other passages, such as Num. 35:30-34 and Deut. 19:11-13, which clearly prescribe the execution of murderers. Second, Coats' reading does not recognize that v. 6 appears to be an older, probably well known, law or proverb which has been inserted to bolster, and further explain, v. 5b's assertion that YHWH requires a reckoning in cases of homicide.[62] The flow of the text leads the reader to expect v. 6 to further describe the divinely appointed reckoning mentioned in v. 5b. Coats, however, argues that v. 6 jumps to describing what the divine reckoning is not, viz. human immolation, without any syntactical markers to support this interpretation. For these reasons, Coats' creative suggestion that Gen. 9:6 denounces human immolation through a rhetoric of irony should be dismissed.

A more satisfactory reading of Gen. 9:6 presents itself once *imago dei* is recognized as a marker of faithful Israel's divine parentage. If only those who obey YHWH's commands bear the divine image, then the killer of האדם in Gen. 9:6 cannot bear the divine image because Torah explicitly forbids this behaviour (Exod. 20:13). The assumption that the killer does not bear the divine image is further strengthened when Gen. 9:6 is read in light of v. 5. Genesis 9:5 states that YHWH requires a reckoning from any person or animal who kills anyone from Noah's family. It follows, then,

---

61. George W. Coats, *Genesis, with an Introduction to Narrative Literature*, Forms of the Old Testament Literature 1 (Grand Rapids: Eerdmans, 1983), 78.

62. Von Rad, *Old Testament Theology*, 1:132–3.

that the killer of Gen. 9:6 may be either human or animal. Whether human or animal, the enigmatic portrayal of the killer in Gen. 9:6 further suggests that this agent does not bear the divine image. The reflection of *imago dei* through faithful adherence to Torah is what makes the life of YHWH's child precious.[63] Therefore, the application of Gen. 9:6 is limited to the killing of YHWH's image-bearing children, and may not be applied to the killing of other humans outside of this category.

Furthermore, in Gen. 9:1 YHWH commissions Noah and his sons as the new humanity to 'be fruitful and multiply and fill the land'.[64] Verses 2-4 proclaim that YHWH has delivered all the animals into the hands of the new humanity, and that 'every moving thing that lives shall be food for them' as long as Noah and his sons do not eat any flesh with the blood still in it. Just as Gen. 9:3-4 addresses the proper slaying and consumption of animals, which do not reflect the divine image, so vv. 5-6 addresses the slaying of the killer whose life is not regarded as precious because he or she does not reflect the divine image. Noah's family are called to reflect the divine image by imitating YHWH's actions in the flood narrative, and purging the land of those who commit murderous violence.

Prior to the cataclysm 'the land was filled with murderous violence (חמס)', and on account of this חמס YHWH determines 'to make an end of all flesh' (Gen. 6:11, 13). Yet, YHWH protects Noah from the cataclysm because he 'finds favour in his eyes' (Gen. 6:8). Similarly, in Gen. 9:6 Noah and his sons, as bearers of the divine image, are called to imitate YHWH by killing any human or animal who kills one of Noah's faithful descendants. Through the immolation of these agents Noah and his sons protect their community against their rivals. In so doing, Noah and his sons struggle to reflect the divine image in the post-cataclysmic world. Moreover, by immolating those who fill the land with חמס, Noah and his sons imitate YHWH's actions in Genesis 6–8 and, in this way, reflect the divine image. This observation raises the possibility that the כִּי clause in the third line of Gen. 9:6 refers to Noah and his sons' imitation of YHWH. In other words, the reference to the divine image in the final כִּי clause not only functions to assign value to the life of האדם, but also notes that because האדם bears the divine image this group must imitate YHWH by purging the land from murderous violence.

---

63. The כִּי clause of the third line is causal and, therefore, cites *imago dei* as the reason the killer of האדם must be immolated. The immolation of the killer, however, does not demand the death of his or her executioner because the killer does not bear the divine image.

64. Roop, *Genesis*, 71; Mathews, *Genesis 1–11: 26*, 399–400.

This reading views Gen. 9:6 in light of its context within the surrounding flood narrative and the rivalry between the faithful Israelite community, who bear the divine image, and their rivals, offspring of the serpent. Genesis 9:6 should not, therefore, be interpreted as assigning inviolability to all human life. It does, however, regard the life of the divine-image-bearing humanity, represented by Noah and his righteous descendants, as precious. The existence of this humanity is threatened by murderous violence. For this reason, faithful Israel must purge murderous violence through the immolation of anyone who kills a divine image-bearer.

3. *Conclusion*

As this chapter has argued, the immolation of other humans is not consistent with the commonly accepted idea that, on account of *imago dei*, all human life is inviolable. Although many point to Gen. 9:6 in support of this idea, the current chapter has presented an alternative reading of Gen. 9:6, which takes into account this passage's place within the flood narrative and the rivalry between the faithful Israelite community and their enemies. I have argued that Gen. 9:6 portrays the life of community members, who bear the divine image through Torah observance, as precious. Moreover, this text commands community members to reflect the divine image by immolating those who threaten to defile the land through acts of murderous violence. In this way, the faithful Israelite community imitate YHWH's actions within the flood narrative. As they fulfil this vocation, the faithful Israelite community, alone, reflects the divine image.

When viewed from this perspective, *imago dei* becomes a marker of communal identity. It also gives the community a common purpose as they actively seek to reflect the divine image through their conduct. This purpose includes the community's struggle against the anti-elect, who actively oppose Torah observance (cf. Gen. 3:15). According to the Pentateuch, these rivals, including those who commit serious breaches of Torah, such as murder, idolatry, blasphemy, and certain sexual offenses, must be immolated. In so doing, the community is drawn together as they reinforce their values and identity by excising those who do not conform to their ideals. By reading this excision through the lens of Réne Girard's mimetic theory, the method employed by the present study generates many fruitful insights concerning the role of human immolation within the Pentateuch. This method, which will be applied to key Pentateuchal texts concerned with human immolation, is explained and defended in the next chapter.

Chapter 3

METHOD

Having recognized *imago dei* and Torah observance as key identity markers that distinguish the faithful Israelite community from their anti-elect rivals, the remainder of this book investigates how this rivalry might influence the practice of human immolation. To this end, the current chapter presents a method for analyzing a possible link between rivalry and human immolation in key biblical passages, such as Lev. 24:10-23 and Num. 15:32-36. By applying this method to a mutual dialogue between Hebrew Bible scholarship and mimetic theory, the present study generates a fresh reading of human immolation within the Pentateuch. Certain malefactors, who fail to reflect the divine image through Torah observance, are portrayed as the faithful community's anti-elect rivals. The community band together to immolate these malefactors, and in so doing, restore peace and order within the community. Through these means, the community also strengthen their self-identification as YHWH's faithful children, who reflect his image. This chapter begins by defining the primary texts for the current study. Next, I shall explain my method for constructing a synchronic reading of these texts within the context of the Pentateuchal narrative. Finally, Girard's theory concerning the scapegoat mechanism is outlined and critiqued, and this study's application of Girard's theory to my synchronic reading of the primary text is developed and explained.

1. *The Primary Text*

This study accepts the source-critical assumption that the final form Pentateuch (Genesis–Deuteronomy) is a complex document, which was composed and redacted from various sources. Although this study presents a synchronic reading of the Pentateuch, it also utilizes the common convention of referring to Julius Wellhausen's Pentateuchal sources of J (for the 'Jahwist'), E (for 'Elohim'), D (for the 'Deuteronomist'), P (for the 'Priestly source'); and H (for the 'Holiness Code').[1] The current study examines the communication of similar concepts across sources, which employ different terminology and aetiology. For example, Deuteronomy justifies the execution of murderers by highlighting that illegitimate bloodshed generates blood guilt (Deut. 19:1-13), while P (or H) prescribes the immolation of murderers as a necessary means of purifying the land (Num. 35:33-34). The present study attempts to go beyond these aetiologies in search of a deeper, perhaps unstated, mechanism which drives human immolation within the Pentateuch.

The present work examines narrative texts that detail human immolation in response to certain offenses, and laws which prescribe human immolation, specifically, casuistic laws containing the מות ימות (infinitive absolute + imperfect *hof'al*) formula. The מות ימות formula, as it is used in texts such as Leviticus 20, refers to human immolation.[2] In P and H human immolation is described by the *hof'al* form of מות, while the *qal* of מות describes divinely mediated death (cf. Lev. 16:2, 13; 22:9).[3] This interpretation is confirmed in texts which also prescribe the mode of immolation to be employed. For example, texts may prescribe communal stoning (e.g. Lev. 24:16; 20:2) or burning (Lev. 20:14; 21:9) as the appropriate mode of execution. For this reason, the current study reads casuistic laws which employ the מות ימות formula as prescribing human immolation, at least within P and H.

Some texts prescribe the כרת-penalty for certain offenses. While some have interpreted the כרת formula as referring to human immolation, this interpretation cannot be sustained,[4] because the כרת formula appears to describe a divinely mediated consequence.[5] Every occurrence of the כרת

---

1. Julius Wellhausen, *Prolegomena to the History of Israel*, trans. John Sutherland Black and Allan Menzies (Atlanta: Scholars Press, 1994).

2. Cf. Lev. 24:16; Num. 15:35; 35:16-18, 21, 31; Jacob Milgrom, *Leviticus 17–22: A New Translation with Introduction and Commentary* (New York: Doubleday, 2000), 1745–7; René Péter-Contesse and John Ellington, *A Handbook on Leviticus* (New York: United Bible Societies, 1990), 301–2; Moshe Greenberg, *Studies in the Bible and Jewish Thought* (Philadelphia: Jewish Publication Society, 1995), 35.

3. Jacob Milgrom, *Studies in Levitical Terminology* (Berkeley: University of California Press, 1970), 5–8. Outside of P and H the formula is also used in other ways (e.g. Gen. 2:17).

4. This approach is seen in Robert McClive Good, *The Sheep of His Pasture: A Study of the Hebrew Noun 'am(m) and Its Semitic Cognates* (Atlanta: Scholars Press, 1983), 87.

5. G. F. Hasel, 'Karat', in *Theological Dictionary of the Old Testament*, ed. G Johannes Botterweck, Helmer Ringgren, and Heinz-Josef Fabry (Grand Rapids: Eerdmans, 2006), 348.

formula within the Pentateuch, expressed in the active voice, takes YHWH as its subject, which suggests that the כרת-penalty is not carried out by a human party, and cannot, therefore, refer to human immolation.[6] For this reason, the present study does not examine the Pentateuchal caustic laws which employ the כרת-penalty, except in cases where they serve to further illuminate other texts which directly refer to human immolation.

2. Reading Method

The current study focuses upon Pentateuchal texts that either explicitly describe or prescribe human immolation. Yet, before continuing I must acknowledge that some scholars deny that the Pentateuch endorses human immolation at all. For example, some have argued that the language of human immolation within the Pentateuch does not describe or prescribe a communal norm, but rather functions as a rhetoric which underlines the importance of certain offenses.[7] The present study does not dispute that Pentateuchal texts that address human immolation may have been interpreted and applied in this way at certain points in Israel's history.[8] This study is, however, concerned with a synchronic reading of the primary text, within the context of the rivalry between faithful Israel and their anti-elect rivals, which is independent of historical interpretations. To this end, the current study presents a synchronic reading of key Pentateuchal texts concerned

---

6. Lev. 17:10; 20:3, 5, 6.

7. Thomas Hieke, 'Das Alte Testament und die Todesstrafe', *Biblica* (2004): 349–74; Louis Stulman, 'Sex and Familial Crimes in the D Code: A Witness to Mores in Transition', *Journal for the Study of the Old Testament* 17, no. 53 (1992): 47–63; Anselm C. Hagedorn, 'Guarding the Parents' Honour – Deuteronomy 21.18-21', *Journal for the Study of the Old Testament* 25, no. 88 (2000): 101–21.

8. The interpretation of human immolation texts will inevitably be shaped by the audience's attitude to capital punishment, and their assumptions surrounding this practice. For this reason, different audiences interpret these texts in different ways. For example, those who accept capital punishment as a divinely sanctioned institution might be inclined to read these texts as a literal call to immolate capital offenders. Alternatively, an audience which rejects capital punishment may read these passages as an exhortation to take certain commands seriously. The Rabbinic tradition takes an interesting approach to these texts. Although this tradition interpreted these texts as a literal call to execute capital offenders, it was also very reluctant to carry out human executions (*m. Makot* 1:10). The Rabbis negotiated this dilemma by demanding an extraordinary burden of proof to reach a guilty verdict in these cases and, in this way, attempted to minimize the practice of capital punishment. Elliot N. Dorff, *For the Love of God and People: A Philosophy of Jewish Law* (Philadelphia: Jewish Publication Society, 2007), 203–4.

with human immolation through Bernard Jackson's narrative approach.⁹ In what follows, I explain Jackson's narrative approach, and how this method will be employed in the current study. I shall then briefly discuss the use of biblical echoes within this book, and support the recognition of these echoes with reference to the work of Richard Hayes and others.

The narrative approach considers the meaning conveyed through subtle literary and thematic echoes across texts. As Jonathan Burnside explains, the narrative approach constructs meaning by paying careful attention to the echo of key stories and imagery across texts:

> The dominant form of sense-construction is narrative and visualisation. Whereas a semantic interpretation asks: 'what is the literal meaning of the words' a narrative approach asks: 'what typical situations do the words of this rule evoke?' or, more straightforwardly, 'what does it make you think of?' It is a picture-oriented or 'imagistic' approach rather than a literal one.¹⁰

Adopting the narrative approach, this study shall pay careful attention to the subtle echo of key stories and imagery employed in the description of capital offences. In this way, the current study shall examine how capital offenses and human immolation are portrayed within the Pentateuch, and how this portrayal might influence and encourage the practice of human immolation.

The narrative approach allows a true synchronic reading of the text, as it reads the Pentateuchal legal material within the context of the overarching narrative. In so doing, this approach pays due attention to the placement of legal texts within the Pentateuchal narrative, and considers how this placement, and the employment of themes and *leitworte*, should influence the text's interpretation.¹¹ As Burnside notes, 'the way in which biblical

---

9. This approach also been effectively utilized by Jonathan Burnside to examine the immolation of the Sabbath Gatherer in Num. 15:32-36. Jonathan Burnside, '"What Shall We Do with the Sabbath-Gatherer?": A Narrative Approach to a "Hard Case" in Biblical Law (Numbers 15: 32-36)', *Vetus Testamentum* 60, no. 1 (2010): 45–62.

10. Ibid., 49.

11. Martin Buber coined the term, *leitwort*, which he describes as 'a word or a word-root that recurs significantly in a text, in a continuum of texts, or in a configuration of texts: by following these repetitions, one is able to decipher or grasp a meaning of the text, or at any rate, the meaning will be revealed more strikingly. The repetition, as we have said, need not be merely of the word itself but also of the word-root; in fact, the very difference of words can often intensify the dynamic action of the repetition. I call it "dynamic" because between combinations of sounds related to one another in this manner a kind of movement takes place: if one imagines the entire text deployed before him, one can sense waves moving back and forth between the words. The measured repetition that matches the inner rhythm of the text, or rather, that

law is structured and organized internally determines the meaning of its content'.[12] The narrative method seriously engages with the final form of the Pentateuch because it does not 'split what authors and compilers have put together'.[13] This method also avoids placing anachronistic, modern legal assumptions upon the text because it remains anchored within the text and 'shows an increased sensitivity to how ideas were constructed in their historical context'.[14] In so doing, the narrative approach also pays careful attention to the addressee of the text and the role played by different parties in the text under consideration.

The narrative approach also allows for the differentiation of different offenses which receive similar consequences.[15] For example, most of the capital offences described in Lev. 20:10-16 necessitate immolation by communal stoning, yet the man who simultaneously marries a woman and her mother must be burned, along with his spouses (v. 14). A narrative approach allows one to explore the different imagery portrayed in Lev. 20:10-16, and to ask how these images communicate different values and ideas. Another advantage offered by this method is the ability to explore the relationship between the Pentateuchal legal and narrative material.[16] For example, the narrative method allows us to investigate the way certain offences, such as 'uncovering the nakedness' of a relative (Lev. 20:11, 17-21), might impact relationships, and how these relationships determine the consequences applied in each case.[17]

---

wells up from it, is one of the most powerful means for conveying meaning without expressing it.' M. Buber, *Werke: Vol. 2: Schriften Zur Bibel* (Munich: Köselverlag, 1964), 1131; translation cited in Robert Alter, *Art of Biblical Narrative*, 2nd edn (New York: Basic Books, 2011), 117.

12. Jonathan Burnside, *God, Justice, and Society: Aspects of Law and Legality in the Bible* (Oxford: Oxford University Press, 2010), 21.

13. Ibid., 14. In a similar vein, Bartor Asnat notes that 'laws play a central role in advancing the main story… [T]he laws respond to the plot, are motivated by it, and serve its aims.' Assnat Bartor, *Reading Law as Narrative: A Study in the Casuistic Laws of the Pentateuch* (Atlanta: Society of Biblical Literature, 2010), 20–1.

14. In the ancient Near East legal concepts were commonly communicated through imagery. Burnside, *God, Justice, and Society*, 26; Bernard S. Jackson, 'Modelling Biblical Law: The Covenant Code', *Chicago-Kent Law Review* 70 (1994): 1745–9, 60–71; Burnside, *God, Justice, and Society*, 11–14.

15. Burnside, *God, Justice, and Society*, 26.

16. Ibid., 27.

17. The person who uncovers the nakedness of his father, by having sexual relations with his father's wife, must be immolated (Lev. 20:11). However, one who uncovers the nakedness of other relatives receives a different consequence, namely, the כרת-penalty (vv. 17-21).

One potential pitfall of this approach, which must be addressed, is the possibility it affords to draw unwarranted, anachronistic allusions between any and every text. The present work addresses this pitfall by drawing upon the work of Richard Hayes, who has discussed criteria for positively identifying intertextual echoes. Some of Hayes' seven criteria for determining intertextual echoes will prove helpful for the current study.[18] Hayes' criteria are: (1) Availability: Were the source texts, which are potentially echoed, available to the readers and writers of the text under examination? (2) Volume: Is there sufficient repetition of terms and syntactical patterns to suggest an intertextual relationship between these texts? (3) Recurrence: How often does an author reference this source? (4) Thematic Coherence: Does the potential echo fit with the author's argument? (5) Historical Plausibility: Could the author have intended this alleged meaning, and would their original audience have understood it? (6) History of Interpretation: Have other interpreters noted this echo? (7) Satisfaction: Does the proposed echo makes sense? The present study draws upon some of these criteria to strengthen its claims concerning intertextual echoes within the Pentateuch.

Mindful of Hayes' first and fifth criteria, availability and historical plausibility, the present work restricts its investigation of intertextual echoes to the Pentateuch itself. Because this study uses the final form Pentateuch as its primary text, it reasonably assumes access to this document in its entirety, and that readers can and should read this text synchronically. Although at times this book draws upon biblical sources beyond the Pentateuch to investigate rare terms and phrases, which are used too sparingly within the Pentateuch to ascertain their sense, discussion of echoes between texts is limited to the final form Pentateuch.[19] Because the final form Pentateuch assumes its own entirety, the textual echoes discussed in the current study satisfy Hayes' first criterion of availability. This study also satisfies Hayes' fifth criterion, historical plausibility, because the editors and redactors of the final form Pentateuch could plausibly expect its audience to recognize echoes within this document.

Cynthia Edenburg has developed Hayes' second criterion, volume, in a way which makes it better suited to identifying echoes within the Hebrew Bible. According to Edenburg, the 'unique recurrence of peculiar formulations...recurrent use of [unique or] rare...expressions may support an argument for literary interrelationship'.[20] Edenburg also notes that a

18. Hayes, *Echoes of Scripture*, 29–32.
19. However, the present study necessarily discusses allusions and echoes which other scholars have noted beyond this field of reference.
20. Edenburg, 'How (Not) to Murder a King', 72.

claimed relationship between texts is further supported by a 'similarity of context or structure'.²¹ For example, Exod. 14:22, 29, 15:19 echoes the Priestly creation account's use of the relatively rare term, תהום (Gen. 1:1–2:3). In both cases, YHWH conquers the תהום and saves people through his provision of dry land. This imagery is also employed in the flood narrative as the fountains of the great תהום burst, drowning every living creature with the exception of Noah, his family, and some select animals who find sanctuary within the ark. Much like Israel's Exodus experience, Noah and his family are delivered from danger through YHWH's provision of dry ground. This echo of rare terminology in a similar context of danger and deliverance suggests a common image is presented in each of these passages.

Hayes' third criterion is not helpful for the study because the Pentateuch has multiple authors and compilers. For this reason, the present study ignores this criterion. However, Hayes' fourth criterion, thematic coherence, is foundational to this study, which interprets all echoes within the context of the unfolding narrative of the Pentateuch. This narrative traces the struggle between YHWH's children, Israel, and their enemies, discussed in the previous chapter. All potential echoes examined within the present study reflect this struggle. In this way, the current work satisfies Hayes' fourth criterion. Additionally, in response to Hayes' sixth criterion, the echoes identified in this study are further supported by the citation of others who have also observed them. Finally, Hayes' seventh criterion, satisfaction, is addressed as all echoes within this book are read synchronically with the rest of the Pentateuch. For example, the previous chapter noted the echo of *imago dei* terminology in Gen. 1:26-28; 5:1-3; and 9:1, 6, and presented a synchronic reading of this echo, which identified the divine image-bearing humanity of 1:26-28 with Seth's lineage through to Noah and his sons. By solely discussing echoes of imagery which are supported by the criteria discussed above, this study hopes to avoid the charge of drawing unwarranted connections between texts.

One possible objection to my employment of the synchronic narrative reading of the Pentateuch could be that this method cuts across all source-critical boundaries, and in so doing ignores the different socio-political settings out of which each source arises. For example, Chapter 2 attempted to read the Priestly texts addressing the image of God (Gen. 1:26-27; 5:1-3; 9:6) alongside the cursing of Noah's grandson, Canaan, which critics commonly assign to a different source. In response to this objection, I would note that the composition of the Pentateuch weaves these sources together in a manner that encourages a synchronic reading of the

21. Ibid.

text. Bearing testimony to this claim is the ongoing debate and discussion surrounding the Pentateuch's composition. Furthermore, both the Jewish and Christian faith traditions have read these texts synchronically for centuries. Although the dissection of the Pentateuch into various, alleged source documents may be necessary for investigating the text's evolution, only synchronic readings can earnestly grapple with the literary artistry and redaction employed in the final form of the Pentateuch. For these reasons, the present study attempts to undertake a synchronic reading of human immolation within the Pentateuch.

In sum, this book reads major Pentateuchal texts concerning human immolation synchronically by employing the narrative method outlined above. This method pays careful attention to the narrative themes and intertextual echoes. To avoid drawing anachronistic links across texts, this study limits the discussion of intertextual echoes to relatively rare terms, which occur within a similar context or structure within the Pentateuch. As discussed in the previous chapter, Israel fulfil their calling as the image-bearing children of YHWH by obeying Torah. However, throughout the Pentateuch faithful Israel struggle to fulfil this vocation on account of their anti-elect rivals. Within the context of this rivalry some Pentateuchal texts command the immolation of faithful Israel's anti-elect rivals. The divinely sanctioned execution of humans within the Pentateuch may be illuminated by applying mimetic theory and Girard's scapegoat stereotypes to a narrative reading of this study's primary text. Through the application of mimetic theory, the current project argues the capital offenders within the Pentateuch become communal scapegoats, as they are executed to restore peace and order within the community.

3. Mimetic Theory and the Scapegoat Mechanism

In this section I briefly introduce and explain mimetic theory, which exposes structures of conflict and scapegoating like those identified between faithful Israel and their anti-elect rivals, in the previous chapter. Next, the scapegoat mechanism and Girard's four scapegoat stereotypes are discussed, along with how these concepts will be applied to my narrative reading of the primary text in subsequent chapters. By employing the narrative approach, this book reads texts concerning human immolation within the context of the rivalry between the faithful Israelite community and their anti-elect rivals. The current study applies Girard's scapegoat stereotypes to this reading of the primary text to reveal the scapegoat mechanism within these passages. This revelation allows a fresh reading of human immolation within the Pentateuch, which is explored in subsequent chapters.

Girard's theory of rivalry and violence is founded upon a unique conception of human desire. In contrast to the romantic notion that each person is an individual who possesses their own unique, autonomous desires, mimetic theory postulates that desire is generated by imitating others. Girard developed this theory through his study of various writers, including Dostoyevsky, Proust, Cervantes, and Shakespeare.[22] In these writings, Girard detected an interesting relationship between imitation, desire, and rivalry. For example, Girard cites the mimetic nature of the relationship between Valentine and Proteus in Shakespeare's *The Two Gentlemen of Verona*. When the time comes for these close friends to study in Milan, Valentine goes, but Proteus remains in Verona because of his love for Julia.

> In spite of Julia, however, Proteus misses Valentine greatly and, after a while, he too goes to Milan. The two friends are reunited in the ducal palace; the duke's daughter, Silvia, is present, and Valentine briefly introduces Proteus. After she departs, Valentine announces that he loves her and his hyperbolic passion irritates Proteus. Once alone, however, Proteus has his own announcement to make: he no longer loves Julia; he too has fallen in love with Silvia…
>
> This is *mimetic* or *mediated* desire. Valentine is its *model* or *mediator*; Proteus is its mediated subject, and Silvia is their common object. Mimetic desire can strike with the speed of lightning; it does not really depend upon the impact made by the object, but only seems to. Proteus desires Silvia not because their brief encounter made a decisive impression on him, but because he is predisposed in favour of whatever Valentine desires.
>
> Mimetic desire is Shakespeare's own idea. We can see this again in Proteus's soliloquy, which keeps minimizing the role of perception in the genesis of his desire for Silvia…
>
> If Silvia is no more desirable objectively than Julia, her only advantage is that Valentine already desires her.[23]

According to Girard, a person (or subject) does not know what to desire until he or she, typically unconsciously, finds a model to imitate.[24] Having found a model, the subject then imitates their model's speech, actions, and desires. This process, which Girard labels 'mimesis', is illustrated in *The Two Gentlemen of Verona* through Proteus' imitation of Valentine's

---

22. James Alison et al., 'General Introduction', in *The Palgrave Handbook of Mimetic Theory and Religion*, ed. James Alison et al. (New York: Palgrave Macmillan, 2017), 1.
23. René Girard, *A Theatre of Envy: William Shakespeare* (Leominster: Gracewing, 2000), 9.
24. Girard, *Violence and the Sacred*, 145–6.

desire for Silvia. If mimesis is allowed to flourish, unchecked, the subject becomes increasingly like their model, and may even come to resemble their model so well that, to the outside observer, these two entities become almost indistinguishable. At this point, the subject and model have become 'doubles' of each other.[25] Valentine and Proteus are portrayed as doubles in *The Two Gentlemen of Verona*. As Girard notes, they 'grow up together, they learn the same lessons, read the same books, play the same games, and agree on just about everything. They also desire the same objects.'[26]

Because doubles share the same desires and goals, they inevitably engage each other in a fierce rivalry over the same object, which generates more mimesis and rivalry, as the two doubles exchange blows with one another.[27] Girard calls this phenomenon 'mimetic rivalry'.[28] This dynamic can be observed in *The Two Gentlemen of Verona*, as Proteus' growing desire for Silvia prompts Valentine to praise Silvia more intensely.[29] The same imitation that was once part and parcel of their relationship now gives birth to a bitter rivalry over the love of a single woman:

> Eros cannot be shared in the same manner as a book, a bottle of wine, a piece of music, a beautiful landscape. Proteus is still doing what he has always done; he is imitating his friend, but the consequences, this time, are radically different. All of a sudden, with no advance warning, the attitude that has always nourished the friendship tears it apart. Imitation is a double-edged sword. At times it produces so much harmony that it can pass for the blandest and dullest of all human drives; at other times it produces so much strife that we refuse to recognize it as imitation.[30]

25. René Girard, Jean-Michel Oughourlian, and Guy Lefort, *Things Hidden since the Foundation of the World*, trans. S. Bann and M. Metteer (Stanford: Stanford University Press, 1987), 26; Schwager, *Must There Be Scapegoats?*, 12–13; Wolfgang Palaver, *René Girard's Mimetic Theory* (East Lansing: Michigan State University Press, 2013), 132.

26. Girard, *A Theatre of Envy*, 9.

27. Girard refers to this type of mimesis as 'internal mediation'. Girard also described another category of mimesis, in which someone imitates a model who cannot reciprocate their mimesis because of the great distance between them. This distance may be because the model is unaware of their imitation, or such a great social or geographical gap exists between these two people that the model does not feel threatened. In this case, no rivalry is generated because the model is too far away. Girard refers to this type of mimesis as 'externally mediated rivalry'. Girard, *Deceit, Desire, and the Novel*, trans. Yvonne Freccero (Baltimore: Johns Hopkins University Press, 1965), 5–9.

28. Girard, *A Theatre of Envy*, 17–18.

29. Ibid., 13–14.

30. Ibid., 9.

If mimetic rivalry is allowed to flourish, unchecked, a mimetic crisis can ensue.[31] Within in a mimetic crisis mimesis spreads throughout the entire community.[32] As everyone imitates everyone else, the differentiation between members of the community dissolves.[33] In this way, every member of the community becomes a double of the other. Inevitably, as the community strive and compete for the same objects, an intense all-against-all mimetic rivalry is generated, one which threatens to destroy the community. Girard cites the example of the Brazilian Kaingang, who were almost wiped out through a mimetic crisis that was spawned through acts of blood vengeance.[34] Yet, a mimetic crisis does not always lead to the annihilation of an entire community. The people may survive if they unite, and vent their mimetic rivalry upon a common enemy, transforming their all-against-all rivalries into an all-against-one rivalry.[35] Girard refers to this phenomenon as the 'scapegoat mechanism'.[36]

In his book, *Permanence and Change*, Kenneth Burke argues that 'the scapegoat mechanism in its purest form' utilizes 'a sacrificial receptacle for the ritual unburdening of one's sins'.[37] According to Burke, the scapegoat ritual arises from internal conflict, 'hence the urgent incentive to be "purified" by "projecting"…conflict upon a scapegoat', upon which all conflict and anger is subsequently vented.[38] Girard argues that the scapegoat mechanism is driven by mimetic rivalry, and prompts the community to vent its collective rivalry upon an individual or subgroup of the community. In this way, peace and order is maintained within the community.[39] The scapegoat mechanism can be identified through four stereotypes: the mimetic crisis, the blaming of the scapegoat, the mark of the victim, and the execution or expulsion of the scapegoat.[40] Girard recognized that these stereotypes are present across various examples of scapegoating in ancient mythology and medieval texts. Two or more of

31. Because the present study does not necessarily accept Girard's assumption concerning the link between imitation and sacrifice, the term 'mimetic crisis' is used to refer to what Girard calls a 'sacrificial crisis'.
32. Palaver, *René Girard's Mimetic Theory*, 136.
33. Girard, *The Scapegoat*, 13.
34. Girard, *Violence and the Sacred*, 52–5.
35. Girard, Oughourlian, and Lefort, *Things Hidden*, 24–7.
36. Palaver, *René Girard's Mimetic Theory*, 152.
37. Kenneth Burke, *Permanence and Change: An Anatomy of Purpose*, 3rd edn (Berkeley: University of California Press, 1984), 16.
38. Kenneth Burke, *The Rhetoric of Religion: Studies in Logology* (Berkeley: University of California Press, 1970), 191.
39. Girard, *Violence and the Sacred*.
40. Girard, *The Scapegoat*, 12–20.

these stereotypes within a given text is sufficient, according to Girard, to identify the scapegoat mechanism.[41] In what follows, I briefly outline Girard's four scapegoat stereotypes, and how they are reflected within the Pentateuchal texts concerning human immolation.

The first stereotype is the mimetic crisis, which is commonly portrayed through violence and/or imagery of natural disasters, including floods and plagues.[42] Excessive mimetic rivalry prompts the community to search for a scapegoat to blame for the crisis. Eventually, blame is assigned, as rampant imitation causes the community's accusations to converge upon a single target. This process divides the community into two groups: the scapegoat or collection of scapegoats, referred to as the outgroup, and the rest of the community, or ingroup. The ingroup corresponds to Kaminsky's elect category, discussed in the previous chapter, while the outgroup corresponds to his anti-elect category. The remainder of this project lays aside Kaminsky's terminology in favour of Girard's dualistic ingroup–outgroup model, which is better suited to the study of human immolation with the Pentateuch.[43] Yet, this book retains the insight, presented in the previous chapter, that throughout the Pentateuch a bitter rivalry rages between the ingroup and the outgroup.

Girard's second stereotype is the blame placed upon a specific scapegoat or outgroup for the mimetic crisis by the rest of their community. This blame is often linked to an assumption that the crisis was caused by the outgroup's unacceptable behaviour. Outgroup members may be accused of violent and/or sexual offences, or simply transgressing social taboos.[44] Within the Pentateuch, many offences of this nature are considered capital crimes. Moreover, these offences are often associated with dire

---

41. Ibid., 24.
42. 'The rising of floodwater, for example, the gradual spreading of the effects of a drought, and especially the spread of contagious disease, resemble mimetic propagation… The fact that flood and epidemic serve as metaphors for mimetic violence does not mean that real floods and epidemics are not objects of religious interpretation, but that they are perceived primarily as the result of the transgression of prohibitions against mimetic behaviour…' Girard, Oughourlian, and Lefort, *Things Hidden*, 13.
43. For the purposes of the present study, Kaminsky's non-elect category is redundant because the texts concerning human immolation within the Pentateuch never involve this category. Human immolation within the Pentateuch involves the elect ingroup killing one of their own, who they identify as an anti-elect outgroup rival. For this reason, Girard's dualistic ingroup-outgroup model is better suited to the examination of human immolation within the Pentateuch.
44. Girard, *The Scapegoat*, 15.

consequences. For example, transgressing certain sexual taboos defiles the people and the land, which makes the land physically sick, and may lead to the community's expulsion from the land (Lev. 18:24-30). By using natural-disaster imagery to portray a mimetic crisis, Lev. 18:24-30 blames outgroup members for the mimetic crisis and, in so doing, satisfies Girard's second stereotype.

The third stereotype cited by Girard is what he refers to as the 'sign of victims'.[45] Although Girard views the scapegoat's selection as 'arbitrary', he also notes that scapegoats often bear a distinguishing mark, such as a limp, skin disease, or a handicap of some sort.[46] Alternatively, the scapegoat may be identified on account of their social status. Scapegoats may be selected because they are either poor or rich, or belong to a despised foreign outgroup.[47] Commonly, the scapegoat is either drawn from outside the community and integrated into the community, or selected from inside the community and depicted as an outsider. In this way, the scapegoat straddles the boundary of the community.[48] Moreover, the scapegoat, who is otherwise like everyone else within the community, is portrayed in an extremely negative light. For example, the Blasphemer's mixed Egyptian/Hebrew lineage in Lev. 24:10-23 portrays this offender as a marginal member of the community. While he is considered an Israelite on account of his Israelite mother, his Egyptian father also identifies him with Israel's primary rival throughout the Exodus narrative.[49] By identifying capital offenders with the Israel's national rivals the Pentateuch portrays these offenders in a negative light and, in so doing, encourages the persecution of this outgroup.

---

45. Girard refers to the scapegoat as the 'surrogate victim', which implies the scapegoat's innocence. According to Girard, although the scapegoat may be guilty of various crimes, they are innocent in the sense that they did not cause the mimetic crisis. To avoid confusion regarding the scapegoat's supposed guilt or innocence, the present study refers to Girard's 'surrogate victim' as the 'scapegoat'. On the concept of the innocent victim in animal and human sacrifice, see ibid. For a criticism of this view see Bruce Chilton, 'René Girard, James Williams, and the Genesis of Violence', *Bulletin for Biblical Research* 3 (1993): 17–29.

46. Girard, *The Scapegoat*, 17–18.

47. Ibid., 18–19.

48. Girard, *Violence and the Sacred*, 270–1.

49. For an explanation of matrilineal descent in the Hebrew Bible, see Shaye J. D. Cohen, 'Was Timothy Jewish (Acts 16: 1-3)? Patristic Exegesis, Rabbinic Law, and Matrilineal Descent', *Journal of Biblical Literature* (1986): 264–7.

The immolation or expulsion of outgroup members, triggered by a mimetic crisis, is Girard's fourth stereotype:

> When a community succeeds in convincing itself that one alone of its number is responsible for the violent mimesis besetting it; when it is able to view this member as the single 'polluted' enemy who is contaminating the rest; and when the citizens are truly unanimous in this conviction – then the belief becomes a reality, for there will no longer exist elsewhere in the community a form of violence to be followed or opposed, which is to say, imitated and propagated. In destroying this target victim, men believe that they are ridding themselves of some present ill… [T]he sudden restoration of peace, seemed to confirm the identification of the guilty party and also the general correctness of the diagnosis. The crisis is seen as a mysterious illness introduced into the community by an outsider. The cure lies in the ridding of the community of the sole malignant element.[50]

With the immolation of the scapegoat the mimetic crisis is halted, and order returns to the community. This process is illustrated in Guillaume de Machaut's *Judgement of the King of Navarre*, which Girard cites as an example of a text displaying all four of his stereotypes.[51]

> After that came a false, treacherous and contemptible swine: this was shameful Israel, the wicked and disloyal who hated good and loved evil, who gave so much gold and silver and promises to Christians, who then poisoned several rivers and fountains that had been clear and pure so that many lost their lives; for whosoever used them died suddenly. Certainly ten times one hundred thousand died from it, in country and in city. Then finally this mortal calamity was noticed.
>
> He who sits on high and sees far, who governs and provides for everything, did not want this treachery to remain hidden; he revealed it and made it so generally known that they lost their lives and possessions. Then every Jew was destroyed, some hanged, others burned, some were drowned, others beheaded with an axe or sword. And many Christians died together with them in shame.[52]

Girard explains his stereotypes by identifying each of them in this text. Girard's first stereotype is seen in the Black Death plague, which represents a mimetic crisis. Guillaume's narrative blames the Black Death of the fourteenth century upon the Jews, claiming that they poisoned the water supply, which satisfies Girard's second stereotype. The third

50. Girard, *Violence and the Sacred*, 81, 83.
51. Girard, *The Scapegoat*, 1–11.
52. Cited in ibid., 2.

stereotype can be observed as the Jews, a minority group with obscure customs and traditions, serve as a potential outgroup.[53] Finally, Girard's fourth stereotype is also present in Guillaume's report that 'every Jew was destroyed, some hanged, others burned; some were drowned, [and] others beheaded'. In this way, the Jewish outgroup was immolated to halt the mimetic crisis.

According to Girard, in addition to being blamed for causing the initial crisis, the scapegoat is also credited with resolving it following their execution.[54] Through this process, which Girard calls 'double transference', the scapegoat mechanism becomes culturally codified, and maintains its transcendence over time. Girard argues that the spontaneous execution of scapegoats eventually gives rise to ritual animal sacrifice, as an animal is substituted for a human victim:

> The original act of violence is unique and spontaneous. Ritual sacrifices, however, are multiple, endlessly repeated. All those aspects of the original act that had escaped man's control – the choice of time and place, the selection of the victim – are now premeditated and fixed by custom. The ritual process aims at removing all element of chance and seeks to extract from the original violence some technique of cathartic appeasement. The diluted force of the sacrificial ritual cannot be attributed to imperfections in its imitated technique. After all, the rite is designed to function during periods of relative calm; as we have seen, its role is not curative, but preventative. If it were more 'effective' than it in fact is – if it did not limit itself to appropriate sacrificial victims but instead, like the original act of violence, vented its force on a participating member of the community – then it would lose all effectiveness, for it would bring to pass the very thing it was supposed to prevent: a relapse into the sacrificial crisis. The sacrificial process is as fully adapted to its normal function as collective murder is to its abnormal and normative function. There is every reason to believe that the minor catharsis of the sacrificial act is derived from that major catharsis circumscribed by collective murder.[55]

While the current project does not assume Girard's theory concerning the origin of animal sacrifice, these comments help frame the mimetic significance of human immolation within the Pentateuch. In line with Girard's comments concerning animal sacrifice, the spontaneous act of human scapegoating may be ritualized, as the community seek to reproduce the catharsis associated with the original collective murder. By specifying

---

53. Ibid., 17–18.
54. Girard, Oughourlian, and Lefort, *Things Hidden*, 99–100.
55. Girard, *Violence and the Sacred*, 102.

the choice of victim and the mode of their execution, the Pentateuch allows the immolation of capital offenders without the random chance, danger, and chaos associated with the activation of the scapegoat mechanism within a mimetic crisis. As I shall argue, the Pentateuch facilitates communal executions by setting capital offenders apart from the rest of the community, and portraying them as a threat. Through the legally sanctioned, collective execution of these malefactors, the community prevents mimetic crises by venting excessive mimetic rivalry. For example, Deut. 22:13-21 prescribes the collective execution of the accused Unchaste Bride, who is blamed for generating a fierce rivalry between her husband and her father. In this case, a husband brings an accusation against his wife, before the elders of the city who must examine the evidence. If the accusations are found to be legitimate, the Unchaste Bride is sentenced to communal stoning at the door of her father's house. The legal procedures and communal stoning in this example establish a transcendent unanimity within the community, which allows the execution of the Unchaste Bride, without generating mimetic violence. In this manner, Pentateuchal texts which prescribe human immolation aim to prevent mimetic crises by producing a similar catharsis to that achieved through spontaneous scapegoating, without the associated danger and unpredictability of a mimetic crisis.

The Pentateuch ascribes the command to execute capital offenders to Moses and YHWH, which allows this command to maintain its transcendence over time. Girard argues that a law or system must be universally acknowledged by the community as transcendent to effectively control mimetic violence: 'As soon as the essential quality of transcendence – religious, humanistic, or whatever – is lost, there are no longer any terms by which to define the legitimate form of violence and to recognise it among the multitude of illicit forms'.[56] The weaving of the command to execute capital offenders into the Pentateuch's legal and ritual material maintains the transcendent quality of human immolation, which might have otherwise been lost. Through these means, the ritual and legal procedures outlined in connection with capital cases throughout the Pentateuch culturally codify the scapegoat mechanism and justify human immolation as a legitimate form of cathartic violence.

4. *Human Immolation and the Scapegoat Mechanism*

In this book, I examine major texts in the Pentateuch that address human immolation and argue that all of these passages exhibit at least two of Girard's four stereotypes. This observation supports my claim

56. Ibid, 24.

that the scapegoat mechanism drives human immolation within the Pentateuch. For example, Num. 25:6-8 displays Girard's four scapegoat stereotypes:

> And behold, one of the people of Israel came and brought a Midianite woman to his family, in the sight of Moses and in the sight of the whole congregation of the people of Israel, while they were weeping in the entrance of the tent of meeting. When Phinehas the son of Eleazar, son of Aaron the priest, saw it, he rose and left the congregation and took a spear in his hand and went after the man of Israel into the chamber and pierced both of them, the man of Israel and the woman through her belly. Thus the plague on the people of Israel was stopped. Nevertheless, those who died by the plague were twenty-four thousand.

In this passage, a lack of differentiation manifests as intermarriage with idolatrous Midianites, and leads to a mimetic crisis in the form of a plague. This crisis satisfies Girard's first stereotype. Girard's second stereotype is also present, as the text blames Israel's idolatry and relationships with 'the daughters of Moab' (Num. 25:1-3) for the plague. Furthermore, the daughters of Moab represent a despised foreign outgroup, which satisfies the third scapegoat stereotype. Finally, Girard's fourth stereotype may be seen as the hero, Phinehas, halts the mimetic crisis by immolating an outgroup member and his foreign wife (25:7-8). Through the immolation of outgroup members the ingroup vent their mimetic rivalries, which halts the crisis, and order is restored.

Significantly, most instances of human immolation within the Pentateuch take place between the Exodus and the Canaanite conquest. In the Exodus narrative Israel's rivalry is directed outwardly against Egypt. Similarly, towards the end of the wilderness narrative, Israel's rivalry is focused upon the Amorites, Moabites, and Midianites (Num. 21:21–25:18; 31), and Deuteronomy directs Israel's national rivalry against the Canaanites. Israel's struggle with enemy nations draws the community together as they focus their collective rivalry upon an external agent. However, during the wilderness period Israel has no external rival, which forces the community to seek another means of venting mimetic rivalry. This situation prompts the Israelites to search for scapegoats from within their own community (e.g. Lev. 24:10-23; Num. 15:32-36). The community then vents their mimetic rivalries through the immolation of these scapegoats and, in this way, the mimetic crises are resolved.

As discussed in Chapter 2, Israel maintains its identity as YHWH's children through Torah observance. In this way, Torah shapes the community's unique identity, and differentiates faithful Israel from other people groups. Moreover, Torah defines the role of individuals within the communal hierarchy, which helps maintain the established social order.[57] Torah's maintenance of national identity and social structure prevents mimetic crises by maintaining differentiation and minimizing mimetic rivalry within the community.[58] For example, the prohibition of sexual relations between close relatives, and the spouses of close relatives, minimizes the potential for rivalry between kinsmen over a sexual partner.[59] However, if these taboos are transgressed, mimetic rivalry over the sexuality of close female relatives will escalate between kinsmen, and a mimetic crisis may ensue.[60] In these situations, Torah also provides a means of venting excessive mimetic rivalry: the execution of the sexual offenders (Lev. 20:10-16). By prescribing the execution of those whose actions threaten the community's unique identity and social structure, Torah helps prevent mimetic crises.

This study argues that the Pentateuch prescribes the immolation of outgroup members as communal scapegoats. To this end, subsequent chapters present narrative readings of key texts concerning human immolation throughout the Pentateuch. By applying Girard's scapegoat stereotypes to these readings, the scapegoat mechanism is revealed within these texts, and a fresh interpretation of human immolation within the Pentateuch is generated. According to this interpretation, human immolation has a cathartic dimension as it purges mimetic rivalry from the community and draws the faithful Israelite community together at the expense of the outgroup. Through the execution of these malefactors, the community also fulfils its role as the image-bearing children of YHWH.

---

57. Saul M. Olyan, *Rites and Rank* (Princeton: Princeton University Press, 2000).

58. As Williams explains, 'those who share their life in common, in community, impinge upon one another mimetically in their similarities and differences. They are impelled to imitate one another, but if the imitation goes too far and the differences melt or are destroyed, then a sacrificial crisis of huge proportions erupts – the mimetic being must have a model or rival to imitate, else he or she will be utterly lost. The dissolution of differences impels the rage to find new differences, and in human culture the most economic way of doing that is to establish the scapegoat as the new point of differentiation. The commandments represent a sort of periphery, an outer edge of the circle that cannot be transgressed without the danger of undifferentiation, of chaos… The commandments are the boundaries forestalling the kind of mimetic crisis and violence that the story of oppression in Egypt and liberation recounts.' Williams, *The Bible, Violence, and the Sacred*, 105.

59. This concept is further explained in Chapter 7.

60. Girard, *Violence and the Sacred*, 219–21.

5. Criticisms of Girard and How the Current Study Addresses these Concerns

Although the method employed by this study draws heavily upon the work of Girard and the role of mimetic rivalry in the scapegoat mechanism, it does not adopt all of Girard's assumptions. This section discusses the difficulties with some of Girard's more problematic assumptions and conclusions, and explains how the current study addresses these problems. Many of these difficulties stem from Girard's attempt to explain the genesis of culture, ritual, and sacrifice solely through mimetic theory. According to Girard, all ancient societies were founded upon an original murder.[61] For example, Girard notes that Romulus founded Rome by killing his brother, Remus, and that Cain murders his brother, Abel, to found the Cainite community.[62] Yet, not all myths fit this framework. When confronted with myths which appear to contradict his theory, Girard claims that the author has deliberately concealed the founding murder. As Guy Lefort explains:

> The founding murder simply cannot be witnessed. This is not then a fortuitous or accidental difficulty but a logical and practical impossibility. As we have said, the only true scapegoats are those we cannot recognise as such.[63]

Unfortunately, this feature makes it impossible to either confirm or disprove Girard's founding-murder theory. Furthermore, Girard's critics have claimed that his theory depends heavily on Greek mythology, and neglects Eastern religions.[64] However, Girard has applied mimetic theory to Eastern religions in his more recent work.[65] Others have also applied

---

61. Girard, Oughourlian, and Lefort, *Things Hidden*, 105–25. For a critique of Girard's conclusions regarding the central role of mimesis and the scapegoat mechanism in the conception of sacrifice and culture, see John Milbank, 'Stories of Sacrifice: From Wellhausen to Girard', *Theory, Culture & Society* 12, no. 4 (1995): 32–44.

62. Girard, Oughourlian, and Lefort, *Things Hidden*, 38–9, 146–7.

63. Ibid., 129.

64. David A. Bernat and Jonathan Klawans, *Religion and Violence: The Biblical Heritage* (Sheffield: Sheffield Phoenix, 2007), 5.

65. René Girard, *Sacrifice René Girard; Translated by Matthew Pattillo and David Dawson*, trans. Matthew Pattillo and David Dawson (East Lansing: Michigan State University Press, 2011). Although this application has also been criticized. Roberto Calasso, *Ardor* (New York: Macmillan, 2014), 348–9.

mimetic theory to speculate on the origin of diverse ancient religions.[66] Yet, in spite of the growing support for Girard's founding murder theory in recent years, this theory remains impossible to verify.[67] For these reasons, the present study does not assume Girard's founding murder theory.

Similarly, this book does not assume Girard's theory on the origin and function of sacrifice. According to Girard, animal sacrifice represents a double substitution.[68] The first substitution is performed when the scapegoat mechanism compels the community to halt the mimetic crisis, and restore peace and order, through the accusation and execution of a single scapegoat. Girard postulates that in time the ritual evolves, and a second substitution is made: an animal is executed and offered in the place of a human scapegoat. He then extrapolates his theory to argue that all sacrifice, across all time and cultures, represents a double substitution.[69] Although Girard's theory of sacrifice appears to resonate well with the substitution of people for animals in select verses of the Hebrew Bible, such as Lev. 17:11, it fails to explain the P source's conception of blood as a detergent which removes impurity.[70] Furthermore, the focus of animal sacrifice within the Hebrew Bible is often the consumption of a meal,

---

66. Wolfgang Palaver and Richard Schenk, *Mimetic Theory and World Religions* (East Lansing: Michigan State University Press, 2017); Brian Collins, 'The Eastern Revolution: From the Vedas to Buddhism, Jainism, and the Upanishads', in Alison et al., eds, *The Palgrave Handbook of Mimetic Theory and Religion*, 111–17.

67. For this reason, Hayden White claims that Girard's application of mimetic theory is unscientific: 'Girard explains too much. What is lacking, in his work…are any criteria of falsifiability, any specification of the kind of data one would have to produce in order to disprove his contentions about the nature of religion, society, sacrifice, myths, and so forth. There is nothing about culture and society that Girard's theories cannot predict. In this respect, they are exactly like any religious system or any metaphysical one. This does not make them useless, but it is fatal to the claim of scientificity.' Hayden White, 'Ethnological "Lie" and Mythical "Truth"', *Diacritics* 8, no. 1 (1978): 7.

68. Girard, *Violence and the Sacred*, 101–2.

69. Ibid., 101–2.

70. For more on the conception of blood as a detergent of disinfectant which removes impurity, see Jacob Milgrom, 'Israel's Sanctuary: The Priestly "Picture of Dorian Gray"', *Revue biblique* 83, no. 3 (1796): 390–9; William K. Gilders, *Blood Ritual in the Hebrew Bible: Meaning and Power* (Baltimore: Johns Hopkins University Press, 2004), 130; Baruch J. Schwartz, 'The Bearing of Sin in the Priestly Literature', in *Pomegranates and Golden Bells: Studies in Biblical, Jewish, and Near Eastern Ritual, Law, and Literature in Honor of Jacob Milgrom*, ed. David P. Wright et al. (Winona Lake: Eisenbrauns, 1995), 4–21.

rather than an act of violent slaughter as Girard assumes.[71] Moreover, like his founding murder theory, Girard's explanation of sacrifice remains impossible to verify. In light of these observations, the present study leaves behind Girard's theory of sacrifice to concentrate upon the role of human immolation within the Pentateuch.

Although at times Girard appears to argue that *all* desire is conceived through mimesis, he does acknowledge the role of other factors in this process.[72] The inability of mimetic theory to explain the genesis of all desire has been noted by Joshua Landy, who cites the example of parents struggling to convince their child to eat Brussels sprouts:

> You can't get a child to want to eat brussels sprouts, because this kind of desire depends on liking, and children just don't like brussels sprouts. They do not get all their desires from parents (even in such a wonderfully closed environment, with so little outside stimulus). They can see their parents eagerly eating healthy food till the cows come home, but they will stand right by their decision to yell for marshmallows.[73]

As Landy notes, the maintenance of desire relies upon the subject favourably experiencing the object in question. If the subject does not enjoy imitating their model, he or she is unlikely to continue this imitation in the absence of another motivation.[74] A child may initially imitate their parents by eating brussels sprouts, but if the child experiences their consumption of the sprouts as unpleasant, any initial desire will be transformed into aversion. Landy's article does not disprove mimetic theory,

---

71. Chilton, 'René Girard, James Williams, and the Genesis of Violence', 26; Luc De Heusch, *Sacrifice in Africa: A Structuralist Approach* (Manchester: Manchester University Press, 1985), 16–17.

72. Cynthia L. Haven, *Evolution of Desire: A Life of René Girard* (East Lansing: Michigan State University Press, 2018), 95; James G. Williams, *The Girard Reader* (New York: Crossroad, 1996), 64; René Girard and Raymund Schwager, *René Girard and Raymund Schwager Correspondence 1974–1991*, trans. Chris Fleming and Sheelah Treflé Hidden (London: Bloomsbury Academic, 2016), 109–10.

73. Joshua Landy, 'Deceit, Desire, and the Literature Professor: Why Girardians Exist', *Republics of Letters* 3 (2012): 9.

74. For example, many people undergo various unpleasant exercises, surgery, and gustatory experiences in pursuit of better health and fitness. In these cases, the desire for the goal must outweigh the unpleasantness of the experience for the subject to continue. The child in Landy's example, however, cannot comprehend the health benefits of brussels sprouts and, for this reason, refuses to imitate their parents.

but cautions against the temptation to laud mimesis as the sole mechanism behind the kindling of *all* desire.⁷⁵

The inability of mimetic theory to explain all desire in isolation from other factors is further highlighted by Toril Moi's critique of Girard's work. Moi offers three central criticisms of Girard's mimetic theory. First, many of Girard's textual analyses focus upon the desires of two male rivals, who struggle with each other for the affection of a female. This framework, which reduces the female to a mere object of desire, overlooks feminine desire.⁷⁶ Second, Moi argues that by explaining the Oedipus complex through his mimetic theory Girard devalues the mother, who he assumes 'cannot possibly be desired for "herself." Her whole value resides in her status as an object for the father. This, of course, is the logical implication of Girard's triangular theory.'⁷⁷ Third, according to Moi, Girard's model cannot explain the pre-oedipal phase of development.⁷⁸ Moi's criticism of Girard's mimetic model highlights that other factors are often at play in the genesis of desire, and that mimetic theory *alone* cannot explain the genesis of all desire. Girard, himself, concedes this point:

> The mimetic is not mono-causal; it is rather a principle of complexity. To people who say 'is there only mimetic desire?' I reply that the answer is probably [sans doute] 'no', and that, in any event, that isn't what interests me. What interests me are the consequences of mimetic desire for the linking [sur les rapports] of individuals and societies.⁷⁹

---

75. Trevor Cribben Merrill too readily dismisses Landy's comments. Merrill claims that Landy's article presents an 'unintentionally humorous double standard that casts doubt on its polemical conclusions: every example of imitation Landy gives applies to docile university professors caught up in trends they fail to perceive as such, while his counter-examples of spontaneous desires uninfluenced by a Girardian "mediator" involve his own predilections for various leisure activities'. Trevor Cribben Merrill, 'Critiques of Girard's Mimetic Theory', in Alison et al., eds, *The Palgrave Handbook of Mimetic Theory and Religion*, 457–8.

76. Toril Moi, 'The Missing Mother: The Oedipal Rivalries of René Girard', *Diacritics: A Review of Contemporary Criticism* 12, no. 2 (1982): 23–5.

77. Ibid., 27.

78. 'If Girard's mimetic theory is applied to the preoedipal stage, one is obliged to posit the woman's desire as original, the mother's desire becomes, paradigmatic of all desire… Given that the first mimetic triangle in one's existence has the power to generate later ones, the application of the mimetic principle to preoedipality obliges us to conclude that all males would be homosexual, as a consequence of their initial imitation of the mother's desire for the father.' Ibid., 27–8.

79. Girard and Schwager, *Correspondence*, 109–10.

The current study does not assume that *all* desire is kindled through mimesis, but acknowledges that other factors, such as personal likes and dislikes, also play a role in mediating desire.[80] That said, this book concentrates upon the role played by mimetic rivalry in the Pentateuch's treatment of human immolation and, in so doing, avoids the danger of falling into reductionism.

Some have criticised Girard's work on a textual basis. For example, Robert Greer Cohn claims that Girard's mimetic theory is based on characters, such as those presented by Dostoevsky and Cervantes, which are either 'unbalanced' or 'exaggerated'.[81] However, while the rivalry between these characters may be somewhat exaggerated, Girard also demonstrates his theory in the work of Shakespeare, whose characters cannot be considered 'unbalanced' or 'exaggerated'.[82] Still others have argued that mimetic theory imposes its own agenda upon the text, to produce the same predictable readings regardless of the text's content. For example, Françoise Meltzer claims that Girard, through his mimetic framework, reads the scandal of scapegoats and substitutions into every text.[83] In a similar vein, Elizabeth Taube argues that through his mimetic framework Girard anachronistically re-assembles mythical fragments to produce readings that are at odds with the cultures in which these myths were forged.[84] These critiques sound a clear warning against anachronistically imposing mimetic theory upon texts. The present study hopes to avoid this error by anchoring itself firmly within the literary context of the Pentateuchal tradition, through the employment of a synchronic, narrative approach to texts concerned with human immolation.

---

80. Robert Greer Cohn criticizes Girard's mimetic theory as 'unidimensional' because it overlooks other factors which play a role in the genesis of desire. Robert Greer Cohn, 'Desire: Direct and Imitative', *Philosophy Today* 33, no. 4 (1989): 319. Yet, many mimetic theorists, like James Warren, acknowledge that genetics and biology also play a role in the genesis of desire. James Warren, *Compassion or Apocalypse, A Comprehensible Guide to the Thought of René Girard* (Washington: Christian Alternative, 2013), 18–19.

81. Cohn, 'Desire: Direct and Imitative', 323.

82. Richard Golsan, 'Girard's Critics and the Girardians', in *Rene Girard and Myth: An Introduction* (New York: Routledge, 2014), 116.

83. Françoise Meltzer, 'A Response to René Girard's Reading of Salome', *New Literary History* 15, no. 2 (1984): 325–32.

84. Elizabeth Traube, 'Incest and Mythology: Anthropological and Girardian Perspectives', *Berkshire Review* 14 (1979): 49.

Another charge levelled at Girard is that his work is overtly evolutionist, ethnocentric, and supersessionist in its slant.[85] For example, critics have labelled Girard supersessionist on account of his assertion that animal sacrifice is obsolete and inferior to modern judicial systems, which, according to Girard, are 'the most effective of all curative procedures'.[86] Girard's critics have also regarded his work as evolutionist and ethnocentric because he argues that the scapegoat mechanism is only clearly unveiled through the Christian Gospels.[87] For Girard, the Gospels' full revelation of mimetic violence is progressively unfolded within the Hebrew Bible, which Girard describes as 'a text in travail'.[88] Although he discerned the outworking of mimetic violence in the scapegoating of both Moses and Job, as Chris Flemming notes, Girard's paradigm assumes that 'the progressive undermining of sacred violence undertaken in the Hebrew Bible is brought to completion in the Gospels'.[89] The current

---

85. Jonathan Klawans, *Purity, Sacrifice, and the Temple: Symbolism and Supersessionism in the Study of Ancient Judaism* (Oxford: Oxford University Press, 2006), 24–5; De Heusch, *Sacrifice in Africa*, 16–17; Traube, 'Incest and Mythology'.

86. Girard, *Violence and the Sacred*, 20–1.

87. Ninian Smart, 'Review of Violence and the Sacred, by Rene Girard', *Religious Studies Review* 6, no. 3 (1980): 174; Bernat and Klawans, *Religion and Violence*, 5. Scubla claims that six hundred years prior to Jesus 'the Orphic tradition condemned with vigor all forms of blood sacrifice and already reproached men with having founded their polis on murder, not only in the myth of the dismemberment of Dionysus by the Titans but also in the story of Orpheus, peace making hero and bard of non-violence, savagely lynched for having denounced the pernicious character of sacrificial rites'. Scubla goes on to argue that while the Orphic tradition is *anti-sacrificial*, Christianity represents 'the first, and perhaps the only, *non-sacrificial* religion of humanity'. Lucien Scubla, 'The Christianity of Réne Girard and the Nature of Religion', in *Violence and Truth: On the Work of Rene Girard*, ed. Paul Dumochel (Stanford: Stanford University Press, 1988), 161, 63.

88. René Girard, 'Generative Scapegoating', in *Violent Origins: Walter Burkert, René Girard, and Jonathan Z. Smith on Ritual Killing and Cultural Formation*, ed. Robert G. Hamerton-Kelly (Stanford: Stanford University Press, 1987), 141.

89. René Girard, *Job, the Victim of His People* (London: Athlone, 1987), and *The Scapegoat*, 178; Chris Flemming, *René Girard: Violence and Mimesis* (Cambridge: Polity, 2004), 124. Within this paradigm, the book of Second Maccabees, which was written in the intertestamental period, could be considered somewhat of a bridge from the Hebrew Bible to the Christian Gospels, as it presents the model of sacrificial martyrdom adopted by the Gospel writers in their presentation of Jesus' death. As both Jon Levenson and Bruce Chilton have argued, the portrayal of Jesus in the Christian Gospels builds upon the concept of martyrdom developed in the Second Maccabees, in which the innocent victim dies to save the community. Bruce Chilton, *Abraham's Curse: The Roots of Violence in Judaism, Christianity, and Islam* (New

project takes a slightly different approach to that adopted by Girard, by reading the Pentateuch as an independent literary tradition in its own right, rather than part of the greater Christian Tradition. By focusing upon mimetic rivalry, excessive levels of which activate the scapegoat mechanism in both the ancient practice of human immolation and modern capital punishment, this study does not elevate the Hebrew Bible (or Christian Gospels) above other ancient texts, but rather examines the Pentateuch as a compilation of source documents, which have been edited and redacted within an ancient, literary context.[90] In so doing, this book hopes to avoid the charges of evolutionism, ethnocentrism, and supersessionism that have been directed towards Girard's work.

6. *Conclusion*

This chapter has presented the method which will be employed in the following chapters to examine human immolation within key texts throughout the Pentateuch. By applying Girard's scapegoat stereotypes to my narrative reading of these texts, the current study argues that outgroup members are immolated within the Pentateuch to vent mimetic rivalry and, in so doing, restore peace and order within the community. An example of this process may be observed in Lev. 24:10-23. In this text, a man who blasphemes and fights with an Israelite ingroup member is immolated by communal stoning, which allows the community to vent their mimetic rivalries. This narrative is examined in the next chapter.

York: Doubleday, 2008); Jon D. Levenson, *The Death and Resurrection of the Beloved Son: The Transformation of Child Sacrifice in Judaism and Christianity* (New Haven: Yale University Press, 1995).

90. For the role of the scapegoat mechanism in the modern practice of capital punishment, see Harding, 'Capital Punishment as Human Sacrifice'; Smith, 'Capital Punishment and Human Sacrifice'.

Chapter 4

THE BLASPHEMER OF LEVITICUS 24:10-23

This chapter applies Girard's mimetic theory to a narrative reading of Lev. 24:10-23. In so doing, I shall identify the Blasphemer of Lev. 24:10-23 as a communal scapegoat, who is immolated to halt a mimetic crisis. This insight generates a fresh reading of Lev. 24:10-23, which is developed over three sections. The first section reveals the scapegoat mechanism within this text through the application of Girard's four scapegoat stereotypes. Second, vv. 15b-16 are examined as a casuistic legal formula arising out of mimetic crisis, which may be applied to future acts of blasphemy, to minimize mimetic rivalry within the community. Finally, vv. 17-22 are investigated as a means of justifying the Blasphemer's immolation. As I shall argue, the Blasphemer's actions threaten the ingroup's ability to faithfully reflect the divine image. For this reason, the ingroup stones the Blasphemer, which restores peace and order to the community.

The text of Lev. 24:10-23 reads:

[10] Now an Israelite woman's son, whose father was an Egyptian, went out among the people of Israel. And the Israelite woman's son and a man of Israel fought in the camp,	וַיֵּצֵא בֶּן־אִשָּׁה יִשְׂרְאֵלִית וְהוּא בֶּן־אִישׁ מִצְרִי בְּתוֹךְ בְּנֵי יִשְׂרָאֵל וַיִּנָּצוּ בַּמַּחֲנֶה בֶּן הַיִּשְׂרְאֵלִית וְאִישׁ הַיִּשְׂרְאֵלִי׃
[11] and the Israelite woman's son blasphemed the Name, and cursed. Then they brought him to Moses. His mother's name was Shelomith, the daughter of Dibri, of the tribe of Dan.	וַיִּקֹּב בֶּן־הָאִשָּׁה הַיִּשְׂרְאֵלִית אֶת־הַשֵּׁם וַיְקַלֵּל וַיָּבִיאוּ אֹתוֹ אֶל־מֹשֶׁה וְשֵׁם אִמּוֹ שְׁלֹמִית בַּת־דִּבְרִי לְמַטֵּה־דָן׃
[12] And they put him under guard, till the will of YHWH should be clear to them.	וַיַּנִּיחֻהוּ בַּמִּשְׁמָר לִפְרֹשׁ לָהֶם עַל־פִּי יְהוָה׃
[13] Then YHWH spoke to Moses, saying,	וַיְדַבֵּר יְהוָה אֶל־מֹשֶׁה לֵּאמֹר׃
[14] 'Bring out of the camp the one who cursed,	הוֹצֵא אֶת־הַמְקַלֵּל אֶל־מִחוּץ לַמַּחֲנֶה

and let all who heard him lay their hands	וְסָמְכוּ כָל־הַשֹּׁמְעִים אֶת־יְדֵיהֶם
on his head, and let all the congregation stone him.	עַל־רֹאשׁוֹ וְרָגְמוּ אֹתוֹ כָּל־הָעֵדָה:
¹⁵ᵃ And speak to the people of Israel, saying,	וְאֶל־בְּנֵי יִשְׂרָאֵל תְּדַבֵּר לֵאמֹר
¹⁵ᵇ Whoever curses his God shall bear his sin.	אִישׁ אִישׁ כִּי־יְקַלֵּל אֱלֹהָיו וְנָשָׂא חֶטְאוֹ:
¹⁶ Whoever blasphemes the name of the LORD	וְנֹקֵב שֵׁם־יְהוָה
shall surely be put to death.	מוֹת יוּמָת
All the congregation shall stone him.	רָגוֹם יִרְגְּמוּ־בוֹ כָּל־הָעֵדָה
The sojourner as well as the native,	כַּגֵּר כָּאֶזְרָח
when he blasphemes the Name,	בְּנָקְבוֹ־שֵׁם
shall be put to death.	יוּמָת:
¹⁷ Whoever takes a human life	וְאִישׁ כִּי יַכֶּה כָּל־נֶפֶשׁ אָדָם
shall surely be put to death.	מוֹת יוּמָת
¹⁸ Whoever takes an animal's life	וּמַכֵּה נֶפֶשׁ־בְּהֵמָה
shall make it good, life for life.	יְשַׁלְּמֶנָּה נֶפֶשׁ תַּחַת נָפֶשׁ:
¹⁹ If anyone injures his neighbour,	וְאִישׁ כִּי־יִתֵּן מוּם בַּעֲמִיתוֹ
as he has done it shall be done to him,	כַּאֲשֶׁר עָשָׂה כֵּן יֵעָשֶׂה לּוֹ:
²⁰ fracture for fracture, eye for eye,	שֶׁבֶר תַּחַת שֶׁבֶר עַיִן תַּחַת עַיִן
tooth for tooth	שֵׁן תַּחַת שֵׁן
whatever injury he has given a person	כַּאֲשֶׁר יִתֵּן מוּם בָּאָדָם
shall be given to him.	כֵּן יִנָּתֶן בּוֹ:
²¹ Whoever kills an animal shall make it good,	וּמַכֵּה בְהֵמָה יְשַׁלְּמֶנָּה
and whoever kills a person shall be put to death.	וּמַכֵּה אָדָם יוּמָת:
²² You shall have the same rule	מִשְׁפַּט אֶחָד יִהְיֶה לָכֶם
for the sojourner and for the native,	כַּגֵּר כָּאֶזְרָח יִהְיֶה
for I am YHWH your God.'	אֲנִי יְהוָה אֱלֹהֵיכֶם:
²³ So Moses spoke to the people of Israel,	וַיְדַבֵּר מֹשֶׁה אֶל־בְּנֵי יִשְׂרָאֵל
and they brought out of the camp the one who had cursed	וַיּוֹצִיאוּ אֶת־הַמְקַלֵּל אֶל־מִחוּץ לַמַּחֲנֶה
and stoned him with stones.	וַיִּרְגְּמוּ אֹתוֹ אָבֶן
Thus the people of Israel did	וּבְנֵי־יִשְׂרָאֵל עָשׂוּ
as YHWH commanded Moses.	כַּאֲשֶׁר צִוָּה יְהוָה אֶת־מֹשֶׁה:

1. *The Blasphemer Prose (Leviticus 24:10-14, 23)*

Scholars have argued that the phrase כגר כאזרח in Lev. 24:16 and 22 suggests that Lev. 24:10-23 addresses, among other things, the question of whether or not foreigners should be subject to laws concerning blasphemy.[1] This assumption has led to Lev. 24:10-23 being labelled a

---

1. Cf. Jacob Milgrom, *Leviticus 23–27*, AB 3B (New York: Doubleday, 2001), 2119; Leigh M. Trevaskis, 'The Purpose of Leviticus 24 within Its Literary Context', *Vetus Testamentum* 59, no. 2 (2009): 295–312; Jonathan Vroom, 'Recasting Mišpāṭîm:

'hard case', which necessitates the divine oracle delivered in vv. 13-14.[2] According to this oracle, whether it is committed by a native Israelite or a foreigner, blasphemy threatens the divine name and the community's wellbeing. Having received this guidance the community can now proceed with the proper course of action, immolating the Blasphemer. The 'hard case' approach to Lev. 24:10-23 assumes that the community are ignorant of how to deal with the Blasphemer on account of his mixed lineage. For example, Bryan Bibb argues that the community 'are not sure what to do in the situation, probably because the offender is not a full Israelite…and hence an alien in the camp, who blasphemes and curses (Yahweh)'.[3]

However, the 'hard case' approach to Lev. 24:10-23 is somewhat problematic. Although the Blasphemer's Egyptian father may place him on the fringe of the community, he is still regarded as a native Israelite, and not a גר, because of his Israelite mother.[4] Verses 10-11 support this reading by referring to the Blasphemer as the 'the Israelite woman's son' three times. These verses also cite the name and tribe of the Blasphemer's mother, which further emphasizes his Israelite lineage. In contrast, the Blasphemer's Egyptian father is mentioned only once with no further details. In this way, Lev. 24:10-11 portrays the Blasphemer as a native Israelite, who happens to have an Egyptian father. Once the Blasphemer is recognized as a native Israelite, Lev. 24:10-23 can no longer be considered a 'hard case' on account of the Blasphemer's legal status. Yet, the Blasphemer's lineage should not be overlooked, especially since Lev. 24:10-11 goes to great lengths to emphasize this detail.[5] Below, I present

---

Legal Innovation in Leviticus 24:10–23', *Journal of Biblical Literature* 131, no. 1 (2012): 27–44; Bryan D. Bibb, *Ritual Words and Narrative Worlds in the Book of Leviticus* (New York: T&T Clark, 2009), 154–5; Rodney R. Hutton, 'Narrative in Leviticus: The Case of the Blaspheming Son (Lev 24, 10-23)', *Zeitschrift für Altorientalische und Biblische Rechtsgeschichte* 3 (1997): 160.

2. Vroom, 'Recasting Mišpāṭîm', 1.

3. Bibb, *Ritual Words and Narrative Worlds*, 154.

4. Shaye J. D. Cohen argues that although the Jewish concept of matrilineal descent (cf. *m. Qidd.* 3:12) can only be traced as far back as the first century CE, in the biblical era Jewish heritage was traced in a matrilineal fashion as long as the child remained part of the Israelite community. Therefore, the Blasphemer, as the offspring of an Israelite woman who lived within the community would have been considered an אזרח. However, according to Cohen, 'when the Israelite woman moved abroad to join her Gentile husband, her children were considered Gentile'. Cohen, 'Was Timothy Jewish?', 264–7.

5. Trevaskis, 'The Purpose of Leviticus 24', 308.

a fresh reading of Lev. 24:10-23 which investigates the importance of the Blasphemer's Egyptian father, while acknowledging the Blasphemer's legal standing as a native Israelite.

1.1. Girard's First Stereotype

In what follows, I apply Girard's four stereotypes to Lev. 24:10-23, and show how the scapegoat mechanism is present in this text. Girard's first stereotype, the mimetic crisis, is indicated by the lack of differentiation and excessive mimetic rivalry within Lev. 24:10-23. This lack of differentiation and excessive rivalry is revealed through a narrative reading of this text, which acknowledges the shared imagery between the events of Lev. 24:10-23 and Exod. 2:11-15. In what follows, I explain how the Exodus narrative, in particular Exod. 2:11-15, portrays a mimetic crisis. By employing the narrative approach I shall then argue that Lev. 24:10-23 echoes this imagery to portray a similar mimetic crisis. In this way, I argue that the narrative of Lev. 24:10-23 assumes a community undergoing a mimetic crisis and that this text satisfies Girard's first stereotype.

As discussed in the previous chapter, mimetic crises are characterized by excessive mimetic rivalry and a lack of differentiation, as the social hierarchy breaks down. These features are all present in the Exodus narrative.[6] Excessive levels of mimetic rivalry are depicted by the natural-disaster imagery of the Exodus narrative.[7] Mimetic rivalry can also be observed in Pharaoh's decree to kill all the Hebrew male infants (Exod. 1:15-22), which is eventually imitated by YHWH on the Passover evening, when all the Egyptian firstborn are slain (Exod. 12:1-30). Furthermore, the eventual emancipation of Pharaoh's Israelite slave force represents a breakdown of the established social order, and heralds a lack of differentiation, as the distinction between slave and master is dissolved. By these means, the Exodus Narrative depicts a nations undergoing a mimetic crisis.

---

6. Simon Skidmore, 'A Mimetic Reading of Exodus 4:24–26', *The Heythrop Journal* (2021): 3–6.

7. As Girard argues, 'the rising of floodwater, for example, the gradual spreading of the effects of a drought, and especially the spread of contagious disease, resemble mimetic propagation… The fact that flood and epidemic serve as metaphors for mimetic violence does not mean that real floods and epidemics are not objects of religious interpretation, but that they are perceived primarily as the result of the transgression of prohibitions against mimetic behaviour…' Girard, Oughourlian, and Lefort, *Things Hidden*, 13.

Propagation of mimetic rivalry may also be seen in Exod. 2:11-15. In this text, Moses 'goes out (יצא) to his people' and sees an Egyptian striking an Israelite (Exod. 2:11). Moses intervenes on behalf of 'his brother', kills the Egyptian, and buries him in the sand (v. 12). Through the ingroup qualifiers 'his people' and 'his brother', the text identifies Moses as part of the Israelite ingroup. The next day, however, Moses witnesses a similar incident, but this time two Israelites are fighting (נצה). Moses rebukes the guilty party, asking 'Why are you striking your neighbour?' (v. 13). Although Moses is willing to slay a hostile Egyptian, he refuses to treat a hostile Israelite in the same manner (vv. 14-15). According to Moses, hostility should never be directed towards fellow ingroup members (v. 13), but only towards outgroup rivals (vv. 11-12). The Hebrew man then directs his rivalry towards Moses by asking: 'who made you a prince and a judge over us? Do you mean to slay me as you slayed the Egyptian?' (v. 14). The willingness of the Israelites to engage in rivalry with both Moses and other fellow Israelites, in a way that mirrors their rivalry with their Egyptian oppressors, portrays the lack of differentiation and excessive mimetic rivalry which characterizes a mimetic crisis.

Leviticus 24:10-23 echoes the imagery of Exod. 2:11-15 to portray a similar mimetic crisis through the employment of multiple shared terms within a similar context.[8] This context is set up by the actions of the Blasphemer in Lev. 24:10, as he 'goes out (יצא) among the people of Israel', which mirrors those of Moses in Exod. 2:11. Next, the Blasphemer is observed fighting (נצה) with an unnamed Israelite man (Lev. 24:10), just as Moses observes two fellow Israelites fighting (נצה) in Exod. 2:13. This fighting portrays a lack of differentiation and an excess of violence within the community, which indicates a mimetic crisis. Furthermore, both texts deal with Moses' role as a judge within the community, albeit in different way. While Moses' fellow Israelites question his role in Exod. 2:14, in Lev. 24:11 the community accept Moses' role, as they seek his judgment concerning the Blasphemer. Moreover, in both passages the protagonists are removed from the community. In Exod. 2:15 Moses flees, and in Lev. 24:23 the Blasphemer is brought outside the camp and stoned. Through these echoes, Lev. 24:10-23 echoes the imagery of Exod. 2:11-15 and communicates the presence of a similar mimetic crisis, which satisfies Girard's first stereotype.

---

8. This observation satisfies Hayes' second criterion for biblical echoes. See Chapter 3.

1.2. *Girard's Second and Third Stereotypes*

Girard's second stereotype sees the community search for a scapegoat to blame for the mimetic crisis. In Lev. 24:11-12 the community bring the Blasphemer to Moses, and place him under guard as they await divine revelation concerning the appropriate course of action. Although at this stage in the narrative the community may be unsure of what to do next, they bring the Blasphemer to Moses because they have identified him as the cause of the crisis. This sentiment is echoed by the Blasphemer's actions, as they are recorded in Lev. 24:10-11. In this text, the Blasphemer is the aggressor and agent of violence, who assaults his fellow Israelite, blasphemes, and curses. Once the crowd identifies the Blasphemer as the cause of the crisis, Moses then confirms the community's judgment through a divine oracle (vv. 13-14). In this way, Lev. 24:10-23 blames the Blasphemer for the mimetic crisis within this text, and satisfies Girard's second stereotype.

Girard's third stereotype may also be seen in the Blasphemer's marginal status, which functions as the sign of the victim. The Blasphemer's mixed lineage portrays him as straddling the boundary of the Israelite community.[9] While the Blasphemer's Israelite mother identifies him with the Israelite community, his Egyptian father serves as a point of separation from the community. Moreover, the Blasphemer's identification with Egypt, Israel's primary nemesis throughout the Exodus narrative, associates him with a despised, foreign outgroup.[10] Furthermore, although the Blasphemer is identified as the son of an Israelite woman, named 'Peace, daughter of my word' (v. 11), his actions are those of a violent outsider. The Blasphemer's portrayal in this text is significant because, according to Girard, a human scapegoat must be 'simultaneously good and evil, peaceable and violent, a life that brings death and a death that brings life'.[11] The Blasphemer's status as both an insider and an outsider,

---

9. Baruch A. Levine, *Leviticus*, The JPS Torah Commentary (Philadelphia: Jewish Publication Society, 1989), 166; Bibb, *Ritual Words and Narrative Worlds*, 153–65; Deborah W. Rooke, 'The Blasphemer (Leviticus 24): Gender, Identity and Boundary Construction', in *Text, Time, and Temple: Literary, Historical and Ritual Studies in Leviticus*, ed. Francis Landy, Leigh M. Trevaskis, and Bryan D. Bibb (Sheffield: Sheffield Phoenix, 2015).

10. As F. V. Greifenhagen notes, 'On the Pentateuch's cognitive map, Egypt thus functions not only as [the] embodiment of that which is adverse and must be repulsed, but also as a mark of the anxiety, ambiguity and contingency of identity itself'. Greifenhagen, *Egypt on the Pentateuch's Ideological Map*, 263.

11. Girard, Oughourlian, and Lefort, *Things Hidden*, 102.

both good and bad, peaceable and violent, places him in a position that straddles these categories, which satisfies Girard's third stereotype, and identifies him as an ideal scapegoat.

The Blasphemer's actions further emphasize his marginal status as they associate him with his Egyptian heritage. Much discussion has taken place over the statement in v. 11, that 'the Israelite woman's son blasphemed (נקב) the name and cursed (קלל)'. As Bryan Bibb notes, 'the irony of blasphemy laws is that one cannot usually define what is meant by the blasphemy due to the text's reluctance to speak plainly about it'.[12] Despite this difficulty, the Blasphemer's actions depict him as a dangerous, foreign influence. Although the נקב and קלל of 'the name' appear to be victimless crimes, they 'strike at the moral and religious fibers which the community as a whole sees as defining its essence and integrity'.[13] Furthermore, as the narrative approach notes, the use of קלל in Lev. 24:11 confirms the Blasphemer's outgroup status, as it echoes YHWH's words to Abraham in Gen. 12:3: 'whoever קלל you I will curse (ארר)'. The term קלל also associates the Blasphemer with the serpent's offspring, who are likewise cursed (Gen. 3:15), and identifies him as a dangerous outgroup rival. This danger is realized when the Blasphemer fights with his nameless rival (v. 10). By attacking this person, the Blasphemer engages in rivalry with anybody and everybody within the Israelite community. Moreover, the Blasphemer's assault upon 'the name', attacks the ingroup and their values. In this way, the Blasphemer threatens the ingroup's ability to faithfully reflect the divine image.

1.3. *Girard's Fourth Stereotype*

Girard's fourth stereotype, the immolation or expulsion of the scapegoat from the community, can be seen in the Blasphemer's stoning (v. 23), which allows the community to vent their mimetic rivalries. Importantly, the Pentateuch describes stoning as a mimetic activity. The mimetic nature of communal stoning is emphasized by Deut. 17:2-7, which commands that if someone 'does what is evil in the sight of YHWH' they must be brought outside the community and stoned. 'The hand of the witnesses shall be first against him to put him to death, and afterward the hand of all the people' (v. 7; see also Deut. 13:9-10). The *Mishnah* further emphasizes

---

12. Bibb, *Ritual Words and Narrative Worlds*, 153–4. For a discussion of the various interpretations of the Blasphemer's actions, see Rodney R. Hutton, 'The Case of the Blasphemer Revisited (Lev. XXIV 10-23)', *Vetus Testamentum* 49, no. 4 (1999): 532–41.

13. Finkelstein, 'The Ox that Gored', 28.

this mimetic element, stating that in cases of blasphemy one of the witnesses must push the offender over a cliff. If he or she does not die through this act, a second witness shall drop a stone onto the offender's heart. This action is then repeated by the entire community until the offender dies.¹⁴ As Girard notes, in the stoning ritual 'all members of the community can and should throw stones at the victim... Everyone participates in the destruction of the anathema... The group alone is responsible. Individuals share the same degree of innocence and responsibility.'¹⁵

In sum, Girard's four stereotypes can be seen in Lev. 24:10-16, 23. The identification of these stereotypes reveals the scapegoat mechanism within this text, which identifies the Blasphemer as a dangerous outgroup member who threatens the ingroup's ability to reflect the divine image. In the midst of a mimetic crisis the ingroup vent their mimetic rivalries upon the Blasphemer, and the crisis is resolved. Out of this event emerges the casuistic legal formula of vv. 15 and 16.

2. *The Casuistic Legal Formula (Leviticus 24:15-16)*

Leviticus 24:15 prescribes the נשא + חטא formula as a consequence for those who curse their god (קלל + אלהיו). Verse 16 parallels this consequence as it commands that those who 'blaspheme the name' (שם + נקב) are immolated by communal stoning. This section applies mimetic theory to a narrative reading of these verses. In so doing, I shall argue that the offences described in vv. 15-16 are illustrated by the Blasphemer in the surrounding prose, and that these verses prescribe the immolation of future scapegoats, whose actions mirror those of the Blasphemer in Lev. 24:10-23. To this end, the following section begins by outlining and critiquing previous interpretations of the נשא + חטא formula that have been offered. Next, I suggest and defend an alternative interpretation of this formula, which describes the Blasphemer's role as a communal scapegoat whose immolation restores order to the community as he 'bears his sin'. In so doing, I also discuss the use of the נשא + חטא formula in connection

---

14. *M. Sanhedrin* 6:4.
15. Girard, *The Scapegoat*, 176–7. Although Girard also claims that stoning avoids physical contact in order to minimize the risk of contamination, there is no risk of contracting impurity contagion through the hand-leaning subrite. The Pentateuch does not assert that blasphemy generates impurity, and even if it did, thanatophoric impurity cannot be contracted through physical contact. The witnesses to the crime of blasphemy can, therefore, carry out the hand-leaning subrite, in accordance with Lev. 24:14, without fear of contamination.

with the priesthood throughout the Pentateuch, and conclude that this formula describes the scapegoat's function of purging mimetic rivalry from the community. A brief discussion will then follow concerning the ritual nature of the Blasphemer's immolation, and how this nature supports the reading of Lev. 24:10-23 presented in the current chapter.

2.1. *Previous Interpretations of the* נשא + חטא *Formula*

In contrast to my reading of Lev. 24:15-16, Jacob Milgrom argues that these verses describe two separate offences with two separate penalties. According to Milgrom, the נשא + חטא formula of v. 15b describes divine retribution for a secret sin, while v. 16 describes human immolation for a publicly witnessed sin.[16] However, this interpretation is somewhat problematic. Verses 15b-16 suggest that this legal formula is drawn directly from the preceding narrative by employing the verbs נקב and קלל, which echo the description of the Blasphemer's actions in v. 11. The verbs נקב and קלל in vv. 15b-16 thus refer to the same act, modelled in the preceding narrative. Furthermore, the actions of the Blasphemer in v. 11 follow his 'going out' among the people of Israel, and are publicly witnessed, ruling out Milgrom's interpretation that v. 15b describes a secret sin and subsequent divine retribution. Therefore, Milgrom's assumption that the נשא + חטא formula of v. 15b represents a separate consequence to that reported in v. 16 is unwarranted.

Within the Pentateuch, the נשא + חטא formula is applied to a diverse set of circumstances, both public and private. For example, this formula is stipulated as a consequence of various cultic infringements, such as failing to keep the Passover (Num. 9:13), the incorrect use of Priestly tithes and 'the holy things' (Num. 18:22, 32), and for moral transgressions, such as sexual misconduct (Lev. 20:20), cursing a god (Lev. 24:15), and harbouring hatred against a fellow Israelite (Lev. 19:17). The נשא + חטא formula is, therefore, employed in connection with a range of offenses spanning both the cultic and moral realms, and the נשא + עון formula is used in a similar way.[17] Some interpret the נשא + עון/חטא formula from the perspective of punitive justice, assuming that, when applied to the offender, this formula describes a divinely appointed penalty for various crimes.[18] However, this approach cannot account for the ritual transformation which the נשא + עון/חטא formula achieves

---

16. Milgrom, *Leviticus 23–27*, 2116–17.
17. Levine, *Leviticus*, 167.
18. Ibid.; Mark F. Rooker, *The New American Commentary: Leviticus* (Nashville: Broadman & Holman, 2000), 296;

in passages such as Lev. 10:17 and 16:22.[19] For this reason, the present study rejects the interpretation of the נשא + עון/חטא formula as a form of punitive justice.

Following A. B. Ehrlich and Walther Zimmerli, Milgrom has suggested an alternative approach to the נשא + עון/חטא formula. Milgrom argues that this formula conveys the concept of bearing responsibility or punishment whenever it takes a human as its subject, but communicates the removal of iniquity when the subject is YHWH.[20] In a similar vein, Baruch Schwartz claims that the נשא + עון/חטא formula 'has two *uses*, but only one meaning'.[21] Schwartz argues that the formulas, נשא + עון, נשא + חטא (and נשא + פשע), may be used to describe guilt as a weight which is borne by an offender. In some cases, this weight may be relieved by another agent.[22] According to Schwartz, the נשא + עון/חטא formula communicates this act when it is applied to a priest.[23] Capital crimes, however, are unique in that the priests cannot relieve the guilt associated with these offences. For this reason, capital offenders must be executed.[24] Likewise, Jay Sklar argues that when the נשא + עון/חטא formula is used in connection with capital offences it should be translated as 'to bear punishment'.[25] Yet, in

---

19. Milgrom, *Leviticus 23–27*, 2116; Jay Sklar, *Sin, Impurity, Sacrifice, Atonement: The Priestly Conceptions* (Sheffield: Sheffield Phoenix, 2005), 20–3. Nobuyoshi Kiuchi, *The Purification Offering in the Priestly Literature: Its Meaning and Function* (Edinburgh: A. & C. Black, 1987), 50–1; Bernd Janowski, *Sühne Als Heilsgeschehen: Studien zur Sühnetheologie der Priesterschrift und zur Wurzel Kpr im Alten Orient und im Alten Testament* (Neukirchen-Vluyn: Neukirchener Verlag, 1982), 53 n. 362; Roy Gane, *Cult and Character: Purification Offerings, Day of Atonement, and Theodicy* (Winona Lake: Eisenbrauns, 2005), 101–5, 264–5.

20. Jacob Milgrom, *Leviticus 1–16*, AB 3A (New York: Doubleday, 1991), 622–3; D. W. Zimmerli, 'Die Eigenart der Prophetischen Rede des Ezechiel. Ein Beitrag zum Problem an Hand Von Ez. 14 1-11', *Zeitschrift für die Alttestamentliche Wissenschaft* 66, no. 1 (1954): 10; Arnold B. Ehrlich, *Randglossen zur Hebräischen Bibel: Textkritisches, Sprachliches und Sachliches, vol. 2* (Leipzig: J. C. Hinrichs, 1909), 37.

21. Schwartz, 'The Bearing of Sin in the Priestly Literature', 9.

22. Ibid., 9–10.

23. Following Schwartz, Roy Gane interprets the Priestly act of נשא + עון as 'removing iniquity', while interpreting the same formula when applied to a sinner as denoting his 'culpability, indicating that he deserves and may suffer consequences'. Gane, *Cult and Character*, 99–103. See also Angel Manuel Rodriguez, 'Substitution in the Hebrew Cultus and in Cultic-Related Texts' (PhD diss., Andrews University 1979 [available via University Microfilms International, 1986]), 131–2.

24. Ibid., 15.

25. Sklar, *Sin, Impurity, Sacrifice, Atonement*, 23.

other cases, the עון/חטא + נשא formula describes the 'remission of the penalty that sin deserves' and, depending on its context, either describes forgiveness or the removal of sin 'so that the sinner no longer needs to suffer the consequences of their sin'.[26]

Although Schwartz's conception of guilt as a burden that may be borne and relieved is helpful, there are some difficulties with the approaches to the עון/חטא + נשא formula outlined above. For example, while Schwartz argues that the burden of sin disappears once it has been assumed by a priestly entity, he offers little evidence to support this claim.[27] Also, Schwartz does not explain how the עון/חטא + נשא formula conveys the assignment of guilt in some contexts, but the removal of guilt in others. These difficulties are addressed in the mimetic interpretation of the עון/חטא + נשא formula offered below, which considers what happens to the burden of sin once it is assumed by a priestly agent. In contrast to the approaches surveyed above, this interpretation attempts to read the עון/חטא + נשא formula consistently across the Pentateuch. In so doing, I suggest that the priestly role of 'bearing sin' is somewhat similar to that played by capital offenders within the Pentateuch.

2.2. *A Mimetic Interpretation of the* חטא + נשא *Formula*

I shall now apply the narrative approach to propose an alternative reading of the עון/חטא + נשא formula in Lev. 24:15 by surveying the use of this phrase throughout the Pentateuch. In Lev. 24:15 the Blasphemer 'bears his sin' (נשא + חטא), as the community purge their mimetic rivalries through his immolation. In this way, the Blasphemer's death achieves a similar transformation to cultic rituals, which also function to vent mimetic rivalry within the community through a Priestly agent (e.g. Lev. 10:17). Like the Blasphemer, the priesthood also 'bears sin' (נשא + עון) as communal scapegoats (Num. 18:1). However, in contrast to capital offenders, the priesthood can 'bear sin' without dying. In what follows, I explain the role of the Priests and Levites as communal scapegoats, who 'bear sin' on behalf of the community, and attempt to show that the transformation described by the עון/חטא + נשא formula in Lev. 24:15 mirrors the priestly vocation of bearing the community's sin. Having done so, these insights will then be applied to Lev. 24:15-16 to argue that the immolation of Blasphemers restores peace and order by purging mimetic rivalry from the community.

26. Ibid, 90, 95.
27. Gane, *Cult and Character*, 103–4.

The Priests and Levites are portrayed as potential scapegoats within the Pentateuch when YHWH claims the Levites as redemption for Israel's firstborn (Num. 3:12).[28] In the Exodus narrative, Israel, YHWH's son, is redeemed from slavery through the substitutionary death of the Egyptian firstborn (cf. Exod. 4:22-23). After the Exodus, however, the Levites replace the Egyptian firstborn as the redemption price for Israel's firstborn (Num. 3:11-13; 8:14-19).[29] In other words, when the Israelite community lack a national rival, towards whom they may direct their mimetic rivalry, their rivalry is directed towards the Levites, who may serve as communal scapegoats. This concept is starkly portrayed in Numbers 16, which describes the cessation of a plague following the death of some rebellious Levites.[30] Likewise, Aaron's sons, Nadab and Abihu, are killed by divinely kindled fire in Lev. 10:1-3, when they offer strange fire to YHWH. As Williams postulates, the divine fire may serve as a cover for mob violence, which culminates in the immolation of Nadab and Abihu as communal scapegoats. Through this act, the peace and order associated with the Israelite cult and the Levitical Priesthood is established.[31] In each of these cases, peace and order is achieved through the death of Levite scapegoats.

---

28. Williams, *The Bible, Violence, and the Sacred*, 106.

29. Whenever the Israelite firstborn outnumber the Levites, the difference is covered through monetary payment (Num. 3:44-48). Furthermore, Williams suggests that Exod. 32:27-29 may describe the slaughter of the Levites as a substitute for the rest of the Israelite community. However, Moses' command to go 'to and fro from gate to gate throughout the camp, and each of you kill his brother and his companion and his neighbor' appears to describe the entire Israelite community as the target of this attack. Ibid., 121–3.

30. Moreover, as Williams notes, 'the censers of the Korah group are to be hammered into plates as a covering for the altar (Num. 17:36-40). The plates will serve as a sign, as a reminder to the children of Israel that only the priests who are descendants of Aaron through Eleazar may approach to burn incense before the LORD. The rebellious, rejected priests are thus represented on the altar itself. Their destruction confirms the differentiation of the priesthood into the Aaronites and the rest of the Levites.' Ibid., 126.

31. Williams suggests that Lev. 10:1-3 serves as an origin story for the Aaronic Priesthood: 'If we recall that God's punishing wrath is the concealed form of collective violence, then the fire from God could be a cover for mob action. If this hypothesis is correct, it would be another part of the picture of the beginnings of the Levitical Priesthood. The Levites were victims or have mythically replaced actual victims who were murdered in acts of collective violence.' Ibid., 124.

The Levite's violent actions in Exod. 32:25-29 further identify this tribe as a group of potential scapegoats.[32] The Levites receive their commission and are blessed when they halt a mimetic crisis by slaughtering their fellow Israelites (Exod. 32:25-29). This mimetic crisis, which is portrayed as a plague (32:35), precipitates from a lack of differentiation as Israel 'break free' (פרע) from Moses' leadership (32:25). However, this crisis is halted when Moses rallies the Levites, who kill three thousand people (vv. 26-28). Once they have restored peace and order to the community, the Levites are commissioned for YHWH's service, 'each one at the cost of his son and of his brother' (v. 29). The peace and order achieved through the Levites' slaughter of their fellow Israelites in this narrative fits the pattern of the scapegoat, who simultaneously survives and halts the mimetic crisis by selecting a victim to die in his or her stead.[33]

The Pentateuch's portrayal of the Levites and the Israelite priesthood shares many similarities with Girard's theoretical reconstruction of sacred kingship. According to Girard, the king is 'nothing more than a victim with a short suspended sentence... [T]he victim is made responsible for the transformation that moves the community from mimetic violence to the order of ritual.'[34] The monarch is venerated, as they await their execution. Yet, if their execution is prolonged, this veneration may be transformed into genuine power. 'At some point this power and the submission of the community would become sufficiently effective and extensive as to make an actual sacrifice of the monarch impossible if not unthinkable.'[35] A substitute must now be executed in the Monarch's place, which for Girard marks the genesis of ritual sacrifice. While this study does not assume Girard's theory concerning the origins of animal sacrifice, the relationship he postulates between sacred kingship and ritual sacrifice appears to be reflected in the Pentateuch's portrayal of the Israelite priesthood. Like Girard's sacred monarch, who avoids their own execution by providing a sacrificial substitute, the Israelite priesthood avoid execution by either killing others or employing various rituals to alleviate the burden of people's sin, which they have assumed. In contrast, the Levites cannot perform these rituals and must, therefore, 'bear their sin' (Num. 18:23) as they act as substitutes for Israel's firstborn (Num. 3:12) and fulfil their crucial ministry concerning the Tabernacle.

32. E.g. Gen. 34; Exod. 32:25-29; Num. 25:1-15; Judg. 19. Ibid., 118, 22–3.
33. Gil Bailie, *Violence Unveiled: Humanity at the Crossroads* (New York: Crossroad, 1995), 147–8.
34. Girard, *Violence and the Sacred*, 52.
35. Ibid., 53.

4. The Blasphemer of Leviticus 24

The Israelite priesthood alleviates the burden of sin, and avoids their own execution, through various means. For example, Phinehas secures his priesthood when he halts a mimetic crisis, in this case depicted as a plague, by driving a spear through two outgroup members.[36] Through this act, Phinehas, the scapegoat priest, immolates two victims in his stead. In so doing, Phinehas restores peace and order to the community, without having to die as a scapegoat himself. If Phinehas had not halted the crisis by executing these people as communal scapegoats, the community would have vented their mimetic rivalries upon others, perhaps even killing Phinehas himself. The priesthood also preserve their own lives, and maintain their offices, by providing cultic channels for the community to vent their mimetic rivalries. For example, on the Day of Atonement the High Priest removes Israel's sin to a remote area by loading it (נשא + עון) upon the scapegoat (Lev. 16:21-22).[37] In so doing, the High Priest 'atones (כפר) for them before YHWH'.[38] In this way, the priesthood prevent and halt mimetic crises by providing a channel to vent mimetic rivalries.

The immolation of outgroup members also purges mimetic rivalries and, in this way, capital offenders 'bear their own sin' (cf. Lev. 24:15).[39]

---

36. As discussed in Chapter 3, this passage satisfies all four of Girard's stereoe types, which confirms the scapegoat mechanism within this text.

37. Klaus Koch, 'עָוֹן', in *Theological Dictionary of the Old Testament*, ed. G Johannes Botterweck, Helmer Ringgren, and Heinz-Josef Fabry (Grand Rapids: Eerdmans, 2004), 560.

38. Keil and Delitzsch interpret the נשא + עון formula in Lev. 24:15 as being synonymous with the concept of atonement. Carl Friedrich Keil and Franz Delitzsch, *Biblical Commentary on the Old Testament* (Edinburgh: T. & T. Clark, 1870), 622.

39. The Rabbinic tradition has also considered the transformational aspect of human immolation. According to *m. Sanh.* 6:2, if one who is about to be executed confesses his sin, or says 'Let my death be atonement for all of my transgressions', his death effectively atones for his wrongs, and assures the offender a peaceful life in the world to come. For the Rabbis, then, the death penalty was not really a punishment at all, but rather a ritual which achieved atonement for a capital offender. David Kraemer, *The Meanings of Death in Rabbinic Judaism* (New York: Routledge, 2002), 145. This interpretation of capital punishment grapples with what it means for an offender to 'bear his own sin'. Although the Rabbinic interpretation exposes the tendency of many scholars to overlook the reparative dimension of human immolation in the Hebrew Bible, this interpretation is impossible to verify. Nowhere in the Pentateuch is a capital offender described as the object of atonement. The Pentateuch does, however, state that immolating manslayers achieves atonement for blood shed upon the land (Num. 35:33), and purges bloodguilt from the people (Deut. 19:11-13). Moreover, immolating an Unchaste Bride purges evil from the community

Although priests achieve this transformation (נשא + עון/חטא) by transferring the sin which they bear to an animal substitute (cf. Lev. 16:21-22), outgroup members are not able to do this and, for this reason, must suffer the consequences of their actions.[40] Through the immolation of capital offenders the community's mimetic rivalries are vented, which both prevents and halts communal crises. The concept of capital offenders 'bearing their sin' is, therefore, similar to the priestly vocation of 'bearing sin' within the Pentateuch. The key difference between these groups is that the priesthood can transfer the sin which they bear to animal substitutes, while outgroup members cannot. Outgroup members 'bear their own sin' (נשא + עון/חטא) through their own immolation, which allows the community to vent their mimetic rivalries.

2.3. *The* נשא + חטא *Formula in Leviticus 24:15-16*

Having argued that the נשא + עון/חטא formula describes the venting of mimetic rivalries through a communal scapegoat, I shall now apply this insight to Lev. 24:15-16. The immediate context of these verses is significant. In Lev. 24:10-23, as I have argued above, the community halt a mimetic crisis by venting their mimetic rivalries upon the Blasphemer. Out of this incident arises the casuistic legal material of vv. 15-16, which prescribes the immolation of blasphemers as a means of purging mimetic rivalry from the community: 'Whoever curses his God shall bear his sin (נשא + חטא). Whoever blasphemes the name of YHWH shall surely be put to death.' The parallelism between the נשא + עון/חטא and מות ימות formulas in these verses suggests that blasphemers 'bear their sin' through

---

(Deut. 22:20-21). The immolation of capital offenders within the Pentateuch benefits the community but not the perpetrator. Just as the Priest bears sin for the good of the people, so outgroup members protect the community as they bear their own sin through their immolation.

40. When the נשא + עון/חטא formula takes the sinner as its subject it is often coupled with negative consequences, such as the כרת-penalty (Num. 9:13), death of an unexplained cause (Exod. 22:9; 28:43), execution (Lev. 24:15), or dying childless (Lev. 20:20). In each case the offender bears the consequence of their sin, while the community remains unaffected. One interesting use of the נשא + עון/חטא formula occurs in Num. 30:16 (Eng. 30:15), which states that a husband who hears and nullifies his wife's vow 'shall bear *her* iniquity'. In this case the husband vicariously bears his wife's sin, while no consequences are recorded. I take this act, which is described by the נשא + עון/חטא formula, as referring to the husband paying a fine on behalf of his wife, similar to those prescribed in Lev. 27. In this way, the husband achieves reparation for his wife's broken vow and, in so doing, mitigates any negative consequences associated with this sin.

their own immolation. In other words, the community achieves peace and order by venting their mimetic rivalries through the immolation of blasphemers.

This idea is further strengthened by the parallels between Lev. 24:10-23 and the Day of Atonement (Lev. 16).[41] The narrative approach acknowledges that the hand-leaning subrite (סמך + יד) and the removal of the Blasphemer to a place 'outside the camp' (יצא + מחוץ למחנה) in v. 14 mirror the subrites concerning the scapegoat and the sin offering performed on the Day of Atonement (Lev. 16:20-22). Furthermore, on the Day of Atonement, Aaron places (נתן) 'the iniquities, transgressions, and sins of the people' upon the head of the live goat through confession and by performing the hand leaning subrite. These iniquities, transgressions, and sins are subsequently removed from the community when the live goat is relocated outside the camp to the wilderness (Lev. 16:22).[42] As the נשא + עון/חטא formula in this verse indicates, the Day of Atonement ritual vents the community's mimetic rivalries. Similarly, when those who witness the Blasphemer's actions place their hands upon the head of the Blasphemer they vent their mimetic rivalries upon him in a remote place away from the Israelite camp.[43]

In sum, Lev. 24:15-16 prescribes the immolation of offenders, who commit similar crimes to that of the Blasphemer in vv. 10-11. Through their immolation, these offenders 'bear their own sin', as the use of the נשא + חטא formula in v. 15 indicates. In this section, I have argued that the נשא + עון/חטא formula describes the role of a scapegoat, through whom the community vents its mimetic rivalries. Although the priesthood also 'bear sin', they remain alive because of their ability to deal with sin through the cult. By contrast, capital offenders 'bear their own sin' by dying. Both capital offenders and the priesthood, therefore, purge mimetic rivalry from the community, as indicated by the use of the נשא + עון/חטא formula in connection with these two groups. The concern for managing mimetic rivalry in vv. 15-16 provides a logical link to the principle of *lex talionis*, which is cited in Lev. 24:17-22.

---

41. As Bryan Bibb also notes this connection: 'The people who heard the blasphemy shall place their hands on his head and then stone him. In this way, the sin will be expunged from the community. Like the scapegoat of Lev 16, the man must bear the iniquity away from the people, accepting back the contagion that he had unleashed in the community.' Bibb, *Ritual Words and Narrative Worlds*, 155.

42. Gane, *Cult and Character*, 261–5; Schwartz, 'The Bearing of Sin in the Priestly Literature', 17–20.

43. Gane, *Cult and Character*, 264–5.

3. Lex Talionis *(Leviticus 24:17-22)*

In this section I argue that the *lex talionis* of Lev. 24:17-22 provides further evidence that the immolation of the Blasphemer in Lev. 24:10-14, 23 purges mimetic rivalry from the community. Although human immolation for the crime of blasphemy seems, at least to modern sensitivities, rather excessive, the *talion* helps explain this consequence by framing it as an act of restorative justice. In so doing, the *talion* provides an important interpretive key to the Blasphemer prose. While at first glance it is unclear why the Blasphemer prose should be interrupted by a section on *lex talionis*, the chiastic pattern evident in vv. 15b-22, and the echo of v. 16 (כגר כאזרח) in v. 22, suggest this interruption is central to interpreting the narrative events and the legal material presented in Lev. 24:10-16, 23.[44] The structure of Lev. 24:10-23 calls the reader to interpret this passage as an application of the *lex talionis* legal principle. As Jonathon Vroom notes in his comments regarding Exod. 21:36, the principle of *lex talionis*, as it is used within the Pentateuch, describes a form of restoration:

> In the case of the talion, the language of corrective justice – restoring balance – is employed in a context of punishment – just desserts. This can be demonstrated by the connection of the verb שלם, which…characterizes the ideals of corrective justice (restoration), with a talionic formula found in Exod 21:36. This verse stipulates that the negligent owner of the ox that killed another ox 'shall surely make restitution [ישלם שלם], an ox for the ox [שור תחת השור]'. This correspondence between שלם and this talionic formula is very telling. Here, the language of reparation and restoration (שלם) is connected with the language of the talion… [T]he talionic formula achieves the ideals of restoration and balance…[and] embodies the ideals of corrective justice – resolving disputes by restoring balance.[45]

By quoting the *lex talionis* of the Covenant Code, Lev. 24:17-21 confirms that the focus of the Blasphemer prose is restorative justice.[46] This shared focus between Lev. 24:17-21 and the Covenant Code is evidenced by the common language used in these texts. In particular, the verb שלם

---

44. Furthermore, the chiastic structure of 15b-22a suggests continuity between the narrative and *lex talionis* in this passage. Hutton, 'Narrative in Leviticus', 151–3.

45. Jonathan Vroom, 'An Eye for an Eye in Context: The Meaning and Function of the Lex Talionis in the Torah' (MA thesis, McMaster Divinity College, 2009), 52–5.

46. Primarily, the *lex talionis* demands reparation for victims through the provision of adequate compensation. Yung Suk Kim, 'Lex Talionis in Exod. 21:22–25: Its Origin and Context', *Journal of Hebrew Scriptures* 6 (2009): 4–5; Raymond

(Lev. 24:18, 21), the מות ימות formula (v. 17), and the preposition תחת (v. 20) all echo the language of the Covenant Code.⁴⁷ In this way, Lev. 24:10-23 claims that the casuistic legal formula of vv. 15b-16 is supported by the legal premise of *lex talionis*, as it is used in the Covenant Code, and confirms that Lev. 24:10-23 is concerned with restorative justice.⁴⁸

According to the *talion*, human immolation is required to achieve reparation for the killing of an ingroup member (Lev. 24:17, 21). The hominoid epithet האדם, which is applied to the victim of homicide in both these verses, confirms that vv. 17 and 21 address the killing of ingroup members.⁴⁹ Verses 17 and 20 also assume the ingroup's role of *imitatio dei*, as they are called to achieve reparation for the homicide of האדם.⁵⁰ Reparation for the injury of האדם is achieved by recompensing the offender with exactly the same injury (vv. 19-20).⁵¹ Similarly, if someone kills an animal the culprit must make reparation for the breach by compensating the animal's owner (vv. 18, 21). The passages discussed in the previous section, which describe the necessity of making reparation

---

Westbrook, 'Lex Talionis and Exodus 21, 22-25', *Revue Biblique* (1986): 52–69; Ludger Schwienhorst-Schönberger, *Das Bundesbuch (Ex 20,22-23,33): Studien zu Seiner Entstehung und Theologie* (Berlin: de Gruyter, 1990), 100–105.

47. The common use of these terms in connection with the *lex talionis* principle satisfies Hayes' second criterion, and confirms that Lev. 24:17-22 echoes Exod. 21:12–22:14.

48. These parallels are noted by Vroom as he argues that Lev. 24:17-21 is dependent upon Exod. 21. Vroom, however, focuses on the significance of the phrase כגר כאזרח, and while he does note the danger which the Blasphemer's actions pose to the community, he does not explore the possibility that the Blasphemer's immolation may have served a reparative function. Vroom, 'Recasting Mišpātîm', 34.

49. See the section on Gen. 9:6 in Chapter 2 for a discussion on the use of האדם as an ingroup identifier within the Pentateuch.

50. See the section on Gen. 9:6 in Chapter 2 for a discussion on *imitaito dei* through human immolation as the role of האדם. Moses carries out this role in Exod. 2:11-12 as he strikes (נכה) and kills the Egyptian, who transgresses the *talion* of Lev. 24:17, 21 by striking (נכה) an Israelite ingroup member. Leviticus 24:17, 21, calls the Israelite ingroup to follow Moses' example in Exod. 2:11-12 by immolating anyone who kills (נכה) a fellow ingroup member (האדם).

51. Although, as many have noted, the injuries associated with the talion are not literal, but figuratively describe the compensation afforded to victims (cf. Exod. 21:22-27). Waldemar Janzen, *Believers Church Bible Commentary*: *Exodus* (Waterloo: Herald, 2000), 298; Nahum M. Sarna, *Exodus*, The JPS Torah Commentary (Philadelphia: Jewish Publication Society, 1991), 126–7; Douglas K. Stuart, *Exodus*, The New American Commentary (Nashville: Broadman & Holman, 2006), 492–5.

through the עון/חטא + נשא formula, parallel Lev. 24:17-21 as they also describe guilty parties whose transgressions are remedied through an act of reparation. This observation, when coupled with the structural unity of Lev. 24:10-23, demands that the narrative of the Blasphemer is read as an application of the reparative principle of *lex talionis*.

Just as the instructions on *lex talionis* in Lev. 24:17-21 aim to achieve reparation through an appropriate offering, so Lev. 24:10-16, 23 outlines the ritual killing of the Blasphemer to achieve reparation for his crime. When the stoning of the Blasphemer in Lev. 24:10-16, 23 is viewed as an act of reparation, then the puzzle of *lex talionis* is no longer a question of which punishment fits the crime, but rather how reparation for this crime can be achieved. For outgroup members who commit capital offences, reparation can only be achieved through their immolation. In Lev. 24:10-23 this reparation is achieved as the community vent their mimetic rivalries on the Blasphemer and, in this way, restore peace and order to the community. The presence of *lex talionis* in vv. 17-21 frames Lev. 24:10-23 as a treatise on making reparation for קלל and נקב. The citation of the *talion* also justifies the casuistic legal material presented in vv. 15-16 as necessary for protecting the community from future mimetic crises.

However, at first glance, it seems problematic to suggest that the *talion* prevents mimetic crises by encouraging victims to mirror their perpetrators' offenses back to them. Yet, this imitation differs from the mimetic rivalry, which characterises mimetic crises, in a number of ways. First, *lex talionis* dictates that rivalry is returned only upon the perpetrator of the original offence. In this way, the *talion* discourages potential offenders by warning them that their actions will be mirrored back to them. Second, the *talion* provides a controlled release of mimetic rivalries by directing them back upon the perpetrator, who is blamed for starting the crisis. Third, the *talion* moderates this release by ensuring an exact mirroring of the initial offense, which prevents the escalation of mimetic rivalry. Through these means, *lex talionis* helps prevent mimetic crises by ensuring a controlled venting of mimetic rivalries upon the original offenders. This observation further explains why the *talion* is cited in Lev. 24:17-22.

4. Conclusion

This chapter has argued that the scapegoat mechanism underlies the stoning of the Blasphemer in Lev. 24:10-23. By portraying the Blasphemer as a dangerous, foreign threat to the ingroup's vocation of reflecting the divine image, Lev. 24:10-16 identifies him as the perfect scapegoat. The immolation of the Blasphemer achieves reparation for his offences, by purging mimetic rivalry and halting the mimetic crisis. This reading is supported by the employment of the חטא + נשא formula in Lev. 24:15b and the citation of the *lex talionis* legal principle in vv. 17-21. Furthermore, the mimetic nature of communal stoning supports the thesis that the scapegoat mechanism underlies the stoning of the Blasphemer in Lev. 24:10-16. The stoning ritual provides an outlet for the venting of mimetic rivalry, as the ingroup bands together against their scapegoat. This mechanism is also observed in another case of human immolation, which is the focus of the next chapter: the stoning of the Sabbath Gatherer in Num. 15:32-36.

Chapter 5

THE SABBATH-GATHERER OF NUMBERS 15:32-36

In Num. 15:32-36 a man is sentenced to death for picking up sticks on the Sabbath. This text shares many similarities with Lev. 24:10-16 in so far as they both describe an offender who violates a communal norm, who is held in custody pending divine revelation, and who is subsequently executed through communal stoning. The present chapter argues that, like the Blasphemer of Lev. 24:10-16, the Sabbath-gatherer of Num. 15:32-36 is immolated as a communal scapegoat to prevent a mimetic crisis. Many of the features that this narrative shares with Lev. 24:10-16, including the mimetic significance of communal execution by stoning, were discussed in the previous chapter. Rather than revisiting these features, the present chapter focuses upon the offender's desecration of the Sabbath in Num. 15:32-36, and why this crime might be considered a capital offence.

A narrative reading of Num. 15:32-36 is presented in this chapter over four sections. The first section begins by exploring the importance of the Sabbath throughout the Pentateuch. Next, I examine the command to execute Sabbath Breakers in Exod. 31:12-17 as an imperative, which is fulfilled in Num. 15:32-36. The insights gleaned from sections 1 and 2 are applied in the third section to produce a narrative reading of Num. 15:32-36. In this reading, the Sabbath-gatherer endangers the community and threatens their ability to reflect the divine image when he violates the core communal value of Sabbath observance. The community then band together and purge their mimetic rivalries by executing the Sabbath-gatherer. This reading is supported by the final section which applies Girard's scapegoat stereotypes to Num. 15:32-36 to reveal the scapegoat mechanism within this text.

1. *The Sabbath*

This section applies the narrative method to argue that the Sabbath principle permeates the entire created order within the Pentateuch. In what follows, I trace this principle through Genesis, Exodus, and Leviticus to argue that the created order is maintained through Sabbath observance. By keeping the Sabbath the ingroup fulfils its role as YHWH's image-bearing children, who continue YHWH's creative work. The Pentateuch opens with the Priestly creation account (Gen. 1:1–2:3) in which YHWH creates 'the sky and the land' (השמים והארץ) over the course of seven days.[1] The narrative's structure of six days of creation followed by Sabbath rest may make Gen. 1:1–2:3 more a 'sabbatogony' than cosmogony.[2] According to the priestly creation account, the Sabbath rhythm is built into the very fabric of creation.[3] In the Babylonian epic, *Enuma Elish*, creation is crowned and consummated with the construction of Marduk's temple, Esagila.[4] The Sabbath plays a similar role in Gen. 1:1–2:3 as it declares and commemorates YHWH's triumph over the primordial elements.[5]

> The Sabbath and the sanctuary represent the same moment in the divine life, one of exaltation and regal repose, a moment free of anxiety. Thus, the account of the construction of the Tabernacle is punctuated by the injunction to observe the Sabbath *in imitatione Dei* (Exod. 31:12-17, 35:1-30). The two institutions, each a memorial and, more than that, an actualisation of the aboriginal creative act, are woven together... Sabbath and sanctuary partake of the same reality; they proceed, *pari passu*, from the same foundational event, to which they testify and even provide access.[6]

This foundational creative act continues through the ingroup's observance of the Sabbath, as seen throughout the book of Genesis. For

---

1. Victor P. Hamilton, *The Book of Genesis: Chapters 1–17* (Grand Rapids: Eerdmans, 1990), 103.

2. Philippe Guillaume, *Land and Calendar: The Priestly Document from Genesis 1 to Joshua 18* (Edinburgh: A. & C. Black, 2009), 41–2.

3. Levenson, *Creation and the Persistence of Evil*, 110–11; Yairah Amit, 'Who Decided to Open the Torah with the Creation of the Sabbath?', in *In Praise of Editing in the Hebrew Bible*, ed. Yairah Amit (Sheffield: Sheffield Phoenix, 2012), 2–11.

4. Jon D. Levenson, 'The Temple and the World', *The Journal of Religion* (1984): 287–8.

5. According to Meredith Kline, YHWH 'has stamped on world history the sign of the sabbath as his seal of ownership and authority'. Meredith G. Kline, *Treaty of the Great King: The Covenant Structure of Deuteronomy: Studies and Commentary* (Eugene: Wipf & Stock, 2012), 19; Levenson, 'The Temple and the World', 287–8; John H. Walton, *Genesis 1 as Ancient Cosmology* (Winona Lake: Eisenbrauns, 2011), 190–2.

6. Levenson, 'The Temple and the World', 288. See also Frank H. Gorman, *The Ideology of Ritual: Space, Time and Status in the Priestly Theology* (Edinburgh: A. & C. Black, 1990), 222.

example, in Gen. 7:4-10 YHWH waits seven days before unleashing the flood waters.[7] Through this act of anti-creation, the land is purified from defilement and corruption.[8] The new creation then emerges as Noah participates in the Sabbath rhythm by waiting seven days before sending out of doves (Gen. 8:10-12). Moreover, in Genesis 29 Jacob works seven years in the hope of marrying Rachel. After Laban deceives him, Jacob works another seven years, eventually attaining Leah and Rachel, through whom the nation of Israel will be birthed. Similarly, in Genesis 41 seven years of plenty are followed by seven years of famine. Out of these cycles of seven comes Egypt's prosperity and the preservation of Israel. Therefore, throughout Genesis, the ingroup continue YHWH's creative work by participating in the Sabbath rhythm.

The Sabbath theme also pervades Exodus and Leviticus. For example, the Festival of Unleavened Bread lasts for seven days (Exod. 12:15; 13:6-7), as does the Priests' consecration and the duration of their service in the Holy Place.[9] Additionally, the number seven features prominently as the number of times blood is sprinkled in various rites and the duration of purification rituals.[10] As Frank Gorman has noted, the seven-day duration of consecration and purification rituals echoes the priestly creation account of Gen. 1:1–2:3.[11] Just as the flood water of Genesis 6–9 purifies the land, and gives birth to a new creation, so seven days of purification mark a new beginning for those previously rendered unclean. Those who observe the Sabbath participate YHWH's creative work,[12] while those who work on the Sabbath 'profane' it (Exod. 31:14).[13] The desecration of YHWH's holy Sabbath constitutes an act of anti-creation.

---

7. Mathews associates the seven-day periods throughout the flood narrative with ancient Israel's sacred calendar. Mathews, *Genesis 1–11: 26*, 372.

8. Harland, *The Value of Human Life*, 167–8.

9. Exod. 29:30, 35-37; Lev. 8:33-35.

10. Lev. 4:17; 8:11; 13:5, 21, 26, 31, 33, 50, 54; 14:7, 8, 51; 16:14, 19.

11. Gorman, *The Ideology of Ritual*, 58, 112–13.

12. As Jon Levenson writes, 'the creative ordering of the world has become something that humanity can not only witness and celebrate, but something in which it can also take part. Among the many messages of Genesis 1:1–2:3 is this: it is through the cult that we are enabled to cope with evil, for it is the cult that builds and maintains order, transforms chaos into creation, ennobles humanity, and realizes the kingship of God who has ordained the cult and commanded it to be guarded and practiced.' Levenson, *Creation and the Persistence of Evil*, 127; see also Gorman, *The Ideology of Ritual*, 39–42.

13. As Propp suggests, Sabbath desecration may cause ritual pollution. William Propp, *Exodus 19–40*, AB 2A (New York: Doubleday, 2006), 492–3. This idea, however, goes beyond what is explicitly mentioned in the text.

The presence of the Sabbath rhythm in the created order is also seen through Israel's practice of gathering manna in the wilderness. Exodus 16 emphasizes the importance of Sabbath rest, as the Israelites are asked to gather only their daily provision of food for the first five days of the week, while gathering double on the sixth, to allow for a Sabbath rest on the seventh. For the first six days of the week, any extra food left 'until morning...bred worms and stank' (v. 20), necessitating six days of gathering. On the Sabbath day, however, the leftover food 'did not stink and there were no worms in it' (v. 24). Furthermore, on the Sabbath day those who went out looking for food found nothing (v. 27). According to Exodus 16, the Sabbath rhythm of creation is also built into the provision and preservation of manna.[14] Through this story, Exodus 16 describes Sabbath desecration as a practice which contravenes YHWH's creative rhythm, and highlights the importance of imitating the Sabbath rhythm described in Gen. 1:1–2:3.

In sum, according to the Pentateuch, the Sabbath rhythm is built into every facet of human life. This rhythm is first introduced in the opening chapter of the Pentateuch (Gen. 1:1–2:3) and continues through the flood narrative (Gen. 6:9–8:19). Jacob and his sons observe the Sabbath throughout the latter chapters of Genesis, as do the people of Israel as they gather manna in the wilderness. Finally, the Sabbath rhythm is also built into Israel's cult and calendar, which allows subsequent generations to enter into this sacred time. As they do so, the faithful ingroup reflect the divine image by continuing YHWH's creative work. In these ways, the Pentateuch presents the Sabbath as a natural rhythm built into the fabric of creation, and implies that faithful Israel must observe this rhythm.

2. *Human Immolation and Sabbath Desecration in Exodus 31:12-17*

The importance of Sabbath observance in maintaining the created order is also assumed by Exod. 31:12-17, which describes the Sabbath as a 'sign'. In so doing, this text supports the argument, presented in the previous section, that ingroup members observe the Sabbath. In what follows I argue that, according to Exod. 31:12-17, Israelites who do not observe the Sabbath sign are considered a dangerous outgroup, and must be immolated to maintain and continue YHWH's creative work. This interpretation of Exod. 31:12-17 lays a foundation for the narrative reading of Num. 15:32-36 presented in the next section.

---

14. Sarna, *Exodus*, 90.

¹² And the YHWH said to Moses,	וַיֹּאמֶר יְהוָה אֶל־מֹשֶׁה לֵּאמֹר:
¹³ᵃ 'You are to speak to the people of Israel and say, "Above all you shall keep my Sabbaths,	וְאַתָּה דַּבֵּר אֶל־בְּנֵי יִשְׂרָאֵל לֵאמֹר אַךְ אֶת־שַׁבְּתֹתַי תִּשְׁמֹרוּ
¹³ᵇ for this is a sign between me and you throughout your generations,	כִּי אוֹת הִוא בֵּינִי וּבֵינֵיכֶם לְדֹרֹתֵיכֶם
¹³ᶜ that you may know that I, YHWH, sanctify you.	לָדַעַת כִּי אֲנִי יְהוָה מְקַדִּשְׁכֶם:
¹⁴ᵃ You shall keep the Sabbath, because it is your holiness.	וּשְׁמַרְתֶּם אֶת־הַשַּׁבָּת כִּי קֹדֶשׁ הִוא לָכֶם
¹⁴ᵇ Everyone who profanes it shall be put to death. Whoever does any work on it, that soul shall be cut off from among his people.	מְחַלְלֶיהָ מוֹת יוּמָת כִּי כָּל־הָעֹשֶׂה בָהּ מְלָאכָה וְנִכְרְתָה הַנֶּפֶשׁ הַהִוא מִקֶּרֶב עַמֶּיהָ:
¹⁵ᵃ Six days shall work be done, but the seventh day is YHWH's solemn, holy Sabbath	שֵׁשֶׁת יָמִים יֵעָשֶׂה מְלָאכָה וּבַיּוֹם הַשְּׁבִיעִי שַׁבַּת שַׁבָּתוֹן קֹדֶשׁ לַיהוָה
¹⁵ᵇ Whoever does any work on the Sabbath day shall be put to death.	כָּל־הָעֹשֶׂה מְלָאכָה בְּיוֹם הַשַּׁבָּת מוֹת יוּמָת:
¹⁶ᵃ Therefore the people of Israel shall keep the Sabbath, observing the Sabbath	וְשָׁמְרוּ בְנֵי־יִשְׂרָאֵל אֶת־הַשַּׁבָּת לַעֲשׂוֹת אֶת־הַשַּׁבָּת
¹⁶ᵇ throughout their generations, as a covenant forever.	לְדֹרֹתָם בְּרִית עוֹלָם:
¹⁷ᵃ It is a sign forever between me and the people of Israel	בֵּינִי וּבֵין בְּנֵי יִשְׂרָאֵל אוֹת הִוא לְעֹלָם
¹⁷ᵇ that in six days the YHWH made heaven and earth, and on the seventh day he rested and was refreshed."'	כִּי־שֵׁשֶׁת יָמִים עָשָׂה יְהוָה אֶת־הַשָּׁמַיִם וְאֶת־הָאָרֶץ וּבַיּוֹם הַשְּׁבִיעִי שָׁבַת וַיִּנָּפַשׁ:

Verses 15a and 17b frame Sabbath observance as imitating YHWH's creative acts as they are narrated in Gen. 1:1–2:3.¹⁵ Just as YHWH created the world in six days, so Israel are called to work for six days, but 'the seventh day is YHWH's solemn, holy Sabbath'.¹⁶ In this way, Israel is invited to imitate YHWH's Sabbath rhythm in their everyday life. Moreover, by linking the Sabbath rhythm to YHWH's actions in the Priestly creation account, Exod. 31:12-17 designates the first six days of the week for tasks such as food production, while the seventh day is set apart as a period of abstinence from these tasks.¹⁷ This reading is

---

15. Umberto Cassuto, *A Commentary on the Book of Exodus* (Jerusalem: Magnes, 1967), 404; Propp, *Exodus 19–40*, 492.

16. I have translated ליהוה as a periphrastic phrase, indicating YHWH's authorship of the Sabbath rhythm, on account of this passage's citation of the Priestly creation account.

17. Like other ancient Near Eastern creation accounts, Gen. 1:1–2:3 focuses upon the creation of elements that are essential to food production, such as rainfall, soil, seasons, and spermatophytes. Walton, *Genesis 1*, 161–2.

supported by Exodus 16, in which Israel violate the Sabbath rhythm by performing acts associated with food production, including gathering, baking, and boiling manna. Boiling or baking manna requires fire, which also explains why Exod. 35:3 prohibits domestic fires on the Sabbath.[18] By abstaining from the tasks involved with food production on the Sabbath, the Israelites imitate YHWH's creative rhythm.[19]

The parallelism between vv. 15a and 17b also suggests that YHWH's experience of being revivified through his holy Sabbath (וינפש) will be shared by those who observe the Sabbath.[20] This revivification directly contrasts the double penalty received by those who desecrate the Sabbath (vv. 14-15). While those who keep the Sabbath are revivified, those who do not are immolated and their נפש is excised from the community through the כרת-penalty (v. 14b). Various interpretations of the כרת-penalty have been offered, including human immolation, excommunication, or some form of divine punishment, such as premature death or the cessation of the offender's lineage.[21] A detailed exploration of these interpretations goes beyond the scope of the present study. That said, each of these interpretations

---

18. Burnside, '"What Shall We Do with the Sabbath-Gatherer?"', 52. Alternatively, some have suggested that the ban on domestic fires outlaws a foreign custom. Cassuto, *Exodus*, 455; Gnana Robinson, 'The Prohibition of Strange Fire in Ancient Israel: A New Look at the Case of Gathering Wood and Kindling Fire on the Sabbath', *Vetus Testamentum* 28, no. 3 (1978): 301–17.

19. Although Exod. 20:10-11 and 31:14-15 prohibits all work on the Sabbath, the passages discussed above focus on food production. Furthermore, Lev. 25:18-22 assures the Israelites that if they observe the Sabbath rhythm, they will have all the food they need. This focus emphasizes the application of the Sabbath law to everyday life, in addition to its observance in Tabernacle construction. Anthony Phillips, *Essays on Biblical Law* (London: T&T Clark, 2004), 237. Hendrix interprets the 'fire' prohibited in Exod. 35:3 as the smelting fire used in the production of metal furniture for the Tabernacle. Ralph E. Hendrix, 'A Literary Structural Overview of Exod 25–40', *Andrews University Seminary Studies* 30, no. 2 (1992): 1. See also Cassuto, *Exodus*, 403–4.

20. Cf. Gerhard F. Hasel, 'The Sabbath in the Pentateuch', in *The Sabbath in Scripture and History*, ed. Kenneth Albert Strand (Washington: Review & Herald, 1982), 25.

21. Milgrom argues that the כרת-penalty could refer to either the excommunication of the offender and their lineage from the community, or the separation of the offender from their ancestors in the afterlife. Others have suggested that the כרת-penalty most likely refers to a premature death. For example, Sklar claims that the offender dies prematurely, when he or she is executed either by the community or YHWH. Yet, as others have noted, this premature death must be divinely administered because only YHWH enforces the כרת-penalty (Hasel, Wenham). See Milgrom,

view the כרת-penalty as the removal of either the offender or their lineage from the community. By entering into YHWH's Sabbath rhythm the Israelite community are revivified, while Sabbath Breakers are excised from the community and executed.

The ingroup's participation in the Sabbath rhythm also maintains their sacred status. Because YHWH is the supreme model of holiness, Israel achieve holiness by imitating YHWH.[22] Part of this imitation includes Sabbath observance (cf. Exod. 31:15-17), which serves as a sign that YHWH sanctifies Israel (Exod. 31:13).[23] The final כי clause of v. 13 links Sabbath observance to holiness, and echoes Exod. 19:5-6, which recalls YHWH's promise to Israel: 'if you will indeed obey my voice and keep my covenant, you shall be my treasured possession among all peoples, for all the earth is mine; and you shall be to me a kingdom of Priests and a holy nation (וגוי קדוש)'.[24] The next כי clause, in Exod. 31:14a, describes the Sabbath as 'your holiness', which suggests that Israel's sacred status is contingent upon Sabbath observance (v. 15b). In addition to the Sabbath, first fruits offerings, tithes, the Nazarites, the incense altar, and the incense burned upon it are described as קדש ליהוה.[25] The plate on the High Priest's turban also bears this phrase (Exod. 28:36; 39:30). In each of these instances, the designation of an object as קדש ליהוה places special restrictions upon the object's function, while reserving it for a unique, often cultic, purpose.[26]

The High Priest, for example, is the only person permitted to perform the necessary rituals in the Holiest of Holies on the Day of Atonement (Lev. 16). His special status also places limits on his participation in other activities, such as customary mourning rites (Lev. 21:1-11).[27] Similarly, first fruits offerings, tithes, and sacred incense were reserved for YHWH and were not to be used for any other purpose. Likewise,

---

Numbers, 405–8; Sklar, *Sin, Impurity, Sacrifice, Atonement*, 20; Hasel, 'Karat', 348; Gordon J. Wenham, *The Book of Leviticus* (Grand Rapids: Eerdmans, 1979), 285–6.

22. Lev. 11:44-45; 19:2; 20:7. David P. Wright, 'Holiness in Leviticus and Beyond: Differing Perspectives', *Interpretation* 53, no. 4 (1999): 352–3.

23. Ibid., 353.

24. Both of these passages assert that Israel will be 'holy' (קדש), if they שמר YHWH's covenant (ברית). These common terms, used with the shared context of a divine address to the people of Israel concerning obedience, satisfies Hayes' second criterion, which identifies Exod. 31:12-17 as a strong echo of Exod. 19:5-6.

25. Exod. 30:10, 37; Lev. 23:20; 27:28-32; Num. 6:8.

26. Stuart, *Exodus*, 635; Sarna, *Exodus*, 183.

27. Rooker, *Leviticus*, 273–4; Levine, *Leviticus*, 142–3.

work is forbidden on the Sabbath because this day is קדש ליהוה. While other objects described as קדש ליהוה, such as the Tabernacle's incense (Exod. 30:37), are sacred icons, the Sabbath constitutes sacred time.[28] By observing the Sabbath, the ingroup enter into a sacred rhythm, which is analogous to High Priest's vocation within the Tabernacle.[29] In this way, Exod. 31:12-17 portrays those who observe the Sabbath as sacred ingroup members, while those who desecrate the Sabbath are identified as a dangerous outgroup. For this reason, Exod. 31:13 and 17 describe the Sabbath as a 'sign' of ingroup identity.[30]

The repetition of verses Exod. 31:13-14 in vv. 16-17 emphasizes the Sabbath's role as a 'sign between' YHWH and Israel.[31] From a mimetic perspective, the sign of Sabbath observance identifies the Israelite ingroup. According to Nahum Sarna, the 'sign' of Sabbath observance signifies faith:

> Its observance is a declaration of faith, an affirmation that Israel is a holy nation not inherently but by an act of divine will; that the relationship between God and Israel is regulated by a covenant; and that the universe is wholly the purposeful product of divine intelligence, the work of a transcendent Being outside of nature and sovereign over space and time.[32]

By observing the weekly Sabbath, the ingroup declare their faith in YHWH and his sovereignty over his creation. As Sarna notes, the basis of this faith is Israel's relationship with YHWH which is 'regulated by a covenant'. This idea is consistent with the command in Exod. 31:16: 'Israel shall keep the Sabbath...as a covenant forever (ברית עולם)'. The phrase ברית עולם is an ingroup signifier, which promises peace and prosperity.[33] A similar use of ברית עולם is observed in the Noachide covenant:

---

28. Like the Sabbath, other holy icons, such as the bread of presence, are also described as ברית עולם. Propp, *Exodus 19–40*, 494.

29. The key terms, עבד and שמר, employed throughout Exod. 31:12-17, further portray the sacred nature of Sabbath observance by linking this activity to Adam's vocation in the Garden (Gen. 2:15) and the Levite's responsibility of 'serving' and 'guarding' the tabernacle (Num. 3:7-8; 18:5-6).

30. S. van den Eynde, 'Keeping God's Sabbath: אות and ברית (Exod 31,12-17)', in *Studies in the Book of Exodus: Redaction, Reception, Interpretation*, ed. Marc Vervenne (Leuven: Peeters, 1996), 509–11.

31. Stuart, *Exodus*, 654–5.

32. Sarna, *Exodus*, 201.

33. Cf. 2 Sam. 23:5; Isa. 55:3; Jer. 32:40; 50:5; Ezek. 37:26.

And God said, 'This is the sign of the covenant (אות־הברית) that I make between me and you and every living creature that is with you, for all future generations: I have set my bow in the cloud, and it shall be a sign of the covenant (לאות ברית) between me and the earth. When I bring clouds over the earth and the bow is seen in the clouds, I will remember my covenant that is between me and you and every living creature of all flesh. And the waters shall never again become a flood to destroy all flesh. When the bow is in the clouds, I will see it and remember the everlasting covenant (ברית עולם) between God and every living creature of all flesh that is on the earth.' God said to Noah, 'This is the sign of the covenant (ברית עולם) that I have established between me and all flesh that is on the earth'. (Gen. 9:12-17)

As signs of the ברית עולם, both the rainbow and the Sabbath serve as reminders of the special relationship between the YHWH and the ingroup, which are built into the created order.[34] Just as the rainbow in Gen. 9:12-17 serves as a reminder of YHWH's covenant promise to keep the destructive flood waters at bay, so the Sabbath testifies to the sacred status of the Israelite ingroup, and that this status is a result of YHWH's sanctification (Exod. 31:13, 17). This idea portrays the ingroup as holy, like the priests who are also sanctified by YHWH (Lev. 21:8), and recalls Israel's designation as a 'kingdom of priests' (Exod. 19:5-6).[35] Therefore, according to Exod. 31:12-17, Sabbath observance identifies the sacred ingroup.[36] Even slaves and animals must be granted Sabbath rest (Exod. 20:10; Deut. 5:14). Furthermore, the emancipation of slaves in the Sabbath year and the return of the Land to its original owners in the year of Jubilee (Lev. 25:1-55) mirror the rest enjoyed by YHWH's people on the weekly Sabbath.[37] In this sense, the Sabbath also signifies Israel's freedom, won through YHWH's liberating actions (Deut. 5:15). Those

---

34. Michael V. Fox, 'The Sign of the Covenant: Circumcision in the Light of the Priestly *'Ot* Etiologies', *Revue Biblique* 81, no. 4 (1974): 576–7.

35. Lev. 21:8, 15, 23; 22:9, 16, 32. Waldemar Janzen links the phrase קדש ליהוה on the High Priest's turban to Exod. 19:6, and interprets this phrase as an expression of 'Israel's status as a *priestly kingdom and a holy nation*'. Janzen, *Exodus*, 357.

36. Cf. Hasel, 'The Sabbath in the Pentateuch', 34–6. In a sense, then, Sabbath observance is both a sign of the covenant and a part of it (cf. Exod. 31:16). Daniel Timmer, 'Creation, Tabernacle and Sabbath: The Function of the Sabbath Frame in Exodus 31:12–17; 35:1–3' (PhD diss., Trinity Evangelical Divinity School, 2006), 73–4.

37. Philip Peter Jenson, *Graded Holiness: A Key to the Priestly Conception of the World* (Edinburgh: A. & C. Black, 1992), 196–7.

who desecrate the Sabbath spurn YHWH's liberation of the Israelites from their Egyptian overlords.[38]

In sum, according to the Pentateuch, the Sabbath rhythm is built into creation. Just as YHWH concluded his creative work by resting on the Sabbath, so the Israelites are called to imitate this rhythm in their daily lives. By abstaining from all work on the Sabbath, including actions associated with food production, the ingroup participate in the Sabbath rhythm, reflect the divine image, and maintain their sacred identity as YHWH's children. Those Israelites who fail to participate in the Sabbath rhythm are considered dangerous outgroup members, who threaten the ingroup's ability to reflect the divine image by undermining the core communal value of Sabbath observance and must, therefore, be immolated. This process is illustrated in Num. 15:32-36, which narrates the story of a man who is killed for 'gathering sticks' on the Sabbath.

3. *The Sabbath-gatherer of Numbers 15:32-36*

[32] While the people of Israel were in the wilderness, they found a man gathering sticks on the Sabbath day.	וַיִּהְיוּ בְנֵי־יִשְׂרָאֵל בַּמִּדְבָּר וַיִּמְצְאוּ אִישׁ מְקֹשֵׁשׁ עֵצִים בְּיוֹם הַשַּׁבָּת
[33] And those who found him gathering sticks brought him to Moses and Aaron and to all the congregation.	וַיַּקְרִיבוּ אֹתוֹ הַמֹּצְאִים אֹתוֹ מְקֹשֵׁשׁ עֵצִים אֶל־מֹשֶׁה וְאֶל־אַהֲרֹן וְאֶל כָּל־הָעֵדָה:
[34] They put him in custody, because it had not been made clear what should be done to him.	וַיַּנִּיחוּ אֹתוֹ בַּמִּשְׁמָר כִּי לֹא פֹרַשׁ מַה־יֵּעָשֶׂה לוֹ:
[35] And YHWH said to Moses, 'The man shall be put to death; all the congregation shall stone him with stones outside the camp'.	וַיֹּאמֶר יהוה אֶל־מֹשֶׁה מוֹת יוּמַת הָאִישׁ רָגוֹם אֹתוֹ בָאֲבָנִים כָּל־הָעֵדָה מִחוּץ לַמַּחֲנֶה
[36] And all the congregation brought him outside the camp and stoned him to death with stones, as YHWH commanded Moses.	וַיֹּצִיאוּ אֹתוֹ כָּל־הָעֵדָה אֶל־מִחוּץ לַמַּחֲנֶה וַיִּרְגְּמוּ אֹתוֹ בָּאֲבָנִים וַיָּמֹת צִוָּה יהוה אֶת־מֹשֶׁה:

In what follows, I draw upon the insights gleaned in the previous two sections to present a narrative reading of Num. 15:32-36. The narrative approach acknowledges that Num. 15:32-36 must be read within its literary context. With this in mind, an examination of the preceding

---

38. Burnside, '"What Shall We Do with the Sabbath-Gatherer?"', 55.

treatise, which outlines the management of שגגה offenses and offences committed ביד רמה (vv. 22-31), is necessary before considering the case of the Sabbath Gatherer.[39] While atonement (כפר) and forgiveness for שגגה offences can be achieved through an offering (Lev. 4:1–5:19; Num. 15:22-29), offences committed with a high hand receive the כרת-penalty:

> But the person who does anything with a high hand (ביד רמה), whether he is native or a sojourner, reviles YHWH, and that person shall be cut off from among his people. Because he has despised the word of YHWH and has broken his commandment, that person shall be utterly cut off; his iniquity shall be on him. (vv. 30-31)

The meanings of שגגה and ביד רמה are debated. To gain a better understanding of these concepts, various interpretations of שגגה and ביד רמה are presented and evaluated below. This survey is followed by an explanation of why the Sabbath-gatherer must be executed. From a mimetic perspective, much like the Blasphemer in Lev. 24:10-23, this malefactor is executed as a communal scapegoat. To confirm this reading, the next section applies Girard's scapegoat stereotypes, revealing the presence of the scapegoat mechanism within this text.

Much debate surrounds the use of the term שגגה in Numbers 15. Some have argued that שגגה offences are committed inadvertently, as opposed to ביד רמה offences which are intentional and may not be expiated.[40] However, this interpretation is somewhat problematic, because the term שגגה may also describe intentional offenses (1 Sam. 26:21; Ezek. 45:20).[41] Furthermore, the purification offering expiates for some intentional offenses (Lev. 5:1-4), and the Day of Atonement achieves expiation for the community's עון, חטא, and deliberate, wanton פשעים.[42] Another interpretation is presented by Baruch Levine, who argues that sins committed ביד רמה contrast inadvertent שגגה offences because they are premeditated. But this theory is inconsistent with the immolation of the Blasphemer in Lev. 24:10-16, whose actions are not premeditated.[43] For these reasons, the current book rejects the idea that שגגה offences are inadvertent, and

---

39. Milgrom, *Leviticus 1–16*, 228; Rooker, *Leviticus*, 108–9; Levine, *Leviticus*, 19.
40. P. P. Saydon, 'Sin-Offering and Trespass-Offering', *The Catholic Biblical Quarterly* 8, no. 4 (1946): 397; Milgrom, *Leviticus 1–16*, 228.
41. Rodriguez, 'Substitution', 84.
42. Gane, *Cult and Character*, 204–5; Rodriguez, 'Substitution', 98, 148.
43. Gane, *Cult and Character*, 210.

can be expiated through sacrifice, while ביד רמה sins cannot because they are deliberate (and premeditated).

Milgrom recognizes and attempts to overcome this difficulty by suggesting that repentance downgrades an inexpiable ביד רמה sin to an expiable שגגה offense.[44] But, if all sins can be expiated through sacrifice and repentance, no distinction remains between שגגה offences and those committed ביד רמה, other than the repentance (or lack thereof) that follows them.[45] Although Milgrom argues that 'all deliberate sins are regarded as presumptuous unless they are tempered by *subsequent* acts of repentance', the Pentateuch provides no example of this dynamic in connection with grave sins, such as those which attract human immolation or the כרת-penalty.[46] For example, in the case of the Sabbath-gatherer no opportunity for repentance is granted.[47] On account of the lack of evidence that repentance downgrades an offence from inexpiable ביד רמה status to expiable שגגה status, this study leaves behind Milgrom's interpretation of the ביד רמה phrase.

Phillips offers another explanation, arguing that expiable שגגה offenses, as opposed to brazen offenses that are committed ביד רמה, are hidden from the community.[48] According to Phillips, by treating undetected שגגה offenses with extreme leniency, the Priestly writer encourages confession from unknown offenders.[49] Yet, this interpretation is also problematic because the כרת-penalty is prescribed in cases of undetected sins, such as illicit sex acts (Lev. 20:17-21). In these cases, human detection is irrelevant because the כרת-penalty is divinely mediated.[50] Furthermore, the secrecy of Achan's sin in Joshua 7 does not save him from being immolated.[51] Therefore, the assumption that שגגה offenses are undetectable, while ביד רמה sins are overt and brazen, does not appear to adequately explain the difference between these two categories.

Adrian Schenker also argues that confession and sacrifice atones for inadvertent and secret offences, while those who are guilty of ביד רמה sins, which are 'Öffentlich' and 'demonstrativ', must be sentenced to death. As Schenker notes, Israel's Exodus from Egypt is also undertaken

---

44. Milgrom, *Leviticus 1–16*, 301–2.
45. Cf. Rodriguez, 'Substitution', 98–9; Rooker, *Leviticus*, 55.
46. Milgrom, *Leviticus 23–27*, 2449; Frank Crüsemann, *Torah: Theology and Social History of Old Testament Law* (Edinburgh: T. & T. Clark, 1996), 318.
47. Phillips, *Essays on Biblical Law*, 258.
48. Ibid., 255–60.
49. Ibid., 259.
50. Gane, *Cult and Character*, 208–9.
51. Ibid.

ביד רמה (Exod. 14:8; Num. 33:3), and in his rebellion Jeroboam 'erhob die Hand gegen gegen der König' (1 Kgs 11:26).[52] Furthermore, the ביד רמה image draws upon the ancient, iconic conception of deities with weapons in their raised hands, which communicated that they were 'triumphantly determined to fight and to win'.[53] This interpretation of the ביד רמה imagery is confirmed by Gen. 14:22, in which Abraham describes his defeat of 'Chedorlaomer and the kings who were with him' as lifting his hand to YHWH (הרימתי ידי אל־יהוה). Acts of defiant warfare waged against an enemy king are commonly described by the phrase ביד רמה. Sins committed ביד רמה against YHWH represent an act of rebellion against YHWH and his covenant.[54]

From a mimetic perspective, sinning with a high hand describes an act which generates mimetic rivalry. Such acts contrast the sins addressed in vv. 22-29, which may be expiated through animal sacrifice, so that the offeror may be forgiven. Herein lies the key difference between שגגה offenses and sins committed ביד רמה. High handed sins cannot be forgiven as they defiantly attack the community's foundation and core values. With the possibility of expiation and forgiveness removed, the high-handed offender must be immolated as a communal scapegoat. On the other hand, reparation for the rivalry generated through שגגה offenses may be achieved through animal sacrifice, which allows the offender to continue living in harmony with other community members.

The placement of the Sabbath-gatherer narrative directly after the legal material of vv. 22-31 suggest that his actions represent an example of rebellion ביד רמה.[55] While the Tabernacle represents sacred space, the Sabbath rhythm functions as sacred time, and Israel is called to continue YHWH's creative work by entering into the Sabbath rhythm. The Sabbath-gatherer collects sticks, presumably to kindle a fire for food preparation, and in so doing violates the sacred Sabbath rhythm

---

52. Adrian Schenker, *Recht und Kult im Alten Testament* (Göttingen: Vandenhoeck & Ruprecht, 2000), 121.

53. C. J. Labuschagne, 'The Meaning of Beyad Rama in the Old Testament', in *Von Kanaan Bis Kerala: Festschrift für J. P. M. Van Der Ploeg*, ed. W. C. Delsman (Leiden: Brill, 1982), 146.

54. Gane, *Cult and Character*, 209.

55. Although the divinely mediated כרת penalty is prescribed for high handed offenses in Num. 15:30-31, the Sabbath-gatherer is immolated through communal stoning. Milgrom resolves this discrepancy by concluding that whoever desecrates the Sabbath receives both penalties. This reading is confirmed by Exod. 31:12-18. Milgrom, *Numbers*, 125–6.

(cf. Exod. 35:3).[56] Through this act, the Sabbath-gatherer desecrates the Israelite community and YHWH's sacred time. This act of rebellion is tantamount to a physical attack upon the Tabernacle. Furthermore, because the Sabbath marks and consummates YHWH's victory over the primordial elements, the Sabbath-gatherer's actions challenge YHWH's supremacy over creation. In this way, the Sabbath-gatherer's actions represent an act of rebellion against YHWH.[57]

Moreover, by gathering wood on the Sabbath, the Sabbath-gatherer spurns YHWH's new Sabbath economy, preferring his period of slavery in Egypt. In Egypt, the Israelites were compelled by their Egyptian rivals to gather (קשש) straw for brick production (Exod. 5:7). The narrative approach recognizes that the Sabbath-gatherer mirrors this action by gathering (קשש) sticks on the Sabbath for food production.[58] As Jonathan Burnside argues, the Sabbath-gatherer's involvement in food production on the Sabbath recalls the Israelites' period of slavery under Pharaoh, who forced them to work continuously for seven days a week without rest:

> Instead of evoking God's rule in Gen 1:1–2:4 the man's behaviour evokes Pharaoh's rule in Exod 5. It reflects a desire to return to the economic conditions associated with Pharaoh and thus signifies the rejection of YHWH's lordship. This reading strengthens the common view that the story is deliberately located in the book of Numbers as an example of the offence that is committed 'with upraised hand' (Num 15:30). The 'upraised hand' (which functions visually as a sign of protest) contrasts with the 'mighty hand' (e.g. Exod 32:11) with which God delivered Israel out of Egypt. The Sabbath-breaker's behaviour thus signifies a desire to return to Egypt. In this sense it thematically repeats the earlier spy-story which includes a statement of the Israelites' desire to return to Egypt (Num 14:4).[59]

---

56. Burnside, '"What Shall We Do with the Sabbath-Gatherer?"', 52–3; Baruch Levine, *Numbers 1–20: A New Translation with Commentary* (New York: Doubleday, 1993), 398–9.

57. Finkelstein, 'The Ox That Gored', 28.

58. Burnside, '"What Shall We Do with the Sabbath-Gatherer?"', 54. This echo is quite strong because the term קשש only occurs in these two instances (Exod. 5:7, 12; Num. 15:32, 33) within the Pentateuch. In both cases a subject gathers an object to aid the production of something else. In the Exodus the Israelites gather straw to produce bricks, while in Num. 15:32-36 the offender gathers wood to produce a meal. This echo, therefore, satisfies Hayes' second criterion because it utilizes an extremely rare term within a shared context.

59. Ibid., 58–9.

In this way, the text portrays the Sabbath-gatherer as a dangerous, foreign influence, who threatens the freedom and sanctity of the Israelite ingroup. Through the Sabbath-gatherer's immolation, the ingroup re-enact their Exodus from Egypt as, once again, they demonstrate their loyalty to YHWH by raising their hand in triumph (cf. Exod. 14:8; Num. 33:3) against the one who raised his hand against YHWH (Num. 15:30). In so doing, the ingroup guard their own sanctity.

In sum, the Sabbath-gatherer's actions constitute an act of rebellion and identify him with Egypt, Israel's rival throughout the Exodus narrative. In this way, Num. 15:32-36 portrays the Sabbath-gatherer as a dangerous rival to the faithful, Israelite ingroup. From a mimetic perspective, the Sabbath-gatherer may serve as a model to others within the community. If others imitate his behaviour, the identity of the community and their sacred status will be jeopardized. For this reason, the Sabbath-gatherer must be executed as a communal scapegoat. Through this act, the community vent their mimetic rivalries, and confirm their commitment to the Sabbath rhythm. This interpretation is confirmed in the next section, through the application of Girard's scapegoat stereotypes to my narrative reading of Num. 15:32-36.

4. *Girard's Four Stereotypes*

The case of the Sabbath-gatherer in Num. 15:30-36 shares many similarities with that of the Blasphemer, discussed in the previous chapter, including the presence of Girard's four stereotypes. Although the presence of Girard's first stereotype, the mimetic crisis, is not as clearly portrayed as it is in Lev. 24:10-16, the potential for a mimetic crisis is suggested in a number of ways. First, as noted above, in Num. 15:32-36 the offender gathers (קשש) sticks. Through this action, the Sabbath-gatherer re-enacts Israel's vocation as slaves in Egypt, and recalls the imagery of the Exodus crisis. With this echo, Num. 15:32-36 threatens a reversal of Israel's liberation from slavery in Egypt, the fulfilment of which is closely linked to the Sabbath within the Pentateuch (Deut. 5:15). This reversal would culminate in a return to slavery, characterized by perpetual work without Sabbath rest, like that experienced by Israel in Egypt under Pharaoh (Exod. 5:5-23). Second, the Sabbath-gatherer's actions contravene the institution of Sabbath observance (Exod. 35:3). This contravention suggests a breakdown of the social order, which is characteristic of a mimetic crisis. Third, this breakdown results in a lack of differentiation between Israel, who observe the Sabbath, and other nations who do not. This lack of differentiation also suggests a mimetic crisis. While the actions of one malefactor does not constitute a mimetic crisis, the crisis threatened here may ensue, if others in the community imitate the Sabbath-gatherer's behaviour. In this way, Num. 15:32-36 at least threatens a mimetic crisis, which is Girard's first stereotype.

Girard's second stereotype may be identified in the blame placed upon the Sabbath-gatherer for the potential mimetic crisis. The Sabbath-gatherer's high-handed actions identify him with Egypt, which places him in direct rivalry with the rest of the Israelite community. As a seditious Israelite, who identifies with Egypt, the Sabbath-gatherer is held in custody pending divine revelation (v. 34). With this action, the community has identified the Sabbath-gatherer as an outgroup member, whose actions threaten to bring a mimetic crisis upon the nation of Israel. Furthermore, when read in concert with Exod. 31:12-17, the Sabbath-gatherer's actions threaten the sacred identity of the faithful Israelite community and, in this way, place the community in jeopardy. Moreover, as an example of someone who sins ביד רמה, the Sabbath-gatherer must bear his sin (Num. 15:31), a statement which assures the ingroup that they will not incur bloodguilt through the immolation of the offender.[60] No bloodguilt is incurred through this act because the offender is regarded as an outgroup member and must, therefore, bear his sin. Through these means, Num. 15:30-36 portrays the Sabbath-gatherer as a communal scapegoat, who is blamed for the potential crisis, which satisfies Girard's second stereotype. Although Girard's third stereotype is not present, his fourth stereotype can be observed through the stoning of the Sabbath-gatherer outside the camp. The presence of these three stereotypes confirms the presence of the scapegoat mechanism in Num. 15:32-36 and supports the narrative reading of this text presented above.

The community is drawn together, as they vent their mimetic rivalries, and restore peace and order at the expense of the Sabbath-gatherer's life. However, communal stoning is only associated with Sabbath desecration in Exod. 31:12-17; 35:2; and Num. 15:32-36, but not other texts which address the Sabbath observance. Israel Knohl assigns Exod. 31:12-17; 35:2; and Num. 15:32-36 to the H source, and argues that H introduces the death penalty for Sabbath desecration in an attempt to elevate the sanctity of the Sabbath. Note that Knohl uses the abbreviation HS in place of H, and PT to describe the Priestly Source:[61]

---

60. Péter-Contesse and Ellington, *Leviticus*, 304; Milgrom, *Leviticus 17–22*, 1746–7; Hieke, 'Das Alte Testament und die Todesstrafe', 356.
61. Israel Knohl, *The Sanctuary of Silence: The Priestly Torah and the Holiness School* (Winona Lake: Eisenbrauns, 2007), 15–18.

> While HS goes to great lengths to stress the importance of Sabbath observance, threatens those who desecrate it with stringent punishments, and goes into the details of forbidden labours, PT nowhere explicitly forbids labors on the Sabbath. The differences in approach become clearest when we contrast the two Sabbath passages in Lev 23:3 and Num 28:9-10. The Leviticus passage, which belongs to HS, is completely concerned with forbidden labours and has nothing to say about any additional sacrifices, whereas the PT passage in Numbers deals only with sacrifices and makes no mention of forbidden labours, despite the fact that throughout the same pericope the labours forbidden on the various festivals are mentioned along with their sacrifices…
>
> The revolutionary project of HS was guided by its vision – to create a broad, all-inclusive framework of faith and cult, in which the multifarious values of the religious experience would be combined: it would express both the reflections of the priests serving in the Sanctuary and the innermost needs of the people in the fields.[62]

Knohl's observations concerning H's unique treatment of the Sabbath have been broadly accepted. However, his claim that H attempted to manufacture an 'all-inclusive framework of faith and cult' remains problematic, because it assumes a structuralist framework in which thought gives birth to ritual. Modern ritual studies have debunked this approach, demonstrating that ritual precedes theological and philosophical speculation.[63] For these reasons, Knohl's attempt to explain why H, as the latest of the major Pentateuchal source documents, uniquely prescribes the death penalty for Sabbath desecration should be rejected.

Mimetic theory suggests a plausible explanation for H's introduction of the death penalty, for those who desecrate the Sabbath. In the midst of a mimetic crisis, the community may have searched for a scapegoat, upon whom they might vent their collective rivalries. Excessive imitation within the community eventually prompts the crowd to converge on a single scapegoat, who is unanimously blamed for the crisis. This person is selected because their refusal to comply with the communal norm of Sabbath observance sets them apart from the rest of their community. As community members vent their collective rivalries upon their scapegoat, they experience a transcendent sense of peace and calm. In time, the community attempt to re-discover this experience by executing others who desecrate the Sabbath. Each subsequent execution is justified by the

---

62. Ibid., 198.
63. Tracy M. Lemos, 'Where There Is Dirt, Is There System? Revisiting Biblical Purity Constructions', *Journal for the Study of the Old Testament* 37, no. 3 (2013): 266–80.

transcendent sense of peace and order experienced by the community. Eventually, H incorporates this practice into its corpus, prescribing the execution of Sabbath breakers (Exod. 31:12-17; 35:2), and including an account of the Sabbath-gatherer's execution in Num. 15:32-36. The Sabbath-gatherer serves as the foundational scapegoat, whose execution inspires the scapegoating of other Sabbath breakers, and H's eventual legislation of this practice.

5. Conclusion

Like the immolation of the Blasphemer in Lev. 24:10-16, the Sabbath-gatherer is executed as a communal scapegoat. Through this act the ingroup vent their mimetic rivalries. The Sabbath-gatherer is selected as a scapegoat because his actions contravene the sacred Sabbath rhythm, threaten the ingroup's ability to faithfully reflect the divine image, and constitute an act of rebellion against YHWH. Through the Sabbath-gatherer's immolation, the ingroup declare their allegiance to YHWH, as they all band together to raise their hands against the Sabbath-gatherer. In this way, Num. 15:30-36 encourages the execution of Sabbath breakers, which draws the ingroup together and maintains their sanctity at the expense of the outgroup. A similar dynamic is also evident in the Pentateuchal texts which address bloodshed (e.g. Num. 35:30-34; Deut. 19:1-13). These texts, which are the subject of the next chapter, employ the concepts of impurity and bloodguilt to portray murderers as a threat to the ingroup's wellbeing.

Chapter 6

HOMICIDE IN THE PENTATEUCH

As discussed in the opening chapter of this book, scholars have offered various explanations for the Pentateuch's prescription of execution in cases of murder. The present chapter applies mimetic theory to a narrative reading of Pentateuchal texts that prescribe the execution of murderers to produce a fresh interpretation of these texts. This reading looks beyond the rhetoric of impurity and danger employed by these texts to reveal the presence of the scapegoat mechanism in each case. Numbers 35:30-34, for example, states that bloodshed pollutes the land, and that atonement (כִּפֶּר) for this pollution can only be achieved through the immolation of the murderer. From a mimetic perspective, the language of impurity and pollution in this text refers to excessive levels of mimetic violence. As Girard writes:

> Two men come to blows; blood is spilt; both men are thus rendered impure. The impurity is contagious, and anyone who remains in their presence risks becoming a party to their quarrel. The only sure way to avoid contagion is to flee the scene of violence…
>
> Violence too long held in check will overflow its bounds – and woe to those who happen to be nearby. Ritual precautions are intended both to prevent this flooding and to offer protection, insofar as it is possible, to those who find themselves in the path of ritual impurity – that is, caught in the floodtide of violence.[1]

When the land becomes defiled with violence the community must vent their mimetic rivalries upon a scapegoat to prevent a mimetic crisis. To this end, Num. 35:30-34 commands the immolation of those who illegitimately shed blood. These offenders are portrayed as an outgroup of potential scapegoats that jeopardize the wellbeing of the faithful

---

1. Girard, *Violence and the Sacred*, 28, 30.

ingroup. Only through the immolation of the murderer outgroup is this danger removed. This concept is repeated in Exod. 21:12-14 and Deut. 19:1-13, albeit without the use of purity language. In this way, the Pentateuch encourages the ingroup to halt dangerous blood feuds within the community by venting mimetic violence, through the immolation of murderers.

This reading is explained and defended over five sections. The first section applies Girard's scapegoat stereotypes to a narrative reading of Gen. 4:1-16, the first homicide reported within the Pentateuch, to reveal the scapegoat mechanism in this text. As the Pentateuchal narrative progresses mimetic violence escalates, culminating in a mimetic crisis, which is described through purity language (Gen. 6:11). Numbers 35:30-34 also employs purity language to describe the danger associated with bloodshed. Yet, before examining this text an appreciation of the key term כִּפֶּר is required. For this reason, the second section of the current chapter examines the use of the term כִּפֶּר within the Pentateuch, and argues that this term describes an act which protects the community from danger. I then apply this interpretation of כִּפֶּר to Num. 35:30-34, in the third section, to argue that by correctly utilizing Asylum Cities and immolating murderers, the ingroup protect the community from the danger associated with mimetic violence. The fourth section investigates the dualistic defiling/purifying nature of bloodshed in Num. 35:30-34, and outlines how mimetic theory helps interpret this dualism. A similar dualism is also identified in the treatment of murderers in Exodus and Deuteronomy in section five. In this section, I argue that a common social mechanism underlies all of these texts. Finally, this dynamic is identified as the scapegoat mechanism through the application of Girard's four stereotypes.

1. *The First Homicide*

The Pentateuch's first reported homicide, in Gen. 4:1-16, recounts the slaying of the ingroup member and divine image-bearer, Abel, at the hand of his brother, Cain. This narrative displays all four of Girard's stereotypes. The first stereotype can be seen as a mimetic crisis grows out of the excessive rivalry between the two brothers, until one slays the other.[2] Cain is then expelled from YHWH's presence and cursed 'from the

---

2. In this text the two brothers struggle over the coveted object of YHWH's acceptance. Warren, *Compassion or Apocalypse*, 132–4.

ground' on account of his fratricide.³ The ground will no longer produce a generous harvest for Cain to enjoy (v. 12). Cain is sentenced to become a 'fugitive and wanderer', which some interpret as a natural consequence of the land's barrenness.⁴ However, the description of Cain as a 'fugitive and wanderer' also describes Cain's expulsion from YHWH's presence. Elsewhere, the Pentateuch links YHWH's presence with blessing and fecundity (cf. Gen. 26:3; Num. 6:22-27), which represents the very antithesis of Cain's cursed existence on a fruitless ground. This exile and famine imagery communicates the presence of a mimetic crisis within the text, which satisfies Girard's first stereotype.

Girard's second stereotype can be seen as the outgroup member, Cain, is blamed for the mimetic crisis. Cain's outgroup status is emphasized as YHWH rejects his offering, while accepting Abel's offering (vv. 3-5). Acknowledging Cain's anger and disappointment, YHWH cautions Cain: 'If you do what is good will you not be accepted? But if you do not do what is good, חטאת is crouching at the door, and it desires you, but you must rule over it' (vv. 6-7). Despite YHWH's warning, Cain fails to rule over חטאת and kills his brother, Abel (v. 8). YHWH responds with the question, 'what have you done?' (v. 10). This question echoes YHWH's words to Cain's parents, Adam and Eve, in the preceding chapter (Gen. 3:13).⁵ Just as Adam and the serpent are blamed for the consequences of their actions, Cain is also blamed for the mimetic crisis which proceeds from his actions.⁶ In this way, Girard's second stereotype is fulfilled.

Girard's third and fourth stereotypes can also be discerned in Gen. 4:1-16 as YHWH expels Cain from his presence and places a 'sign' upon

---

3. The מן in v. 11 could be interpreted as comparative: 'you are *more* cursed than the ground'. However, in light of vv. 12 and 14 the phrase ועתה ארור אתה מן־האדמה should be interpreted as the ground cursing Cain by yielding a poor harvest of crops. William Reyburn and Euan McGregor Fry, *A Handbook on Genesis* (New York: United Bible Societies, 1997), 115.

4. Sarna, *Genesis*, 34; Herbert Edward Ryle, *The Book of Genesis* (Cambridge: Cambridge University Press, 1921), 75.

5. Due to the proximity of these two echoes to each other an audience could be reasonably expected to hear YHWH's words to Cain as a repetition of the words spoken to Cain's parents in Gen. 3:13, strongly satisfying Hayes' fifth criterion. Moreover, these phrases both take place in the shared context of YHWH responding to a human defying his warnings, which satisfies Hayes' second criterion. And, Hayes' sixth criteria is also fulfilled because others have noted this echo. Mathews, *Genesis 1–11: 26*, 275. These observations support the claim that Gen. 4:13 echoes 3:10.

6. On the placement of blame upon the Adam and the serpent in Gen. 3:14-19, see ibid, 243-54.

him, 'lest anyone who finds him should attack him' (vv. 14-15).[7] This 'sign' constitutes the preferential sign of the victim, and satisfies Girard's third stereotype,[8] and is later passed on to Cain's descendants, who become metalsmiths and musicians. These people were marginalized and feared because of the magical abilities ascribed to smiths and artisans, and intermarriage with these outgroups was considered strictly taboo.[9] Finally, YHWH rejects Cain and expels him from his presence, which fulfils Girard's fourth stereotype, the expulsion of the scapegoat. The presence of Girard's four scapegoat stereotypes in Gen. 4:1-16 reveals the scapegoat mechanism within this text.

Although Cain's expulsion is attributed to YHWH in Gen. 4:1-16, the presence of the scapegoat mechanism in this text suggests that the community expelled Cain from their midst during a mimetic crisis. By banding together and expelling Cain from their presence, the community experience catharsis as they purge their collective mimetic rivalries. The confusion of the mimetic crisis, coupled with the catharsis accompanying its resolution, leads the community to project their own violence onto YHWH. The community which expels a scapegoat from its midst will often attribute this act to a deity, because they see themselves as completely passive throughout the crisis and its resolution.[10] For this reason, the community's expulsion of Cain from their midst is attributed to YHWH in Gen. 4:1-16. The community's expulsion of the first murderer in Gen. 4:1-16 differs from the treatment of other murderers throughout the Pentateuch.

Although other Pentateuchal texts command that those who commit murder be handed over to the avenger of blood for execution (Num. 35:21; Deut. 19:12), Cain is merely expelled from his community. When Cain complains, asserting that 'whoever (כל) finds me will kill me', the

---

7. Although this passage is difficult to interpret, YHWH's promise of a seventy-fold vengeance upon Cain should be read within the context of Lamech's poem in vv. 23-24. Genesis 4 describes Cain and his descendants as ruthless outgroup of unkillable killers. This outgroup engage in rivalry with the faithful ingroup, who are represented by Abel, Seth, and his descendants (see Chapter 2).

8. James G. Williams argues that the sign portrays Cain as 'a kind of God whom others may not harm'. Williams, *The Bible, Violence, and the Sacred*, 36. In this way, Cain's sign portrays him as a formidable adversary who is virtually impossible to kill. The sign of Cain may serve to explain why the faithful Israelite ingroup have failed to eradicate the offspring of the serpent and are locked in a perpetual rivalry with this outgroup.

9. Paula M McNutt, 'In the Shadow of Cain', *Semeia* 87 (1999): 45–64.

10. Palaver, *René Girard's Mimetic Theory*, 153.

community responds, 'if anyone (כל) slays Cain, vengeance shall be taken on him sevenfold' (Gen. 4:14-15). Significantly, the term כל in these verses does not refer to the avenger of blood, but to others who have no right to kill Cain because they are not legitimately avenging the blood of their relative. When viewed from a mimetic perspective, these potential murderers have contracted Cain's violent contagion, which has been propagated throughout the community. Cain fears that he will be killed in the resulting blood feud. Yet, the community listens to his protest and protects Cain by placing a sign upon him. In this way, the Genesis narrative reveals an appreciation of the mimetic threat which murderous violence poses to the community.

Through this sign, those who would seek to kill Cain are warned that their actions will precipitate a lethal cycle of violence. By these means, the community attempts to stall the cycle of violence. This cycle is also threatened in Lamech's promise of vengeance (Gen. 4:23-24). However, in spite of these threats, mimetic violence eventually corrupts and fills the land (Gen. 6:11).[11] Acknowledging this process, the narrative approach reveals that Gen. 4:1-24 testifies to the contagious nature of violence, and may pave the way for subsequent Pentateuchal texts, which prescribe the execution of murderers. Even though Cain is quarantined from the rest of the community, his violence continues to spread, ultimately leading to the cataclysm narrated in Genesis 6–8. When read within this context, the community's decision to spare Cain's life represents a failed legal experiment, one which allowed murderous violence to spread and corrupt the land (Gen. 6:11). In response to these events, a new command is conceived in the wake of the flood: 'whoever sheds the blood of אדם, by אדם shall his blood be shed' (Gen. 9:6). This principle is repeated throughout the rest of the Pentateuch (Exod. 21:12-14; Num. 35:30-34; Deut. 19:1-13). From Gen. 9:6 onwards, the Pentateuch seeks to purge and manage mimetic violence through Asylum Cities and the execution of murderers at the hand of the avenger of blood (Num. 35:21; Deut. 19:12).

2. *Interpreting* כִּפֶּר

According to Num. 35:30-34, bloodshed defiles and pollutes the land. A mimetic interpretation of 35:30-34 will be presented in the third section of this chapter. However, before considering this text, a brief discussion of the verb כִּפֶּר, which is a key term in Num. 35:30-34, is necessary. This section surveys the recent literature regarding the use of this term within

---

11. Warren, *Compassion or Apocalypse*, 134–6; Bailie, *Violence Unveiled*, 138–9.

the Hebrew Bible, and argues that כִּפֶּר describes the effective removal of the danger posed by either impurity or sin. I then apply this interpretation of כִּפֶּר to a mimetic reading of Num. 35:30-34 in the next section. Through this exercise, I argue that the immolation of murderers prescribed in Num. 35:30-34 protects the community from the cycle of blood vengeance and prevents mimetic crises by venting mimetic violence in a controlled manner.

Although כִּפֶּר is an important concept within the Pentateuch, the meaning of this term is widely debated. Two basic suggestions have been offered concerning the etymology of the term כִּפֶּר, which is often translated 'atone'. The first suggestion is that the *piel* stem, כִּפֶּר, like the *qal* stem, כָּפַר, is derived from the Arabic cognate, *kafara*, which conveys the idea of covering over something (e.g. Gen. 6:14). Those who subscribe to this theory argue that כִּפֶּר conceals either sin or impurity from YHWH's sight.[12] For example, Mary Douglas argues that acts of כִּפֶּר cover over breaches in the divine–human relationship: 'When the covering of the universe has been rent, it is not the person who did the deed who needs urgently to be washed but the covering that needs repair... Repairing the covering is what atonement [viz. כִּפֶּר] achieves...'[13] However, this theory does not account for texts, such as Lev. 4:26, which use the term כִּפֶּר to describe the removal of impurity and/or sin from a person.[14]

A second etymology that has been suggested for the term כִּפֶּר better explains its use in passages such as Lev. 4:26. This approach claims that כִּפֶּר was derived from its Akkadian cognate, *kuppuru*, which conveys the idea of wiping something clean.[15] The link between the Akkadian concept of wiping (*kuppuru*) and cultic purification is illustrated in the text of

---

12. David Hoffmann, *Das Buch Leviticus*, vol. 1 (Berlin: Poppelauer, 1905), 123; D. Mangum et al., *The Lexham Theological Wordbook: Electronic Edition* (Bellingham: Lexham, 2014); Mary Douglas, 'Atonement in Leviticus', *Jewish Studies Quarterly* 1, no. 2 (1993): 116.

13. Douglas, 'Atonement in Leviticus', 123.

14. Gane examines the use of the term, כִּפֶּר, with the מִן preposition, and concludes that in each instance the מִן is privative, demonstrating that in these texts impurity (and/or sin) is removed from the offerer and not the sanctuary. This observation suggests that, with the exception of Azazel's goat in Lev. 16, all offerings benefit the offerer and, contra Douglas, do not address the rent universe. Gane, *Cult and Character*, 106–43, 93.

15. William K. Gilders, *Blood Ritual in the Hebrew Bible: Meaning and Power* (Baltimore: Johns Hopkins University Press, 2004), 28–9; Baruch A. Levine, *In the Presence of the Lord: A Study of Cult and Some Cultic Terms in Ancient Israel* (Leiden: Brill, 1974), 59–63; Milgrom, *Leviticus 1–16*, 1080; Janowski, *Sühne als Heilsgeschehen*, 27–102.

the Babylonian Akitu festival. On the fifth day of the Akitu festival the priest purifies the cella of Nabu by wiping (*kuppuru*) the temple walls with the carcass of a ram (line 354). This carcass acts somewhat like a sponge or detergent, absorbing impurity, and thereby cleansing the temple.[16] The importance of cleansing the temple was well appreciated by Israel and her ancient Near Eastern neighbours. If the biblical concept of כִּפֶּר is related to its Akkadian cognate, *kuppuru*, then it describes an act of ritual purification. Jacob Milgrom famously proposed a model for the conception of כִּפֶּר as purification with reference to Oscar Wilde's novel, *The Picture of Dorian Gray*. In Wilde's novel, the chief protagonist, Dorian Gray, leads a debaucherous lifestyle which mars a painted image of his likeness but not his physical appearance. Much like the marring of Gray's portrait, Milgrom argues that 'sin may not leave its mark on the face of the sinner, but it is certain to mark the face of the sanctuary, and unless it is quickly expunged, God's presence will depart'.[17] However, as Roy Gane has demonstrated, with the exception of Azazel's goat (Lev. 16) כִּפֶּר removes sin and/or impurity from the offerer and not the sanctuary.[18] Thus, although Milgrom correctly recognizes the cultic importance of כִּפֶּר, his focus on the sanctuary overlooks the effect of כִּפֶּר upon the offerer.

A more expansive view of כִּפֶּר is offered by Nobuyoshi Kiuchi, who argues that כִּפֶּר functions as a *supernym* of טהר, קדש, חטא, and נשא עון, and enables the transformation of a person or object from one state to another, such as from impure to pure, profane to holy, or impure to holy.[19] These transformations, however, do not fully explain the use of כִּפֶּר in passages such as Lev. 17:11:

[11a] For the life of the flesh is in the blood,	כִּי נֶפֶשׁ הַבָּשָׂר בַּדָּם הוּא
[11b] and I have given it for you on the altar to make atonement for your lives	וַאֲנִי נְתַתִּיו לָכֶם עַל־הַמִּזְבֵּחַ לְכַפֵּר עַל־נַפְשֹׁתֵיכֶם
[11c] for it is the blood that makes atonement by the life.	כִּי־הַדָּם הוּא בַּנֶּפֶשׁ יְכַפֵּר

Leviticus 17:11 describes the substitution of the life contained within sacrificial blood for the offerer's life. This substitution is described as

---

16. William K. Gilders prefers to refer to blood as a ritual 'disinfectant', in place of the more commonly used term 'detergent', because 'blood remains on the sancta to which it is applied, and…destroys impurity', rather than simply removing it. Gilders, *Blood Ritual*, 130.

17. Milgrom, 'Israel's Sanctuary', 398.

18. Gane, *Cult and Character*, 106–43.

19. Kiuchi, *The Purification Offering*, 97–9. See also Sklar, *Sin, Impurity, Sacrifice, Atonement*, 125–7.

an act of כִּפֶּר.[20] Janowski argues that the concept of כִּפֶּר as substitution, presented in Lev. 17:11, provides the key to correctly understanding כִּפֶּר throughout the entire Hebrew Bible.[21] Yet, one difficulty with this approach is that some passages, such as Num. 17:9-15, describe the act of כִּפֶּר without the substitutionary death of any animal. Furthermore, the conception of כִּפֶּר as substitutionary atonement, presented in Lev. 17:11, should not be imposed on texts ascribed to other sources, which literary critics date to an earlier period.[22] Despite these difficulties, the possibility that כִּפֶּר may, at times, convey connotations of substitution or ransom cannot be dismissed. While some texts employ כִּפֶּר to describe the purging or removal of sin and/or impurity, other texts, such as Lev. 17:11, appear to employ כִּפֶּר as a synonym for ransom, which presents the interpreter with a puzzling dualism.

In grappling with this dualism some have argued that the idea conveyed by the term כִּפֶּר is dependent upon the preposition that follows it. According to this theory, the phrase כפר על-נפשכם should be interpreted as an idiomatic phrase meaning 'to act as a ransom for your lives'.[23] This idea appears to be conveyed by the כפר על-נפשכם phrase in passages such as Exod. 30:11-16 and Num. 31:48-54. By contrast, when כִּפֶּר appears without the על-נפש phrase it refers to purification. The advantage of this approach is the flexibility it affords for interpreting כִּפֶּר as 'ransom' in texts which employ the כפר + על-נפש formula, while retaining the interpretation of כִּפֶּר as 'purification' in other texts. The weakness of this approach is that the כפר + על-נפש formula is not used in every case which employs כִּפֶּר to communicate the idea of ransom. For example, the כפר +על-נפש formula is absent from Gen. 32:21 (Eng. 32:20), in which Jacob hopes to כִּפֶּר his brother with a מנחה. Jacob's מנחה in this verse serves as a ransom for his life even in the absence of the כפר + על-נפש formula. Similarly, although the כפר + על-נפש formula is absent from Prov. 16:14, the idea of ransom is conveyed by the wise man who achieves כִּפֶּר for the king's wrath. Therefore, the presence or absence of the כפר + על-נפש formula is not a reliable indicator of the meaning of כִּפֶּר.

---

20. Janowski, *Sühne als Heilsgeschehen*, 359; Kiuchi, *The Purification Offering*, 105–6; Levine, *In the Presence of the Lord*, 68; Rodriguez, 'Substitution', 256.
21. Janowski, *Sühne als Heilsgeschehen*, 359.
22. Gilders, *Blood Ritual*, 170–6.
23. Levine, *In the Presence of the Lord*, 67–8; Milgrom, *Leviticus 1–16*, 707–8; Baruch J. Schwartz, 'The Prohibitions Concerning the "Eating" of Blood in Leviticus 17', in Anderson and Olyan, eds, *Priesthood and Cult in Ancient Israel*, 55–6; Gilders, *Blood Ritual*, 170–4.

Another interpretation of כִּפֶּר is proposed by Jay Sklar. Rather than differentiating between the ideas of purification and ransom, Sklar argues that כִּפֶּר conveys the dual function of purging impurity and ransoming one's life from death.[24] According to Sklar, both sin and impurity place an individual, and in some cases the entire community, in jeopardy.[25] Sklar argues that in the context of sin, the act of כִּפֶּר describes a ransom for life and, therefore, removes any imminent danger (e.g. Gen. 32:21).[26] Even in contexts which employ כִּפֶּר to describe the purgation of impurity, Sklar claims that כִּפֶּר represents an act of ransom because effective purification removes any danger associated with impurity.[27] Sklar's thesis finds some support in Num. 35:30-34, which discusses both the removal of pollution (חנף) and the ransoming of the community through human immolation.[28] Even the use of כִּפֶּר within the context of consecration is regarded by Sklar as an act of ransom, achieved through a type of super-cleansing, which is necessary to protect the lives of the Priests, Levites, and Nazarites from the danger posed by their respective offices.[29]

Sklar's work provides an elegant solution to the puzzle surrounding the use of כִּפֶּר in the Pentateuch. According to Sklar, כִּפֶּר describes an act which effectively removes danger. The ultimate aim of removing danger is common to all the interpretations of כִּפֶּר surveyed above. Whether an individual text appears to use כִּפֶּר to communicate an act of purification or ransom, the key aim of removing danger, and securing the wellbeing of the community, is always a function of כִּפֶּר. The presence and management of this danger can also be explained by applying mimetic theory. In what follows, I offer a mimetic interpretation of the Israelite cult's role of protecting the community, and I argue that the term כִּפֶּר describes an act which safeguards the community from the danger of a communal crisis by managing mimetic rivalry.

---

24. Sklar, *Sin, Impurity, Sacrifice, Atonement*.

25. This interpretation is similar to that offered by William Gilders, who translates the term כִּפֶּר as 'effecting removal of whatever causes a disruption in the proper workings of the divine–human relationship'. Gilders, *Blood Ritual*, 165. See also Gane, *Cult and Character*, 194–5.

26. Sklar, *Sin, Impurity, Sacrifice, Atonement*, 81–101.

27. Ibid., 130–3.

28. Ibid., 54–5.

29. The close relationship between כִּפֶּר and כֹּפֶר (ransom payment) in Num. 35:30-34 suggests that, at least in this passage, כִּפֶּר communicates the concept of rescue from imminent danger. Cf. Milgrom, *Numbers*, 370.

Girard argues that 'religion is nothing more than this immense effort to keep the peace' by managing mimetic violence.[30] According to Girard, the archaic sacred is birthed through the scapegoat mechanism, which prompts the community to band together and execute a single scapegoat in the midst of a mimetic crisis.[31] For the community, the scapegoat represents both absolute good and absolute evil.[32] The scapegoat is considered evil because they are blamed for the crisis, but also good on account of the catharsis experienced in their death. Girard postulates that this double transference leads the community to worship the scapegoat, which they have executed, as a god:

> If, as a present and living member of the community the victim brought death, and if, once dead, the victim brought life to the community, one will inevitably be led to believe that its ability to transcend the ordinary limits of the human in good and evil extends to life and death. If the victim possesses a life that is death and a death that is life, it must be that the basic facts of the human condition have no hold on the sacred. In this we witness the first outlines of religious transcendence.[33]

Although the current study does not assume Girard's theory concerning the origin of the sacred, his concept of double transference, in which the deity is perceived as both absolute good and absolute evil, helps explain why the Pentateuch portrays YHWH as both beneficent and maleficent. James Warren explains the concept of double transference by likening the Israelite cult to a nuclear power plant.[34] Spatially, these plants are designed around a core of dangerous radioactive material, just as the Tabernacle is designed around the adytum, which houses YHWH's dangerous yet potentially beneficent presence.[35] The graded holiness and dress of the cult's High Priest, Priests, Levites, and laity defines these people's place and role in relation to the adytum, much like workers in a nuclear power plant are trained, equipped, and dressed to occupy different spaces and carry out specific roles in relation to its radioactive core.[36] When these boundaries are transgressed in Num. 16:1-35, a mimetic crisis breaks out. This crisis, which sees many in the community killed,

---

30. Girard, Oughourlian, and Lefort, *Things Hidden*, 32.
31. Ibid., 35.
32. Palaver, *René Girard's Mimetic Theory*, 153.
33. Girard, Oughourlian, and Lefort, *Things Hidden*, 41.
34. Warren, *Compassion or Apocalypse*, 144–57.
35. Ibid., 146–7.
36. Ibid., 147–8.

is portrayed through the natural-disaster imagery of a deadly earthquake. In response to the people's complaining, YHWH then attempts to destroy the community with a plague, which also suggests a mimetic crisis (Num. 17:6-10). Aaron, however, achieves כִּפֶּר and stays the plague by offering incense (Num. 17:11-15).

Numbers 17:9-15 (in our English Bibles, 16:44-50) is particularly interesting because, unlike other acts of כִּפֶּר within the Pentateuch, it does not involve the slaying of an animal or the manipulation of blood. For this reason, Num. 17:9-15 serves as a useful text for exploring the meaning of the term, כִּפֶּר. In response to the plague of Num. 17:9-15, Moses commands Aaron to take his censer, 'put fire on it from the altar, lay incense on it, carry it quickly to the congregation, and make atonement for them (וכפר עליהם), for wrath has gone out from YHWH; the plague has begun' (17:11). The destruction threatened by YHWH's wrath parallels the devastating potential of radioactive material when handled carelessly.[37] Yet, when Aaron follows Moses' instructions, as the priest who is specifically trained and equipped to deal with these crises, he successfully stops the plague and achieves 'כִּפֶּר for the people' by placing an apotropaic incense barrier 'between the dead and the living' (17:12-13).[38]

The lack of purification terminology and animal blood suggests that כִּפֶּר, as it is used in Num. 17:9-15, communicates neither purification nor substitutionary atonement. Although Levine concedes that כִּפֶּר 'does not mean to "cleanse"' in this passage, he claims that the '*result* [of Aaron's incense rite] is a kind of purification'.[39] This interpretation is confusing. What Levine describes as 'a kind of purification' in this passage is not the cultic transformation from impure to pure, but rather the protection of the community from danger. Sklar's understanding of כִּפֶּר as the removal of danger explains the use of כִּפֶּר in Num. 17:9-15 in a way that the other approaches discussed above cannot. The present study, therefore, builds upon Sklar's conception of כִּפֶּר to interpret this term as a removal of danger, which may be achieved through various means, including animal substitution (Lev. 17:11), purification (Lev. 4:26), consecration (Exod. 29:36-37), and other apotropaic acts (Num. 17:9-15).

---

37. Ibid., 148–9.
38. Levine, *Numbers 1–20*, 420–1.
39. Ibid., 420. Italics in the original quote. Similarly, Milgrom subtly amends his regular translation of כִּפֶּר as 'purification' to 'make appeasement'. The appeasement of YHWH's wrath through Aaron's actions highlights the apotropaic dimension of כִּפֶּר in this text.

In sum, the Pentateuch uses the term כִּפֶּר to describe various transformations including purification, substitutionary atonement, and ransom payment. From a mimetic perspective, all of these transformations are necessary to protect the Israelite community from mimetic violence. Within this framework, כִּפֶּר is best understood as a broad supernym describing various acts that protect the community from the danger of a mimetic crisis by effectively managing mimetic rivalry. The narrative approach recognizes that this concept remains consistent across various texts, whether they describe the negative effects of mimetic violence through natural disaster or plague imagery (Gen. 6–9; Num. 17:9-15), in terms of bloodguilt (Deut. 19:1-13), or through purity language (Num. 35:30-34).

3. *Numbers 35:30-34*

According to Num. 35:30-34, the impurity associated with bloodshed pollutes and defiles the land. The mimetic approach employed in the current section interprets this pollution and defilement as excessive mimetic violence. In so doing, I do not wish to argue that the original authors and audience of Num. 35:30-34 would have equated impurity with mimetic violence, but rather that this text employs purity language to communicate the danger associated with illegitimate bloodshed and explain how this danger may be averted.[40] Through a narrative reading of this text, I argue that the concrete danger, which underlies the rhetoric of purity in Num. 35:30-34, is the spread of mimetic violence, which may precipitate a mimetic crisis. According to this reading, Asylum Cities attempt to stop the spread of mimetic violence and, in so doing, seek to avoid mimetic crises, like the one narrated in Genesis 6–9. Next, I argue that the immolation of murderers in Num. 35:30-34 also prevents mimetic crises by venting mimetic violence in a controlled manner. Numbers 35:30-34 describes this process as an act of כִּפֶּר which, as discussed above, protects the community from mimetic violence:

40. As Stephen F. Bigger writes, 'Pollution restrictions were not directly concerned with moral questions and most have no bearing on morality, but in some cases (such as in sexual matters) morality was in practice encouraged by fear of pollution... Any event, attitude or action that threatened social order was viewed with suspicion since social stability was paramount in the uncertain days of the settlement. Their fears of anything threatening life or order merged to form a wide-ranging mystical-yet very real-danger which we, for convenience, call "pollution". Stephen F. Bigger, 'The Family Laws of Leviticus 18 in Their Setting', *Journal of Biblical Literature* 98, no. 2 (1979): 195.

³⁰ If anyone kills a person,	כָּל־מַכֵּה־נֶפֶשׁ
the murderer shall be put to death on the evidence of witnesses.	לְפִי עֵדִים יִרְצַח אֶת־הָרֹצֵחַ
But no person shall be put to death on the testimony of one witness.	וְעֵד אֶחָד לֹא־יַעֲנֶה בְנֶפֶשׁ לָמוּת:
³¹ Moreover, you shall accept no ransom	וְלֹא־תִקְחוּ כֹפֶר
for the life of a murderer,	לְנֶפֶשׁ רֹצֵחַ
who is guilty of death,	אֲשֶׁר־הוּא רָשָׁע לָמוּת
but he shall be put to death.	כִּי־מוֹת יוּמָת:
³² And you shall accept no ransom	וְלֹא־תִקְחוּ כֹפֶר
for him who has fled to his city of refuge,	לָנוּס אֶל־עִיר מִקְלָטוֹ
that he may return to dwell in the land	לָשׁוּב לָשֶׁבֶת בָּאָרֶץ
before the death of the High Priest.	עַד־מוֹת הַכֹּהֵן:
³³ᵃ You shall not pollute the land	וְלֹא־תַחֲנִיפוּ אֶת־הָאָרֶץ
in which you live,	אֲשֶׁר אַתֶּם בָּהּ
for blood pollutes the land,	כִּי הַדָּם הוּא יַחֲנִיף אֶת־הָאָרֶץ
³³ᵇ and no atonement can be made for the land	וְלָאָרֶץ לֹא־יְכֻפַּר
for the blood that is shed in it,	לַדָּם אֲשֶׁר שֻׁפַּךְ־בָּהּ
except by the blood of the one who shed it.	כִּי־אִם בְּדַם שֹׁפְכוֹ:
³⁴ You shall not defile the land	וְלֹא תְטַמֵּא אֶת־הָאָרֶץ
in which you live,	אֲשֶׁר אַתֶּם יֹשְׁבִים בָּהּ
in the midst of which I dwell,	אֲשֶׁר אֲנִי שֹׁכֵן בְּתוֹכָהּ
for I the LORD dwell in the midst of	כִּי אֲנִי יְהוָה שֹׁכֵן בְּתוֹךְ
the people of Israel.	בְּנֵי יִשְׂרָאֵל:

3.1. *Asylum Cities and Bloodshed*

Because Num. 35:30-34 concludes the priestly law on Asylum Cities (Num. 35:9-34), these cities must be considered as part of a narrative approach to Num. 35:30-34. Asylum Cities control the practice of blood vengeance by providing a safe space, beyond the reach of the 'avenger of blood' (גאל הדם), to which the accused murderer may flee.[41] To avenge the death of his kin the avenger of blood seeks to kill the murderer.[42] This

---

41. Marilyn J. Lundberg, 'Cities of Refuge', in *Eerdmans Dictionary of the Bible*, ed. David Noel Freedman, Allen C. Myers, and Astrid B. Beck (Grand Rapids: Eerdmans 2000); N. H. Ridderbos, 'Cities of Refuge', in *The New Bible Dictionary, Third Edition*, ed. D. R. W. Wood and Ian Howard Marshall (Westmont: Inter-Varsity, 2001), 205; Moshe Greenberg, 'The Biblical Conception of Asylum', *Journal of Biblical Literature* (1959): 125–32.

42. Pamela Barmash, *Homicide in the Biblical World* (Cambridge: Cambridge University Press, 2005), 50–2. Some, however, have argued that the גאל הדם was not the victim's kin, but rather a state official who was responsible for avenging illegitimate killing. Anthony Phillips, *Ancient Israel's Criminal Law: A New Approach*

act of vengeance, however, causes the original murderer's kin to rise up and seek vengeance for their blood. In turn, vengeance for this killing is sought as a third avenger of blood arises. Following each murder another avenger of blood is drawn into the cycle of violence as each one imitates the murderous violence that was inflicted upon their relative. If left unchecked, this cycle may generate a mimetic crisis into which the whole community is drawn.

Asylum Cities limit mimetic violence, and thereby stall mimetic crises, by protecting accused murderers from the avenger of blood (cf. Exod. 21:12-14; Deut. 19:6). By contrast, outgroup members are not accepted into these cities, but are handed over to the avenger of blood for immolation, because they ambush and kill 'out of hatred... or enmity' with weapons (Num. 35:16-21).[43] Through this description, Num. 35:16-21 depicts the murderer outgroup as dangerous rivals to the ingroup. In contrast, ingroup members, who have killed someone 'without enmity' or the malicious use of a weapon, and without ambushing them, are accepted into Asylum Cities (vv. 22-29).[44] In this way, Asylum Cities control the venting of mimetic violence by handing over dangerous outgroup members for immolation, while protecting ingroup killers. This process prevents the avenger of blood from perpetuating a cycle of reciprocal violence (vv. 25-26), and helps achieve a controlled venting of mimetic violence against outgroup members, to prevent mimetic crises.[45]

The flood narrative of Genesis 6–9 describes a mimetic crisis that precipitates from the proliferation of mimetic violence. In Gen. 6:1-7, the land is corrupted and filled with murderous violence (חמס) as Cain's descendants proliferate and propagate mimetic violence. These events culminate in a mimetic crisis, which is depicted as a cataclysm (6:5,

---

to the Decalogue (New York: Schocken, 1970), 103; Mayer Sulzberger, *The Ancient Hebrew Law of Homicide* (Philadelphia: J. H. Greenstone, 1915), 53–4. However, the language of relationship and 'hot anger' associated with the גאל הדם suggests this individual was a close relative of the deceased (Deut. 19:6), rather than an impartial official (cf. 2 Sam. 3:30). Burnside, *God, Justice, and Society*, 255.

43. Burnside, *God, Justice, and Society*, 262.

44. The remainder of this chapter uses the term 'murderer' to refer to the specific outgroup whose violent actions are described in Num. 35:16-21. In contrast, the term 'killer' is reserved for ingroup members, who kill someone 'without enmity', ambush, or the malicious use of a weapon (Num. 35:22-29).

45. On the Asylum City's role in protecting the accused killer from the avenger of blood, see Jeffrey H. Tigay, *Deuteronomy*, The JPS Torah Commentary (Philadelphia: Jewish Publication Society, 1996), 179–80; Barmash, *Homicide in the Biblical World*, 24–5.

11-12).⁴⁶ Only the small ingroup of Noah and his family survives the flood because, in contrast to the rest of his generation, Noah was righteous (צדיק) and 'found favour in the eyes of YHWH' (vv. 8-9).⁴⁷ Following the flood, the land's fecundity returns and Noah becomes a successful farmer (Gen. 9:20-21). The imagery of a restored, post-cataclysmic creation, combined with Noah's neo-Adamic commission in Gen. 9:1-7, signals the end of the mimetic crisis.⁴⁸ The land has been successfully purified from mimetic violence, but the cost is high.⁴⁹ Every living creature outside the ark has been destroyed, while the ingroup, which consists of Noah and his family, survives inside the ark. This narrative and the story of Cain and Abel in Gen. 4:1-16 describe the catastrophic potential of mimetic violence when it is left unchecked. Asylum Cities and the immolation of murderers aim to avoid these crises by providing a controlled venting of mimetic violence.

3.2. *Impurity and Danger in Numbers 35:30-34*

The threat posed to the ingroup by the murderer outgroup is communicated through a rhetoric of impurity and danger in Num. 35:30-34. According to this text, the community must not allow the land to become polluted (חנף) or defiled (טמא) through mimetic violence. The terms חנף and טמא in Num. 35:33-34 depict murderers and their actions as a threat to the faithful ingroup. This threat is further portrayed through the violent participles מכה, רצח, and שפך, which are employed in Num. 35:30-34.⁵⁰ These participles separate the murderer from the addressee of the text, who is addressed through second-person imperatives. Through these means, Num. 35:30-34 emphasizes the dichotomy between its addressees who, as ingroup members, bear the divine image and the dangerous

---

46. Warren traces the escalation of violence from Cain's slaying of his brother in Gen. 4 to its climax in the flood narrative of Gen. 6–9. Warren, *Compassion or Apocalypse*, 134–6.

47. Harland, *The Value of Human Life*, 65–6.

48. In Gen. 9:1 Noah and his sons are portrayed as the ideal humanity when YHWH blesses them and echoes Gen. 1:28 with the phrase 'be fruitful and multiply and fill the earth'. Mathews, *Genesis 1–11: 26*, 388–9. A. W. Pink also notes that, like Adam, Noah worked the soil and suffered the uncovering of his nakedness. Pink, *Gleanings in Genesis*, 120. See also Sailhamer, *The Pentateuch as Narrative*, 129–30.

49. Harland argues that the flood cleanses the land from the defilement and corruption caused by murderous violence. Harland, *The Value of Human Life*, 28–44.

50. Assnat Bartor argues that in this passage the רֹצֵחַ participle assigns the guilt of murder to the offender, as distinct from other killers who give no indication that their actions were intentional and pre-meditated. Bartor, *Reading Law as Narrative*, 83.

murderer outgroup. The danger posed by the murderer is further emphasized through the effect of bloodshed upon the land.

Numbers 35:34 implies that bloodshed defiles (טמא) the land. However, Eve Levavai Feinstein argues that, according to Num. 35:30-34, the land is 'depraved' (חנף) by acts of bloodshed (v. 33), and the defilement mentioned in v. 34 is caused by the 'miscarriage of justice'.[51] Feinstein's reading of Num. 35:33-34, nevertheless, has several difficulties. First, there is nothing in the text to link the defilement referred to in v. 34 to a miscarriage of justice. Second, Ps. 106:38-39, the only other text in the Hebrew to employ the חנף and טמא word pair, links this phrase to the shedding of innocent blood, without any subsequent miscarriage of justice. This observation suggests that Num. 35:33-34 uses the חנף and טמא word pair in the same manner.[52] Furthermore, this reading is supported by the parallelism between חנף and טמא in vv. 33 and 34, which Feinstein overlooks.[53] Third, כִּפֶּר does not purge pollution (חנף) in the Hebrew Bible, but rather impurity (טמא). The כִּפֶּר achieved through the immolation of the murderer in v. 33, therefore, presupposes the land is defiled (טמא) by bloodshed, and not by any subsequent miscarriage of justice, as Feinstein supposes.

The כי clause of v. 34 clarifies the importance of maintaining the land's purity by noting that YHWH dwells 'in the midst of the people of Israel'. YHWH's presence is incompatible with the impurity generated through bloodshed.[54] Although Num. 35:30-34 attaches no specific danger to the defilement of the land, the incompatibility of YHWH's presence with impurity suggests that the pollution and defilement of the land (חנף and טמא) may force either YHWH's exit (cf. Ezek. 5:11; 9:7) or Israel's

---

51. Eve Levavi Feinstein, *Sexual Pollution in the Hebrew Bible* (Oxford: Oxford University Press, 2014), 179.

52. Although Ps. 106:38-39 is outside the Pentateuch, there are good reasons to suspect that this reference echoes Num. 35:30-34. First, the shared terminology and context common to both these texts strongly satisfies Hayes' second criterion. Psalm 106:38-39 echoes Num. 35:30-34 by claiming that the Israelites חנף and טמא the ארץ when they וישפכו דם נקי. Second, the qualifier נקי (cf. Deut. 19:10, 13) and the involvement of the Israelite 'sons and daughters' in זנה as 'they זבח to the idols of Canaan' (cf. Exod. 15–16) strongly suggests that the author(s) of Ps. 106:38-39 had access to a very late version of the Pentateuch, satisfying Hayes' first and fifth criteria.

53. The phase ולא־תחניפו את־הארץ אשר in Num. 35:33 clearly parallels the phrase ולא תטמא את־הארץ אשר in v. 34.

54. As Milgrom writes, 'It is a basic theological postulate that the divine Presence cannot abide in a land polluted by murder; the offense leads to the pollution of earth and the abandonment by God of His sanctuary and people'. Milgrom, *Numbers*, 291.

expulsion from the Land (Lev. 18:24-28). In Ps. 106:34-41, both the land and the people are described as חנף and טמא, which leads to the people's expulsion from YHWH's presence. Furthermore, just as Cain was expelled from the presence of YHWH after slaying his brother (Gen. 4:16), so illegitimate bloodshed threatens Israel's expulsion from the land. The Tannaitic commentary on Num. 35:33-34 also reflects this thinking:

> You shall not defile the land in which you live, in the midst of which I dwell; for I the Lord dwell in the midst of the people of Israel: Scripture indicates that blood shed imparts uncleanness to the land and drives God's presence away, and because of blood-shed the house of the sanctuary was destroyed.[55]

According to Num. 35:30-34, the danger associated with illegitimate bloodshed is averted through the murderer's immolation. In contrast to the biblical tradition, other ancient Near Eastern law codes allow a murderer to compensate for their crime through a ransom payment.[56] Numbers 35:33, however, states that 'blood pollutes the land, and no כֹּפֶר can be made for the land for the blood that is shed in it, except by the blood of the one who shed it'. In other words, only the murderer's immolation can save the community from the danger associated with bloodshed.[57] From a mimetic

---

55. CLXI:III.1 Translation from Jacob Neusner, *A Theological Commentary to the Midrash: Sifré to Numbers and Sifré to Deuteronomy* (Lanham: University Press of America, 2001), 41.

56. Milgrom, *Numbers*, 295. Timothy M. Willis, *The Elders of the City: A Study of the Elders-Laws in Deuteronomy* (Atlanta: Society of Biblical Literature, 2001), 106–9; Barmash, *Homicide in the Biblical World*, 171–4; Samuel Rolles Driver and John C. Miles, *The Babylonian Laws, vol. 1* (Oxford: Clarendon, 1952), 501–2.

57. Koch argues similarly, explaining that the death of the capital offender achieves כֹּפֶר for the community, but not for the offender, himself. Klaus Koch, 'Sühne und Sündenvergebung um die Wende von der Exilischen zur Nachexilischen Zeit', *Evangelische Theologie* 26, no. 5 (1966): 231–2. The idea of human death as כֹּפֶר for bloodshed in Num. 35:9-34 is also investigated in the Talmud. The Talmud states that כֹּפֶר for some bloodshed can also be achieved through the death of the High Priest. As discussed above, although those who are granted refuge in Asylum Cities have shed blood, these people are still considered ingroup members. Yet, these ingroup members are detained in the Asylum City until the death of the High Priest (Num. 35:25). From this detail, the Talmud concludes that the death of the High Priest achieves כֹּפֶר for the ingroup members who have killed another person (*Lev. Rab.* 10.6; see also Milgrom, *Numbers*, 294). This interpretation is supported by the observation, made in Chapter 4, that the priesthood functions as a group of scapegoats as they vicariously bear Israel's sin (cf. Num. 18:1). The High Priest performs his final act as communal scapegoat by achieving כֹּפֶר for ingroup killers through his death. This process serves as another example of an outgroup member who dies to benefit the ingroup.

perceptive, blood feuds conceived through mimetic violence threaten to generate a mimetic crisis within the community. The sanctioned execution of the murderer outgroup allows the avenger of blood to exact vengeance for the death of his kin, while also bringing a stop to the cycle of blood vengeance. Numbers 35:30-34 recognizes the potential of mimetic violence to destroy the community, and prescribes the immolation of the murderer outgroup as a means of carefully managing mimetic violence to prevent a mimetic crisis.

4. *The Dualistic Nature of Bloodshed*

The Pentateuch presents a dualistic conception of bloodshed, one in which ingroup blood defiles and outgroup blood purifies. At first glance, this idea appears paradoxical. If bloodshed pollutes and defiles the land, how can more bloodshed purify it? Genesis 9:6 claims that whoever sheds דם האדם must, in turn, be immolated by האדם. In Chapter 2 this text was explained through the realization that in Gen. 9:6 the phrase דם האדם refers to ingroup blood that is shed by an outgroup rival. In what follows, I employ a narrative approach to read Num. 35:30-34 in conversation with Gen. 9:6, and apply a mimetic critique to this reading in order to resolve the apparently paradoxical dualism of bloodshed within the Pentateuch.

Although Num. 35:30-34 does not employ the term, דם האדם, this text echoes Gen. 9:6, and, for this reason, the narrative approach frames Num. 35:30-34 as an explanation of the terse statement presented in Gen. 9:6.[58] According to Num. 35:33, the immolation of murderers prescribed in Gen. 9:6 is necessary because 'דם pollutes the land, and no כֹּפֶר can be made for the land for the דם that is shed in it, except by the דם of the one who shed it'. If Num. 35:33 is read as an explanation of Gen. 9:6, then דם in Num. 35:33 must be read as an abbreviation of the term, דם האדם, employed in Gen. 9:6. This reading interprets the term דם in Num. 35:33 as the blood of the ingroup, who bear the divine image, and not a universal reference to all human blood. Only the blood of the ingroup, therefore, defiles the land, while the blood of the murderer outgroup purifies. This apparent paradox can be explained from a mimetic perspective.

From a mimetic perspective, Num. 35:30-34 aims to prevent mimetic crises by venting mimetic rivalry upon those who defile the land by illegitimately shedding ingroup blood. This venting keeps mimetic violence in

---

58. This echo satisfies Hayes' second criterion because these texts both address the שפך of דם, while assuming that this act has a defiling effect upon the land. Furthermore, in both these texts YHWH commands the ingroup to execute murderers.

check and, in so doing, stalls the cycle of blood vengeance. Without this control mimetic violence spreads and threatens the entire community. The controlled killing of outgroup members does not defile or pollute the land because mimetic violence is directed outwardly from the ingroup, and vented in a controlled manner upon another party. For this reason, internal rivalries pollute the land with mimetic violence, but external rivalries cleanse the land. This dynamic explains why ingroup blood pollutes and defiles, while the immolation of the murderer outgroup purifies the land. The dualistic nature of human blood is also found in Exodus and Deuteronomy, which also prescribe the immolation of murderers.

5. *Homicide in Deuteronomy and Exodus*

This section examines the treatment of murderers in Exodus and Deuteronomy. I begin this section by analyzing Deut. 19:1-13, which, like Num. 35:9-34, addresses Asylum Cities and the immolation of murderers. In this discussion I apply a narrative approach to argue that Deut. 19:1-13 communicates the danger associated with illegitimate bloodshed, albeit through different terminology to that employed in Num. 35:30-34. Having done so, I argue that both Deut. 19:1-13 and Num. 35:9-34 communicate the same danger, namely the dangerous cycle of blood vengeance, which is fuelled by mimetic violence. Furthermore, both of these texts prescribe the appropriate use of Asylum Cities and the immolation of murderers as a means of limiting this danger. A narrative approach is then applied to Exod. 21:12-14 to reveal that this text also prescribes the execution of murderers to ensure the community's wellbeing. Girard's scapegoat stereotypes are then applied to demonstrate that the scapegoat mechanism underlies the treatment of murderers in these three texts.

5.1. *Homicide in Deuteronomy*

According to Deut. 19:10, the purpose of Asylum Cities is to avoid incurring the bloodguilt associated with shedding 'the blood of the innocent' (דם נקי). This phrase refers to the death of an ingroup member who accidentally kills his or her 'neighbour' (vv. 4-5).[59] The terms דם נקי and 'neighbour' identify both the killer and their neighbour as ingroup members.[60] Accidental killers are regarded as ingroup members because they harboured no enmity towards their neighbour prior to the incident

---

59. Tigay, *Deuteronomy*, 182; Burnside, *God, Justice, and Society*, 259–60.

60. The term 'neighbour' restricts the application of legal material to ingroup members throughout the Pentateuch. For example, the phrase ברעך in Exod. 20:16 qualifies the commandments of vv. 13-16: 'You shall not murder, commit adultery

(v. 6). Because accidental killers belong to the ingroup, shedding their blood brings bloodguilt upon the community (v. 10) and may precipitate a mimetic cycle of blood vengeance. To prevent this cycle, accidental killers must be protected from the avenger of blood.

Conversely, anyone who intentionally slays their neighbour must be handed over to the avenger of blood 'so that he may die' (Deut. 19:12). In contrast to the unintentional killer of vv. 4-10, the intentional murderer 'hates his neighbour, ambushes him, attacks him, and fatally strikes him so that he dies' (v. 11).[61] This violent sequence of verbs portrays the intentional murderer as a dangerous rival to the ingroup. The community are reminded that they must execute murderers so that 'it may go well' for them, and are warned against allowing their feelings and emotions to jeopardize this goal (Deut. 19:11-13).[62] While shedding the דם נקי brings bloodguilt upon the people, the immolation of the murderer secures the community's wellbeing by removing bloodguilt.[63] Therefore, although they employ different terminology, Deut. 19:1-13 and Num. 35:30-34 both assume the same dualistic conception of bloodshed.

The shared dualistic conception of bloodshed in these texts is further emphasized by the narrative approach, which reads Deut. 19:1-13 and Num. 35:30-34 in conversation with Deut. 21:1-9. Deuteronomy 21:1-9 addresses the discovery of a corpse, which has been 'pierced' (חלל), indicating that this person was murdered.[64] Yet, the murderer remains unknown and, therefore, in lieu of the murderer's immolation a special rite must be performed to purge the guilt of innocent bloodshed (דם נקי):

> [After breaking a cow's neck] the elders of that city nearest to the slain man shall wash their hands over the cow whose neck was broken in the valley, and they shall testify, 'Our hands did not shed this blood, nor did our eyes see it shed. Atone (כפר), O YHWH, for your people Israel, whom you have redeemed, and do not set דם נקי in the midst of your people Israel, so that their blood might be atoned (כפר) for. (vv. 6-8)

with, steal from, or bear testimony against your neighbour'. John Hartung, 'Love Thy Neighbor', *Skeptic* 3, no. 4 (1995): 86–99.

61. As Barmash notes, when compared with other ancient Near Eastern texts the biblical texts express a unique 'anxiety over articulating a distinction between intentional and accidental homicide. They are trying to provide concrete illustrations of the distinction.' Barmash, *Homicide in the Biblical World*, 125.

62. Bartor, *Reading Law as Narrative*, 154.

63. David Daube, *The Culture of Deuteronomy* (Ibadan: University of Ibadan Press, 1969), 48–9.

64. Eugene H. Merrill, *Deuteronomy*, New American Commentary (Nashville: Broadman & Holman 2001), 288.

Significantly, Deut. 21:1-9 describes a rite which seeks כִּפֶּר for bloodguilt when the murderer is unknown. By seeking כִּפֶּר this rite aims to protect the community from the danger associated with דם נקי, when it cannot be purged through the procedures outlined in Deut. 19:1-13.[65] Although various interpretations of this ritual have been suggested, an examination of these interpretations goes beyond the scope of the present chapter.[66] More pertinent to the present discussion is the observation that the rite described in Deut. 21:1-9 addresses the ingroup's inability to achieve כִּפֶּר and purge דם נקי through the usual means of immolating the murderer. In this way, Deut. 21:1-9 recognizes the purgation of דם נקי through human immolation as an act of כִּפֶּר, which strengthens the claim that this text also holds a dualistic conception of bloodshed. From a mimetic perspective, both of these texts warn that blood vengeance threatens to generate mimetic crises. To nullify this threat, Deut. 19:1-13 and Num. 35:30-34 both prescribe the immolation of the murderer outgroup.

5.2. Homicide in Exodus 21:12-14

The call to execute murderers is also sounded in the Exod. 21:12-14, which states that anyone who intentionally ambushes and slays another person must be executed.[67] This action satisfies the need for blood vengeance and,

---

65. Tigay, *Deuteronomy*, 472–3; Willis, *The Elders of the City*, 156.

66. While some have argued that the subrite of slaying the cow achieves כִּפֶּר as a substitute for the murderer, others have argued that the cow subrite achieves כִּפֶּר as a type of sacrifice. Anthony Phillips, *Deuteronomy* (Cambridge: Cambridge University Press, 1973), 138–9; Samuel Rolles Driver, *A Critical and Exegetical Commentary on Deuteronomy* (Edinburgh: T. & T. Clark, 1902), 241–2; Janowski, *Sühne als Heilsgeschehen*, 166; Henry McKeating, 'The Development of the Law on Homicide in Ancient Israel', *Vetus Testamentum* 25, no. 1 (1975): 62–3; Ziony Zevit, 'The 'Egla Ritual of Deuteronomy 21:1-9', *Journal of Biblical Literature* 95, no. 3 (1976): 377–90; S. H. Hooke, 'The Theory and Practice of Substitution', *Vetus Testamentum* 2, no. 1 (1952): 10–11. Another approach envisages this subrite as symbolizing the fate of the elders, if their testimony is false. If the elders have lied about their ignorance, they will, like the cow, be executed. Don C. Benjamin, *Deuteronomy and City Life: A Form Criticism of Texts with the Word City ('Ir) in Deuteronomy 4:41–26:19* (Lanham: University Press of America, 1983), 298. Alternatively, the cow subrite may aim to eliminate the impurity or bloodguilt associated with דם נקי. David P. Wright, 'Deuteronomy 21:1-9 as a Rite of Elimination', *The Catholic Biblical Quarterly* 49, no. 3 (1987): 387–403. Each of these interpretations see the ritual of Deut. 21:1-9 as a means of seeking כִּפֶּר for bloodshed when the murderer cannot be executed.

67. Burnside, however, follows Jackson, and cautions that these verses could also be interpreted as providing permission to execute murderers, rather than commanding it: 'The proper sense of verse 14 may actually be one of encouragement: "he should

in so doing, achieves reparation for illegitimate bloodshed. Achieving reparation for various actions is central to the Covenant Code, a theme which is summarized in the *lex talonis* legal principle (Exod. 21:23-25).[68] For example, the verses preceding Exod. 21:12-14 prescribe the emancipation of female slaves, whose master has dealt treacherously with them, as reparation (vv. 8-11). Furthermore, Exod. 21:18–22:15 prescribes various modes of reparation required for actions which inflict harm upon others. In each case, these acts of reparation, including monetary payment or letting a slave go free, minimize mimetic rivalry by restoring relationships between ingroup members. Outgroup members, however, must be immolated for their offenses.

By immolating murderers the ingroup secure their wellbeing. According to Exod. 21:12-14, members of the murderer outgroup slay 'their neighbours' through cunning (ערמה) methods (v. 14). As the narrative approach acknowledges, the term ערמה links the intentional murderer to the serpent of Genesis 3, which is also described as ערום.[69] In this way, Exod. 21:14 identifies murderers with the offspring of the serpent outgroup. In contrast, those who are killed are described with the epitaph 'neighbour', which identifies these victims as ingroup members. Therefore, like Deut. 19:1-13, Exod. 21:12-14 prescribes the immolation of a dangerous outgroup rival who intentionally slays an ingroup member (cf. Gen. 9:6). The immolation of this outgroup achieves reparation for their offenses by satisfying the need for blood vengeance and, in this way, stalls the cycle of mimetic violence, restoring peace and order to the community. The next section confirms this reading of homicide within the Pentateuch through the application of Girard's scapegoat stereotypes.

5.3. *Homicide and the Scapegoat Mechanism*
Girard's first stereotype can be seen when a narrative approach is applied to Exod. 21:12-14, Num. 35:30-34, and Deut. 19:1-13. The narrative approach reads these passages in light of other texts, such as Genesis 6–9, which narrates the destructive effects of blood vengeance. As discussed above, blood vengeance is a mimetic process that, if left unchecked, could precipitate a mimetic crisis. A narrative reading of Exod. 21:12-14,

---

[normally] be put to death." Unfortunately for us, biblical law does not have any clear or regular way of distinguishing between different modalities, such as "may," "must," and "it should be a good idea."' Burnside, *God, Justice, and Society*, 258.

68. See Chapter 4.

69. Genesis 3:1 and Exod. 21:14 are the only two passages in the Pentateuch that employ the root ערם. This observation strongly satisfies Hayes' second criterion for biblical echoes.

Num. 35:30-34, and Deut. 19:1-13, therefore, recognizes that homicide threatens to generate a mimetic crisis within the community. In this way, Girard's first stereotype, the mimetic crisis, is threatened by homicide. Girard's second stereotype is also present as these texts blame murderers for mimetic crises through a rhetoric of impurity (Num. 35:30-34), bloodguilt (Deut. 19:1-13), and danger (Exod. 21:12-14). Thus, Girard's first and second stereotype are satisfied in the Pentateuch's treatment of homicide.

Although Girard's third stereotype is not present in these texts, his fourth stereotype can be observed in Exod. 21:12-14, Num. 35:30-34, and Deut. 19:1-13. Each of these texts commands the ingroup to execute murderers. This act stops the mimetic cycle of blood vengeance, and allows the avenger of blood to exact vengeance for the death of his kin. The avenger of blood's unique claim upon the life of the murderer explains why murderers are not immolated through communal stoning, which is prescribed for other offences, including blasphemy and desecrating the Sabbath (Lev. 24:10-16; Num. 15:32-36). In contrast to the seemingly victimless crimes of blasphemy and Sabbath desecration, homicide injures the family of its victims, which demands reparation. This reparation (or vengeance) is achieved when the avenger of blood executes the murderer. In this way, Israel secures its wellbeing as it 'purges the guilt of innocent blood' from its midst (Deut. 19:13), and achieves כִּפֶּר for the land (Num. 35:30-34). A narrative reading of the Pentateuch's treatment of homicide, therefore, satisfies three of Girard's scapegoat stereotypes. This observation suggests that the common social mechanism underlying the immolation of murderers within the Pentateuch is the scapegoat mechanism.

6. Conclusion

This chapter argued that Num. 35:30-34 calls the faithful ingroup to immolate dangerous murderers by employing a rhetoric of impurity and danger. Through this rhetoric, Num. 35:30-34 portrays the murderer as a potential scapegoat. According to Num. 35:30-34, while bloodshed defiles the land, the immolation of outgroup murderers achieves purification for their actions. The same dualistic conception of bloodshed was also demonstrated in the treatment of murderers in Exod. 21:12-14 and Deut. 19:1-13. The narrative approach applied within this chapter demonstrated that if the ingroup fails to manage bloodshed correctly, the land will become polluted and defiled by mimetic violence, and the community will be placed in danger of a mimetic crisis (cf. Gen. 6–9). By immolating outgroup murderers the ingroup avoids this danger, as they vent their mimetic rivalries in a controlled manner. The next chapter investigates a similar dynamic in Leviticus 20, which prescribes the immolation of outgroup members who place the community in danger through the impurity generated by their offences.

Chapter 7

THE MANAGEMENT OF MIMETIC RIVALRY IN LEVITICUS 18 AND 20

In this chapter I examine Leviticus 18 and 20, which address the defiling nature of various offences and prescribe the execution of offenders to avoid the danger associated with their crimes. According to Lev. 18:24-25, certain offences have the potential to defile both the Land and its people. This defilement forces the Land to 'vomit out its inhabitants' (Lev. 18:24-30). From a mimetic perspective, this natural-disaster imagery depicts a mimetic crisis that culminates from excessive rivalry within the community. To ensure the community's wellbeing, this rivalry must be vented through the execution of a scapegoat. As this chapter argues, Leviticus 18 and 20 identify those who commit certain sexual taboos as potential scapegoats through a rhetoric of disgust, impurity, and danger. Leviticus 20 then prescribes the immolation of these scapegoats as a means of venting mimetic rivalry. In this way, the ingroup guards the Land's purity and, thereby, prevents mimetic crises. This mimetic reading of Leviticus 18 and 20 will be explained and defended throughout the chapter.

To start, I present the dynamics of the scapegoat mechanism in Leviticus 18 through the application of Girard's scapegoat stereotypes. Although Leviticus 18 does not prescribe human immolation for those who transgress sexual taboos, its assertion that the transgression of sexual taboos defile the Land helps explain why these offences attract the death penalty in Leviticus 20.[1] Next, Leviticus 20 is discussed in the second

---

1. Although there has been much discussion surrounding the relationship between Lev. 18 and 20, this chapter adopts a synchronic approach by assuming these chapters share common vocabulary and ideas. This approach is supported by the similar content, prohibition language, and style employed in these two chapters. Although the differences between Lev. 18 and 20 suggest that these chapters were composed by separate authors, and that neither text is dependent upon the other, they were most likely based on a common tradition. Milgrom, *Leviticus 17–22*, 169.

section, beginning with a mimetic reading of the treatment of Molech worshippers in Lev. 20:1-5.[2] After this discussion, the concept of holiness and separation, as it is described in Lev. 20:6-9, 22-26, is examined within the context of the Land's defilement at the hands of those who transgress communal taboos. The prescription of different consequences for various sexual offences listed in Lev. 20:10-21 is then explained as a means of managing mimetic rivalry within the community. In closing, I argue that the consequences prescribed for various offences in Leviticus 20 restore peace and order to the community by venting the mimetic rivalry generated through these offences.

1. *Leviticus 18:24-30*

Leviticus 18:1-5 warns its readers not to follow the conduct of the Egyptians and the Canaanites, but to adhere to YHWH's 'statutes and rules'. Verses 6 to 23 lists various offenses, such as incest, sexual relations with a menstruant, adultery, bestiality, and Molech worship, which are all presented as abominable, foreign customs.[3] The chapter then concludes as follows:

[24] 'Do not defile yourselves by any of these things,	אַל־תִּטַּמְּאוּ בְּכָל־אֵלֶּה
for by all these the nations I am driving out before you have become unclean,	כִּי בְכָל־אֵלֶּה נִטְמְאוּ הַגּוֹיִם אֲשֶׁר־אֲנִי מְשַׁלֵּחַ מִפְּנֵיכֶם:
[25] and the Land became unclean,	וַתִּטְמָא הָאָרֶץ
so that I punished its iniquity,	וָאֶפְקֹד עֲוֹנָהּ עָלֶיהָ
and the Land vomited out its inhabitants.	וַתָּקִא הָאָרֶץ אֶת־יֹשְׁבֶיהָ:
[26] But you shall keep my statutes and my rules	וּשְׁמַרְתֶּם אַתֶּם אֶת־חֻקֹּתַי וְאֶת־מִשְׁפָּטַי
and do none of these abominations, either the native or the stranger who sojourns among you	וְלֹא תַעֲשׂוּ מִכֹּל הַתּוֹעֵבֹת הָאֵלֶּה הָאֶזְרָח וְהַגֵּר הַגָּר בְּתוֹכְכֶם:
[27] (for the people of the Land, who were before you, did all of these abominations,	כִּי אֶת־כָּל־הַתּוֹעֵבֹת הָאֵל עָשׂוּ אַנְשֵׁי־הָאָרֶץ אֲשֶׁר לִפְנֵיכֶם
so that the Land became unclean),	וַתִּטְמָא הָאָרֶץ:
[28] lest the Land vomit you out when you make it unclean, as it vomited out the nation that was before you.	וְלֹא־תָקִיא הָאָרֶץ אֶתְכֶם בְּטַמַּאֲכֶם אֹתָהּ כַּאֲשֶׁר קָאָה אֶת־הַגּוֹי אֲשֶׁר לִפְנֵיכֶם:

---

2. Leviticus 20 presents similar material to Lev. 18, but in a casuistic form which specifies the correct mode of reparation for each offence. Feinstein, *Sexual Pollution in the Hebrew Bible*, 168.

3. Deuteronomy 18:9-14 also describes many of these practices as abominable, foreign customs.

²⁹ For everyone who does	כִּי כָּל־אֲשֶׁר יַעֲשֶׂה
any of these abominations,	מִכֹּל הַתּוֹעֵבוֹת הָאֵלֶּה
the persons who do them shall be cut off	וְנִכְרְתוּ הַנְּפָשׁוֹת הָעֹשֹׂת
from among their people.	מִקֶּרֶב עַמָּם:
³⁰ So keep my charge	וּשְׁמַרְתֶּם אֶת־מִשְׁמַרְתִּי
never to practice any of these abominable customs	לְבִלְתִּי עֲשׂוֹת מֵחֻקּוֹת הַתּוֹעֵבֹת
that were practiced before you,	אֲשֶׁר נַעֲשׂוּ לִפְנֵיכֶם
and never to make yourselves unclean by them:	וְלֹא תִטַּמְּאוּ בָּהֶם
I am the YHWH your God.'	אֲנִי יְהוָה אֱלֹהֵיכֶם:

Leviticus 18:24-30 serves as a conclusion and justification for the apodictic material presented in vv. 1-23.⁴ Much like Num. 35:30-34, Lev. 18:24-25 assumes that certain behaviours have the potential to defile the Land.⁵ However, in Num. 35:30-34 illegitimate bloodshed defiles the Land directly, while according to Lev. 18:24-25 certain sexual practices defile the people, who in turn defile the Land.⁶ Despite this minor difference, Lev. 18:24-25 shares with Num. 35:30-34 a concern for the Land's purity. The assertion that certain taboos defile both the Land and the people in Lev. 18:24-25 identifies those who transgress these taboos as impure and dangerous.⁷ Although Num. 35:30-34 is not specific about the danger associated with the Land's impurity, Lev. 18:24-28 explicitly warns its readers of the consequences threatened by the Land's defilement.

1.1. *Girard's Four Stereotypes*

In what follows I argue that the scapegoat mechanism can be discerned in Leviticus 18 by observing Girard's first, second, third, and fourth stereotypes in this text. This observation supports the hypothesis that human immolation for these offences, as prescribed in Leviticus 20, functions to protect the community from a mimetic crisis by venting excessive mimetic rivalry. Girard's first and second stereotype may be observed

---

4. Leviticus 18:24-30 employs the terms, עשה, שמר, חקת and משפטים, which link this passage back to vv. 1-5, while the terms, טמא and תועבה echo vv. 6-23. Feinstein, *Sexual Pollution in the Hebrew Bible*, 167.

5. Wright, 'Holiness in Leviticus and Beyond', 357.

6. Feinstein, *Sexual Pollution in the Hebrew Bible*, 122; Milgrom, *Leviticus 17–22*, 1579.

7. Christophe Nihan, 'Forms and Functions of Purity in Leviticus', in *Purity and the Forming of Religious Traditions in the Ancient Mediterranean World and Ancient Judaism* (Leiden: Brill, 2013), 351–5. Although there is some debate over whether these prohibitions address marriage or sexual intercourse, these alternatives are the same because in ancient Israelite law couples who engage in sexual relations must marry (Exod. 22:15-16; Deut. 22:28-29). Milgrom, *Leviticus 17–22*, 1532.

in the mimetic crisis threatened by the actions of certain outgroup members in Lev. 18:24-28. According to this text, the Land that becomes defiled by certain sexual transgressions expels its inhabitants. The Land's expulsion of the Canaanites is cited as empirical support for the link between the transgression of these sexual taboos and the danger of being expelled. The message is clear: if the Israelites follow the practices of the Canaanites, they will be likewise expelled from the Land.[8] From a mimetic perspective, the natural-disaster imagery of the Land 'vomiting out' its inhabitants depicts a mimetic crisis. However, if Israel guards its own purity and the purity of the Land by following YHWH's 'statutes and rules', it will avoid mimetic crises and enjoy a blessed life in the Land. The community's welfare in the Land, therefore, depends upon Israel observing YHWH's 'statutes and rules' and not following Egyptian and Canaanite customs (Lev. 18:3). In this way, Leviticus 18 blames those who transgress specific taboos for the potential mimetic crisis described in vv. 24-28, which satisfies Girard's first and second stereotypes.

One may also observe Girard's third stereotype in Leviticus 18, namely, the sign of the victim. This chapter identifies various offences with Israel's most dangerous rivals throughout the Pentateuch, the Egyptians and the Canaanites. Although the Egyptians were somewhat accepting of marriage between close kin, there is little external evidence to suggest that any of the other prohibited acts listed in Leviticus 18 were regarded as normative in either Egypt or Canaan.[9] Furthermore, throughout Mesopotamia most of the practices listed in Leviticus 18 were regarded as taboo.[10] Therefore, the labelling of sexual taboos as foreign customs in Leviticus 18 probably does not reflect the normative behaviour of the Egyptians, Canaanites, or Mesopotamians. Rather, this labelling functions as a rhetoric of xenophobia, which portrays certain taboos as dangerous and foreign. As the narrative approach acknowledges, Egypt is presented as Israel's first national rival in Exodus, while Deuteronomy casts the Canaanites as Israel's final rival within the Pentateuch. The reference to these two groups in Lev. 18:3 functions as a merism, which refers to all of Israel's rivals: past, present, and future. In this way, Leviticus 18 links offenders who transgress the taboos listed in this passage with Israel's despised, foreign rivals, which fulfils Girard's third stereotype.

Moreover, Leviticus 18 and 20 ostracize this despised outgroup through repeated references to uncovering 'nakedness' (עֶרְוָה). The narrative approach employed in this study recognizes that the Pentateuch attaches

---

8. Nihan, 'Forms and Functions of Purity in Leviticus', 339–40.
9. Feinstein, *Sexual Pollution in the Hebrew Bible*, 126–7.
10. Ibid., 127–8.

a negative connotation to the concept of uncovering nakedness. Although Adam and Eve are both naked in the garden (Gen. 2:25), the revelation of this nakedness precedes their expulsion from YHWH's presence (3:6-24). Leviticus 18 states that Israel will also be expelled from YHWH's presence if they, like Adam and Eve, illegitimately uncover one another's nakedness. Furthermore, after the Genesis flood narrative Canaan is cursed on account of the actions of his father, Ham, who uncovers Noah's nakedness (9:22-25).[11] This text links the act of uncovering another's nakedness to Israel's rival, the Canaanites. Those who illegitimately uncover another's nakedness within the Pentateuch are, therefore, regarded as dangerous, cursed outgroup members.[12]

Leviticus 18 also employs a rhetoric of disgust to further ostracize those who transgress sexual taboos. In addition to their dangerous, foreign, defiling nature, these taboos are also referred to as תועבת five times in Lev. 18:22-30. The fivefold use of the term תועבת in this short passage, which is often translated as 'abominations', assigns shame and stigma to those who commit these offenses.[13] Furthermore, according to Lev. 18:25-28, תועבת defile the Land. This defilement causes the Land to vomit out (קיא) its inhabitants.[14] Through the use of this imagery, Lev. 18:25-28 aims to convince the ingroup that they should feel disgust when confronted with sexual taboos and those who transgress them.[15] By employing this rhetoric of disgust, Leviticus 18 facilitates the persecution of these outgroup members, and helps justify the penalties imposed upon them in Leviticus 20.

Girard's fourth stereotype, the expulsion of the scapegoat, can be observed through the prescription of the כרת-penalty in Lev. 18:29 for 'anyone who does any of these abominations'. Although the כרת-penalty

---

11. For a discussion of Ham's actions in this text, see Frederick W. Bassett, 'Noah's Nakedness and the Curse of Canaan a Case of Incest?', *Vetus Testamentum* 21, no. 2 (1971): 232–7.

12. Furthermore, the idea of nakedness in these verses may communicate concepts such as 'being dominated, controlled, inferior in status, physically ineffective and defenseless, exposed, unacceptable, isolated, abandoned, and degraded...' Lyn M. Bechtel, 'Shame as a Sanction of Social Control in Biblical Israel: Judicial, Political, and Social Shaming', *Journal for the Study of the Old Testament* 49 (1991): 67.

13. Bartor, *Reading Law as Narrative*, 80–1. On the use of תועבת to generate disgust, see Thomas Kazen, 'The Role of Disgust in Priestly Purity Law', *Journal of Law, Religion and State* 3, no. 1 (2014): 9; Feinstein, *Sexual Pollution in the Hebrew Bible*, 20–1.

14. As Feinstein notes, the term תבל in Lev. 18:23 and 20:12 also functions as a rhetoric of disgust. Feinstein, *Sexual Pollution in the Hebrew Bible*, 118.

15. Ibid., 130.

is particularly difficult to interpret, this penalty separates outgroup members from the ingroup. This separation restores peace and order to the community. Just as Asylum Cities and human immolation protect the Land from the mimetic violence associated with illegitimate bloodshed in Num. 35:9-34, so the כרת-penalty protects the people and the Land from the mimetic rivalry associated with the transgression of certain taboos. In so doing, the prescription of the enigmatic כרת-penalty in Lev. 18:29 satisfies Girard's fourth stereotype.

In sum, Leviticus 18 satisfies all four of Girard's scapegoat stereotypes, which reveals the scapegoat mechanism within this text. This observation supports the hypothesis that human immolation in Leviticus 18 and 20 aims to prevent mimetic crises by venting mimetic rivalry. Leviticus 20 further satisfies Girard's fourth stereotype as it expands upon the legislation of Leviticus 18 to prescribe human immolation and the כרת-penalty for certain offenses.

2. *Leviticus 20*

Leviticus 20 addresses many of the same taboos as Leviticus 18. However, while Leviticus 18 presents these taboos as apodictic prohibitions, the casuistic legislation of Leviticus 20 provides guidance on how to manage the mimetic rivalry generated by these offences. This section examines the prescription of human immolation for the offenses listed in Leviticus 20, which are listed in the table below.

Offenses	Lev. 18	Lev. 20	Formula of Immolation in Lev. 20
Molech Worship	18:21	20:2-5	מות יומת
Cursing a parent	-	20:9	מות יומת... דמיו בו
Adultery	18:20	20:10	מות יומתו
Incest[16]	18:6-16	20:11-12	מות יומתו... דמיהם בם
Male homosexual coitus	18:22	20:13	מות יומתו... דמיהם בם
Coitus with a mother and her daughter	18:17	20:14	באש ישרפו אתו ואתהן
Bestiality	18:23	20:15-16	מות יומתו... דמיהם בם
Necromancy	(19:31)	20:27	מות יומתו באבן ירגמו דמיהם בם

---

16. For a discussion of these laws from an anthropological perspective, see ibid., 100–121; Madeline Gay McClenney-Sadler, *Recovering the Daughter's Nakedness: A Formal Analysis of Israelite Kinship Terminology and the Internal Logic of Leviticus 18* (London: T&T Clark, 2007).

As this table shows, some of the laws listed in Leviticus 20 that prescribe human immolation end with the phrase בו/דמיהם בם. Although it is unclear why this phrase is attached to some laws and not others, the employment of this phrase throughout Leviticus 20 is important for two reasons. First, the בו/דמיהם בם phrase confirms that the מות יומת formula in Leviticus 20 refers to literal human immolation. This phrase provides assurance that whoever immolates the offender will not incur bloodguilt.[17] Such reassurance would be unnecessary if the מות יומת formula did not refer to a literal execution. Further confirmation of this reading is found in v. 27, which prescribes immolation via communal stoning for all mediums and necromancers. Second, as the narrative approach recognizes, the image of the offender's blood being 'upon them' recalls the act of sacrificial blood manipulation. Just as the Israelite priesthood achieves important transformations through the correct manipulation of sacrificial blood, so the community transform the chaos of a mimetic crisis into peace and order, by venting excessive mimetic rivalry through the immolation of outgroup members.

In contrast to outgroup members, ingroup members must never be immolated. The prohibition of Lev. 20:1-5 guards against the sacrifice of ingroup offspring (זרע). The narrative approach acknowledges that the use of the term זרע in Lev. 20:2-4 emphasizes the precious nature of the lives of Seth's descendants, the faithful ingroup, who engage in rivalry with the cursed offspring of the serpent throughout the Pentateuch (Gen. 3:15). Conversely, those who transgress the taboos listed in Leviticus 20 are associated with the cursed offspring of the serpent. Deuteronomy 27:20-23 draws out this association, as it pronounces curses (ארר) upon those who transgress many of the sexual taboos listed in Leviticus 18 and 20.[18] Furthermore, when Lev. 20:1-5 is read within the context of vv. 22-23, which label the offences listed in this chapter as abhorrent (קוץ) foreign customs, it portrays these offenders as a despised, foreign outgroup who threaten the ingroup's wellbeing. Leviticus 20, therefore, assumes the same ingroup–outgroup categories, which this book has observed throughout the Pentateuch.

Sarah J. Melcher takes an alternative approach to the use of the term זרע in Lev. 20:2-4, claiming that this term emphasizes the importance

---

17. Péter-Contesse and Ellington, *A Handbook on Leviticus*, 304; Milgrom, *Leviticus 17–22*, 1746–7; Hieke, 'Das Alte Testament und die Todesstrafe', 356.

18. 'Cursed be anyone who lies with his father's wife, because he has uncovered his father's nakedness... Cursed be anyone who lies with any kind of animal... Cursed be anyone who lies with his sister, whether the daughter of his father or the daughter of his mother...' (Deut. 27:20-23).

of maintaining a pure patrilineal community and provides a rationale for the prohibitions outlined in the remainder of Leviticus 20.[19] There are, however, a few difficulties with Melcher's interpretation. First, the term זרע occurs only in vv. 2-4. The absence of this term in vv. 5-21 weakens Melcher's claim that the whole chapter is concerned with maintaining a pure lineage. Second, most of the prohibitions listed in vv. 10-21 involve relations between a man and the wife of his close relative, such as his brother's wife (Lev. 18:16; 20:21). This practice is similar to Levirate marriage (Deut. 25:5-10), in which a widow provides patrilineal descendants for her deceased husband by engaging in sexual relations with his brother.[20] This observation suggests that the prohibition of sexual relations with one's brother's wife cannot be justified as an attempt to preserve patrilineal descent. Third, one would expect these verses to be more concerned about relations with foreigners more so than close relatives, if they were truly concerned with purity of descent. However, intermarriage with foreigners is not prohibited in Leviticus 18 or 20. Fourth, some prohibitions in Lev. 20:10-21, such as vv. 13-16, are concerned with unions which cannot produce offspring and cannot, therefore, be explained as an attempt to guard patrilineal descent.[21] For these reasons, this chapter adopts an alternative approach, one which considers the management of mimetic rivalry as the rationale for the prohibitions presented in Leviticus 20.

2.1. *Molech Worship (Leviticus 20:1-5)*

In what follows I apply a narrative approach to interpret the concern for holiness and purity expressed in Leviticus 20 as an attempt to avoid the negative consequences threatened in Lev. 18:24-30. As noted in the previous section, the natural-disaster imagery utilized within this passage threatens a mimetic crisis. According to Lev. 18:24-30, this crisis unfolds

---

19. Sarah J. Melcher, 'The Holiness Code and Human Sexuality', in *Biblical Ethics and Homosexuality: Listening to Scripture* (Louisville: Westminster John Knox, 1996), 87–102. See also Milgrom, *Leviticus 17–22*, 1530.

20. Within the Jewish traditions various attempts have been made to reconcile these two legal traditions; see Tigay, *Deuteronomy*, 232. Jonathan R. Ziskind has argued that Lev. 18 and 20 promote a social reform, which outlaws Levirate marriage as taboo. Jonathan R. Ziskind, 'The Missing Daughter in Leviticus XVIII', *Vetus Testamentum* 46, no. 1 (1996): 125–30. This chapter, however, accepts Stephen F. Bigger's argument that the females in view here are married and, therefore, Lev. 20:10-21 addresses a different situation to Levirate marriage. Bigger, 'The Family Laws of Leviticus 18 in Their Setting', 199.

21. Cf. Deborah L. Ellens, *Women in the Sex Texts of Leviticus and Deuteronomy: A Comparative Conceptual Analysis* (London: T&T Clark, 2008), 98–9.

because the Land is defiled through the transgression of certain taboos. In this way, Leviticus 18 employs a similar rhetoric of impurity and danger to that observed in Num. 35:30-34. While Num. 35:30-34 argues that killing the faithful ingroup defiles (טמא) and pollutes the Land (חנף), Lev. 20:2-4 states that killing one's זרע in Molech worship defiles (טמא) the sanctuary and profanes (חלל) YHWH's holy name. According to the Pentateuch, the Israelite priests must separate the holy (קדש) from the profane (חלל), the pure (טהר) from the impure (טמא), and teach the people to do likewise (Lev. 10:10-11). Through Molech worship this separation breaks down with the immolation of the Israelite ingroup, which alone reflects the divine image.

Leviticus 20:2-5 presents Molech worship as a rival cult to the one promoted throughout P and H, with its own priests who are portrayed as monstrous doubles of the Aaronic Priests.[22] In mimetic theory, the term 'double' refers to two people or groups who are locked in mimetic rivalry with each other. This rivalry grows increasingly fierce as the two doubles imitate each other, and any apparent differences between them dissolve.[23] To the outside observer, these doubles seem like mirror images of each other, but each double views his or her counterpart as their enemy or 'monstrous double'.[24] By inverting the portrait of the Israelite Priest presented in Leviticus 21, Lev. 20:2-5 portrays the Molech priesthood as the monstrous double of the Aaronic priesthood.[25] For example, while the Aaronic priests perform approved sacrifices by fire and guard their own purity as well as that of the sanctuary and YHWH's holy name (Lev. 21:1-6, 12, 23), the priests of Molech defile the sanctuary and profane YHWH's holy name as they sacrifice ingroup children by fire (Lev. 20:3).[26] Moreover, the burning of a priest's daughter, who profanes (חלל) both herself and her father through זנה (Lev. 20:9), echoes the actions of the Molech priesthood, which חלל YHWH's holy name through

---

22. Burnside notes the rivalrous relationship between these two priesthoods. Jonathan P. Burnside, 'The Medium and the Message: Necromancy and the Literary Context of Leviticus 20', in *Leviticus in Its Contexts: Method, Rhetoric and Theology*, ed. Francis Landy, Leigh M. Trevaskis, and Bryan D. Bibb (Sheffield: Sheffield Phoenix, 2010), 48.

23. Girard, *Violence and the Sacred*, 146–8.

24. Schwager, *Must There Be Scapegoats?*, 12–13; Palaver, *René Girard's Mimetic Theory*, 132.

25. Burnside also notes this mirroring, describing the Molech priests as an 'inversion' or 'negative image' of the Aaronic priesthood. Burnside, 'The Medium and the Message', 48.

26. Ibid., 49.

זנה (Lev. 20:3, 5).[27] In this way, Leviticus 20 portrays the priesthood of Molech, who commit זנה by immolating sacred ingroup children, as the monstrous double of the Aaronic priesthood.

In Lev. 20:2-5, the priestly writer(s) employ(s) the language of holiness and purity to paint their rivals as a monstrous threat, which must be nullified through immolation. As discussed in Chapter 6, the sanctuary can be likened to a nuclear power plant—it must be handled and maintained with extreme care to harness YHWH's beneficent power, while avoiding the deadly consequences of negligent management. Such negligence places the community at risk of being expelled from the Land (Lev. 18:24-28; 20:22). This observation explains why, according to Lev. 20:2, both natives and foreigners must abstain from Molech worship. To avoid expulsion from the Land, the offender who defiles and profanes YHWH's sanctuary through Molech worship must be immolated (20:2-3). In this way, the ingroup prevent the Molech worshipper from serving as a model for others within the community to imitate. Furthermore, immolating Molech worshippers purifies the sanctuary from the defilement caused by the shedding of ingroup blood in Molech worship; it also reconsecrates YHWH's name as holy. These transformations portray an underlying belief, similar to that expressed in Gen. 9:6 and Num. 35:30-34, namely, that while the shedding of ingroup blood defiles, the immolation of the offender responsible for this defilement has a purifying effect.[28] From a mimetic perspective, this catharsis is achieved by venting the fierce rivalry between the Aaronic and the Molech priesthoods.

While most of the laws in Leviticus 20 either prescribe the כרת-penalty or the communal stoning of the offender, Lev. 20:1-3 prescribes both of these consequences for the Molech worshipper.[29] Milgrom explains this double penalty by arguing that killing one's child necessitates the immolation of the offender and that, as an act of idolatry, Molech worship also commands the divinely mediated כרת-penalty.[30] However, this interpretation is undermined by the realization that elsewhere within the Pentateuch

---

27. Ibid. The use of these common terms within the shared context of the priesthood satisfies Hayes' second criterion for biblical echoes.

28. As Nihan notes, 'deliberate transgressions contaminate the inner-sanctum *and* the land'. While the Day of Atonement purifies the Tabernacle, human immolation and the application of כרת-penalty for the transgressions listed in Lev. 20 purges the impurity associated with these transgressions from the Land. Nihan, 'Forms and Functions of Purity in Leviticus', 349.

29. The offender's family (מִשְׁפָּחָה) also receives the כרת-penalty. Burnside, *God, Justice, and Society*, 358–9.

30. Milgrom, *Leviticus 17–22*, 1729–30.

idolatry receives the death penalty (Deut. 13). Furthermore, as noted above, Milgrom's assumption that Molech is the name of a deity finds little support in the biblical or archaeological evidence.[31] Alternatively, Molech worship may describe a rival Yahwistic cult that practiced child sacrifice.[32] Because of the uncertainty surrounding Molech worship, Milgrom's classification of this practice as a form of idolatry, and his attempt to explain the double penalty attached to this offence, should be treated with caution. The present study is content to view Molech worship as a rival religious practice to the cult officiated by the Aaronic priesthood. This approach leaves open the question of the exact nature of Molech worship.

The double penalty in cases of Molech worship can be explained by the extreme severity of the offence.[33] This explanation is supported by the observation that Leviticus 20 lists offences, and their associated consequences, in descending order of severity. Molech worship, which receives both the death and כרת penalties (20:1-5), heads up this list, followed by various sexual transgressions that only attract the death penalty (vv. 10-16). The list concludes with lesser transgressions, for which the כרת-penalty is prescribed (vv. 17-21).[34] While this penalty is sufficient to protect the community from some transgressions, others require the offender's immolation. From a mimetic perspective, Molech worship receives the double penalty because it involves a rival priesthood, which acts as a double to the Aaronic priesthood.[35] The fierce

---

31. Bennie H. Reynolds, 'Molek: Dead or Alive?', in *Human Sacrifice in Jewish and Christian Tradition*, ed. Karin Finsterbusch, Armin Lange, and Diethard Römheld (Leiden: Brill Academic, 2007), 133–50. Despite this lack of evidence, others have also interpreted the term 'Molech' as the name of a deity. George C. Heider, *The Cult of Molek: A Reassessment* (Sheffield: JSOT, 1985); John Day, *Molech: A God of Human Sacrifice in the Old Testament* (Cambridge: Cambridge University Press, 1989); Jonathan P. Burnside, 'Strange Flesh: Sex, Semiotics and the Construction of Deviancy in Biblical Law', *Journal for the Study of the Old Testament* 30, no. 4 (2006): 393.

32. Otto Eissfeldt, *Molk als Opferbegriff im Punischen und Hebraischen und das Ende des Gottes Moloch* (Halle: Max Niemeyer, 1935); Reynolds, 'Molek: Dead or Alive?'

33. Burnside, 'Strange Flesh', 393.

34. However, v. 6, which prescribes the כרת-penalty for those who engage with soothsayers and necromancers, resists this schema. Milgrom, *Leviticus 17–22*, 1730. Burnside argues that this list is not 'arranged in increasing order of seriousness'. Burnside, 'Strange Flesh', 416.

35. Assuming that Molech worship represents as act of idolatry, Raymond Schwager argues that Molech worship is particularly heinous because it unites idolatry and violence in a single act of worship. Schwager, *Must There Be Scapegoats?*, 90.

mimetic rivalry between these two groups must be purged through the communal stoning of Molech worshippers. Additionally, the divinely mediated כרת-penalty, imposed upon the offender and their family (Lev. 20:5), aims to limit the spread of Molech worship. Because imitation is most intense within the family unit, the families of those who engage in Molech worship are the people most likely to imitate this practice. The enforcement of the divinely mediated כרת-penalty upon the family of Molech worshippers removes from the community those who are most likely to repeat this offence. In this way, peace and order are maintained and the Aaronic priesthood is bolstered. Furthermore, those who remain faithful to the Aaronic priesthood are confirmed as the image-bearing children of YHWH.

2.2. *Holiness and Separation (Leviticus 20:6-9)*

Leviticus 20:6-9 sandwiches a call for the community to pursue holiness (vv. 7-8) between a prohibition against using mediums and necromancers (v. 6) and a command to immolate those who curse (קלל) their parents (v. 9). In what follows I argue that these verses charge the ingroup to pursue holiness, and secure their identity as the image-bearing children of YHWH, by adhering to YHWH's commands. This goal is threatened by those who 'turn to mediums and necromancers to זנה after them' (v. 6). In so doing, these offenders turn away from the Aaronic priesthood. When viewed from this perspective, mediums and necromancers also represent rivals to the Aaronic priesthood.[36] The rivalry between these two groups is described as impurity in Lev. 19:31, which asserts that those who engage mediums and necromancers defile (טמא) themselves.[37] A narrative reading

---

36. Some scholars have argued that necromancy was actually part of Molech worship. Burnside, 'The Medium and the Message', 42–3; Karel Van der Toorn, 'Echoes of Judaean Necromancy in Isaiah 28, 7-22', *Zeitschrift für die alttestamentliche Wissenschaft* 100, no. 2 (1988): 204; Heider, *The Cult of Molek*, 401; Milgrom, *Leviticus 17–22*, 1771. If this interpretation is correct, then Lev. 20:6 and 27 also address the rivalry, which is generated through Molech worship.

37. Milgrom argues that this defilement is metaphoric because no purification rites are prescribed. *Leviticus 17–22*, 1702. This interpretation is, however, problematic. First, due to their ambiguous nature terms such as 'literal' and 'metaphoric' are of little help when discussing the nature of impurity. Klawans, *Impurity and Sin in Ancient Judaism*, 32–3. Second, the defilement of the Land and people described in Lev. 18:24-30 threatens Israel's expulsion from the Land. This threat suggests that the defilement discussed in Lev. 18:24-30, whether literal and metaphoric, must be addressed to secure the community's wellbeing. Third, Milgrom's claim that this impurity cannot be remedied through purification rites overlooks the possibility that the כרת-penalty and immolation of offenders may represent acts of purification and sanctification.

of Lev. 19:31 acknowledges that the impurity generated through these acts contaminates the Land and its inhabitants, and may precipitate a mimetic crisis (Lev. 18:24-30). To maintain the community's purity and safety the כרת-penalty is applied to these offenders (Lev. 20:6).[38] This reading is supported by vv. 7 and 8:

[7] Consecrate yourselves and be holy for I am the YHWH your God.	וְהִתְקַדִּשְׁתֶּם וִהְיִיתֶם קְדֹשִׁים כִּי אֲנִי יְהוָה אֱלֹהֵיכֶם:
[8a] Keep my statutes and do them; [8b] I am the YHWH who sanctifies you	וּשְׁמַרְתֶּם אֶת־חֻקֹּתַי וַעֲשִׂיתֶם אֹתָם אֲנִי יְהוָה מְקַדִּשְׁכֶם:

Although Israel itself is not intrinsically holy, by keeping YHWH's statutes the community attains and maintains its holiness.[39] This call to holiness is reiterated in vv. 22-26, which exhorts the ingroup to separate themselves from the practice and practitioners of the sexual taboos listed in Leviticus 20. In these verses, the dangerous and disgusting nature of foreign customs is reinforced, by recalling the image of the Land vomiting out the Canaanites (vv. 22-23) that was originally presented in Lev. 18:24-30. Following this caution, Lev. 20:24-26 encourages Israel to pursue holiness:

> But I have said to you, 'You shall inherit their Land, and I will give it to you to possess, a Land flowing with milk and honey'. I am YHWH your God, who has separated (בדל) you from the peoples. You shall therefore separate (בדל) the clean beast from the unclean, and the unclean bird from the clean. You shall not make yourselves detestable by beast or by bird or by anything with which the ground crawls, which I have set apart (בדל) for you to hold unclean. You shall be holy to me, for I YHWH am holy and I have separated (בדל) you from the peoples, that you should be mine.

Leviticus 20:22-26 encourages the ingroup to separate themselves from outgroup members in a numbers of ways. First, vv. 22-23 reinforce the disgusting nature of the Canaanites, which contrasts Israel's chosen and holy status (vv. 24-26). Second, the reference to Canaan as a 'Land flowing with milk and honey' in v. 24 situates this passage in the Exodus narrative, and recalls the promise of Israel's liberation from their Egyptian

---

38. Donald J. Wold, 'The Kareth Penalty in P: Rationale and Cases' (paper presented at the Society of Biblical Literature Seminar Papers, 1979), 2.
39. Milgrom, *Leviticus 17–22*, 1739–40; Jan Joosten, *People and Land in the Holiness Code: An Exegetical Study of the Ideational Framework of the Law in Leviticus 17–26* (Leiden: Brill, 1996), 132; Wright, 'Holiness in Leviticus and Beyond', 353; Nihan, 'Forms and Functions of Purity in Leviticus', 341.

overlords in passages such as Exod. 3:8.⁴⁰ In so doing, this phrase recalls the other major rival of Israel within the Pentateuch, the Egyptians, and recapitulates the call of Lev. 18:1-5. Third, the fourfold use of the root בדל reinforces the distinct separation between Israel and their rivals, which is conceived and maintained through both divine and human agency.⁴¹ Although YHWH has separated Israel from its rivals, Israel must be careful to maintain this separation by making divinely appointed distinctions between the clean and the unclean (v. 25).⁴² In this way, the ingroup continue YHWH's work of separation, attaining and maintaining their holy status.

Israel's sanctification is also achieved in Lev. 20:9 through the immolation of anyone who curses (קלל) their parents (cf. Exod. 21:17). The narrative approach reads this command within the context of other texts that also employ the term קלל. Throughout the Pentateuch, outgroup members are cursed when they attempt to קלל the blessed ingroup. For example, Israel is blessed when their rival Balak, the foreign Moabite king, seeks to קלל the Israelite community (Num. 22–24; Deut. 23:4). On another occasion the ingroup member Abraham is promised blessing, while those who קלל him will be cursed (Gen. 12:1-3). In each of these cases an outgroup member's attempt to קלל the Israelite ingroup backfires. Likewise, the outgroup member who קלל his or her parents must be executed (Exod. 21:17; Lev. 20:9) because they have engaged in rivalry with the Israelite ingroup. In so doing, this person identifies themselves as the offspring of the serpent, who are cursed and engage in perpetual rivalry with the faithful ingroup (Gen. 3:14-15). These malefactors must be executed to allow the ingroup to faithfully reflect the divine image. From a mimetic perspective, these executions draw the ingroup together,

---

40. The description of Canaan as a Land of 'milk and honey' echoes the Canaanite description of Baal's reign, during which 'the heavens rain fat/oil and the wadis flow with honey' (*KTU* 1.6 III: 12-13). The echo of this verse in Exod. 3:8 portrays YHWH as a rival to Baal. P. Stern, 'The Origin and Significance of "the Land Flowing with Milk and Honey"', *Vetus Testamentum* 42 (1992): 555–6.

41. The use of בדל in Lev. 20:20, 22-26 also recalls the employment of this term in Gen. 1:1–2:3. According to Milgrom, this recollection shows that the 'separation of Israel from the nations is a sine qua non for the maintenance of order *within the human world*...just as God created order out of chaos in the *natural* world by his act of separation (*hibdîl*, Gen. 1:4, 7, 14, 18), so the separation of Israel from the nations is essential not just for Israel's survival, but for an orderly *human* world'. Milgrom, *Leviticus 17–22*, 1762, 1764.

42. Walther Zimmerli, '"Heiligkeit" Nach Dem Sogenannten Heiligkeitsgesetz', *Vetus Testamentum* 30, no. 4 (1980): 502.

and confirm their identity as YHWH's children, as the community vent their collective rivalries upon the outgroup.

In sum, Lev. 20:7-8 calls the people of Israel to 'consecrate themselves' by avoiding unclean practices, people, and objects, such as those listed in Leviticus 20. By observing these commands, the ingroup separates itself from the outgroup and maintains its holiness (vv. 7-8a). Through this process, YHWH sanctifies the ingroup by separating it from the outgroup. This dynamic can be seen as YHWH applies the כרת-penalty to those who זנה after mediums and necromancers (v. 6). Furthermore, mediums, necromancers, and those who קלל their parents must be immolated (vv. 6, 27). From a mimetic perspective, the recognition, separation, and immolation of these outgroup members protects the ingroup from mimetic crises by venting mimetic rivalry.

2.3. *Sexual Offences and Mimetic Rivalry (Leviticus 20:10-21)*

Leviticus 20:10-21 lists multiple sexual taboos and the appropriate consequences for each offence. In what follows I argue that the consequences prescribed in Lev. 20:10-21 aim to manage the mimetic rivalry associated with each offence. The first of these offences, committing adultery (נאף) with a neighbour's wife (את־אשת רעהו), is recompensed with human immolation (v. 10). By specifying the adulteress as 'his neighbour's wife', Lev. 20:10 addresses נאף committed against a fellow Israelite.[43] Significantly, the 'neighbour' qualifier is not applied to the adulterer and adulteress in this verse because they are considered outgroup members. Engaging in נאף with an ingroup member's wife constitutes an act of open defiance, which may generate jealousy and rivalry, because in ancient Israel a husband was thought to exercise authority over his wife's sexuality.[44] This rivalry is vented, and peace and order restored to the community, through the immolation of the adulterer and adulteress. This reading is supported by the wording of this law, which suggests communal execution.[45]

When read within the context of vv. 11-21, which address the issue of sexual relations between relatives, v. 10 appears to prescribe immolation

---

43. In Lev. 19:18 the term 'sons of your people' parallels 'your neighbour', suggesting that רעה functions as an ingroup identifier: 'You shall not take vengeance or bear a grudge against the sons of your own people (את־בני עמך), but you shall love your neighbor (לרעך) as yourself...' See Milgrom's discussion of רעה in Milgrom, *Leviticus 17–22*, 1654–6. See also *Sanh.* 52b.

44. Feinstein, *Sexual Pollution in the Hebrew Bible*, 110; Melcher, 'The Holiness Code and Human Sexuality', 91–2.

45. Milgrom, *Leviticus 17–22*, 1748.

for those who commit נאף with the wife of a fellow Israelite who is outside the family unit.[46] Significantly, the term נאף is not used to describe any of the offences listed in vv. 11-21, which suggests that these taboos were considered a different category of offence. As Jonathan R. Ziskind argues, Lev. 20:11-21 probably addresses an audience which condoned these acts, and did not consider them as נאף.[47] This insight, when combined with a mimetic approach, explains why different consequences are prescribed throughout Lev. 20:10-21. In what follows I examine the laws of Lev. 20:11-21, which narrow the focus of illegitimate sexual relations with fellow Israelites to primarily address sexual taboos involving family members.[48]

Some have argued that the prohibitions listed in Lev. 20:11-21 attempt to preserve patrilineal descent.[49] However, this interpretation is problematic, as argued above with reference to the work of Melcher. This critique need not be repeated here. Another approach considers the sociological importance of sexual taboos for the family unit. For example, Ibn Kaspi argues that these taboos attempt to keep peace within the household, and Shadal adds, 'it is well known that the hostility between relatives is greater than the hostility between strangers'.[50] Maimonides argues that the prohibitions of Leviticus 18 and 20 reflect the access that males had to females within their households:

> All illicit unions with females have one thing in common: namely, that in the majority of cases these females are constantly in the company of the male in his house and that they are easy of access for him and can easily be controlled by him – there being no difficulty in making them come to his presence; and no judge could blame the male for their being with him. Consequently if the status of the woman with whom union is illicit were that of *any unmarried woman*, I mean to say that if it were possible and that the prohibition with regard to them were only due to their *not being the man's wives*, most people would have constantly succumbed and fornicated with them.[51]

---

46. Ibid., 1747; Burnside, 'Strange Flesh', 400.
47. Ziskind, 'The Missing Daughter in Leviticus XVIII'.
48. Leviticus 20:13, 15, 16, 18 are exceptions to this theme.
49. Melcher, 'The Holiness Code and Human Sexuality', 91–9; Milgrom, *Leviticus 17–22*, 1530–1.
50. Cited in Milgrom, *Leviticus 17–22*, 1530. See also Joshua Roy Porter, *Leviticus* (Cambridge: Cambridge University Press Archive, 1976), 145; Bigger, 'The Family Laws of Leviticus 18 in Their Setting'.
51. *Guide for the Perplexed* 3.49, cited in Milgrom, *Leviticus 17–22*, 1535.

For Maimonides, then, these prohibitions specifically address relations with close female relatives simply because they are close to hand. These women may become desired by multiple kin within the same household. According to mimetic theory, if one male demonstrates a desire for a close female relative, another close relative may imitate this desire. This shared desire may culminate in a vicious rivalry, as the two kinsmen struggle for possession of the coveted object: the close female relative.[52] Girard argues that incest prohibitions can be explained as an attempt to limit mimetic rivalry between close relatives, who might otherwise struggle together over a single woman:

> The sentence weighs on all the women who figured as prizes in the rivalry; that is, on all women who live within a group – not because they are intrinsically more desirable, but because they are near at hand and therefore likely objects of rivalry. The prohibition always covers the closest instances of consanguinity, but its outer limits are not necessarily defined to blood relations...
>
> It would be untrue to say that they were designed to deal with an imaginary situation; on the contrary, they serve to prevent people from being caught up in violent mimesis... The reason is clear: the prohibitions were dictated by violence in itself, by the violent manifestations of a previous crisis, and they are fixed in place as a bulwark against similar outbursts.[53]

Girard notes that the closer a person becomes to his or her rival, and the coveted object, the fiercer the rivalry between them becomes.[54] This observation may explain why 'uncovering the nakedness' of close male relatives attracts human immolation in Lev. 20:11-12. A male who desires to have sexual relations with his close relative's wife engages in mimetic rivalry with his close relative as they struggle over her sexuality. The prohibitions listed in Leviticus 18 and 20 emphasize the closeness of these relationships: 'she is your mother... it is your father's nakedness... their nakedness is your own nakedness... she is your sister... she is your

---

52. As Ken Stone's work suggests, the desired object in these cases may be power over a rival male, which is obtained by gaining possession over the coveted woman's sexuality. For the sake of simplicity I have framed the woman as the desired object in heterosexual relations. Stone's insights are explained and applied to the Pentateuch's prohibition of homosexual coitus between two men below. For Stone's conclusions regarding the impact of heterosexual relations upon male power and honour, see Ken Stone, *Sex, Honor and Power in the Deuteronomistic History: A Narratological and Anthropological Analysis* (Sheffield: JSOT, 1996), 135–7.

53. Girard, *Violence and the Sacred*, 219.

54. Girard, *Deceit, Desire, and the Novel*, 84–5.

father's close relative... she is your mother's close relative... she is your aunt... she is your son's wife... it is your brother's nakedness... they are close relatives'. As Assnat Bartor notes, 'the declarations that are directed personally to the addressee...illustrate the illicit relationship...this is not just "any" sister, mother, or aunt, it is *your* sister, *your* mother, *your* aunt'.[55] If these rivalries occur in multiple families across the community, a mimetic crisis may ensue much like the one described in Lev. 18:24-30. These crises are prevented by the prohibiting the object of desire, in this case, sexual relations with the wives of close male relatives.[56]

Because the intensity of rivalry increases as rivals become closer, rivalries between close male relatives must be vented through the offender's execution. For example, v. 11 prescribes the immolation of the man who has sexual relations with his father's wife. The justification offered for his immolation is that 'he has uncovered his father's nakedness'.[57] As the narrative approach recognizes, uncovering the nakedness of one's father echoes Canaan's actions in Gen. 9:22-25.[58] Through this echo Lev. 20:11 identifies those who uncover their father's nakedness as belonging to the offspring of the serpent outgroup. Similarly, because Reuben had sexual relations with his father's concubine he was denied the firstborn's inheritance (Gen. 49:3-4).[59] According to Lev. 20:12, the inversion of this transgression, sexual relations with one's son's wife, also receives the death penalty. This observation highlights that the short distance between the rivals is the primary concern of these verses. Because sons are born in the 'image' of their father (cf. Gen. 5:1-3), these rivals could easily become doubles of each other, between whom the fiercest and most dangerous of all rivalries rage. Conversely, those

---

55. Bartor, *Reading Law as Narrative*, 82.

56. Girard, *Violence and the Sacred*, 219–21.

57. Ziskind, 'The Missing Daughter in Leviticus XVIII', 127–8. Furthermore, as Ziskind notes, Leviticus 18 and 20 employs cumbersome, seemingly obsolete, formulas to designate their relationship to a close male relative. For example, one's sister is described as 'a daughter of his father or a daughter of his mother' (20:17). Ibid., 129. From a mimetic perspective, these formulas attempt to link these unmarried females to a potential male rival for would-be suitors to discourage sexual relations with these female family members.

58. Both these texts portray a son seeing his father's nakedness (ערוה) as a Canaanite custom, satisfying Hayes' second criterion. Hayes' sixth criterion is also satisfied as others have also noted this echo. Milgrom, *Leviticus 17–22*, 1537–8.

59. Kenneth A. Mathews, *Genesis 11:27-50:26* (Nashville: Broadman & Holman, 2005), 886. Uncovering the nakedness of one's father could also constitute an act of sedition against the patriarch (cf. 2 Sam. 16:20-22). Burnside, 'Strange Flesh', 402.

who uncover the nakedness of more distant relatives are not executed, but either receive the כרת-penalty (Lev. 20:17-18) or die childless (ערירי, vv. 20-21).[60] The different consequences prescribed for different offences reflect various relationships between the subject, model, and object in cases of sexual rivalry.

According to Lev. 20:17, uncovering the nakedness of one's sister incurs the כרת-penalty. This penalty may be explained by the unmarried status of the sister.[61] The sister's unmarried status in Lev. 20:17 is revealed in that the offender uncovers *her* nakedness, and not that of another male (cf. Lev. 20:11-12, 20-21). Because there is no husband in this case, there is no jealous male to engage in rivalry. Similarly, although no specific penalty is prescribed for a man who uncovers the nakedness of his unmarried aunt, beyond the נשא + עון formula (20:19), Lev. 18:12-13 lists this offence as being punishable by the כרת-penalty (cf. Lev. 18:29).[62] Furthermore, the כרת-penalty is also prescribed for those who uncover a presumably eligible female's nakedness by engaging in sexual relations with a menstruant (Lev. 20:18).[63] In each of these cases, uncovering a

---

60. Some have suggested that sexual relations with an uncle's wife was prohibited because she represents a matriarchal figure. Feinstein, *Sexual Pollution in the Hebrew Bible*, 110; Milgrom, *Leviticus 17–22*, 1544. However, this interpretation does not explain the prohibition against sexual relations with the wife of one's brother. These prohibitions are better explained as a means of restricting mimetic rivalry and, thereby, preventing a communal crisis.

61. Ziskind also argues that the females, whose nakedness is uncovered in Lev. 20:17, 19 are unmarried. Ziskind, 'The Missing Daughter in Leviticus XVIII.'

62. Burnside argues that the offence addressed in v. 19 is at 'the limit of what is classified as wrongdoing. This means that is it hard to find the right punishment, and so none is given.' Burnside, *God, Justice, and Society*, 360.

63. Although menstrual impurity is tolerated within the Pentateuch, strict protocols are prescribed to control the spread of this contagion (Lev. 15:19-24). According to Lev. 15:24, any man who has sexual relations with a menstruant contracts a contagious, though apparently tolerated, impurity for seven days. The offender is quarantined for this period, until he is no longer considered unclean and, therefore, poses no threat to others or the sanctuary. Wright, *The Spectrum of Priestly Impurity*, 155–7. In contrast, Lev. 20:18 prescribes the כרת-penalty for those who transgress this taboo. Leigh Trevaskis has offered a source-critical explanation for the different treatment of the man who has sexual relations with a menstruant in Lev. 15:24, which belongs to the P sources, and 20:18 which stems from H. Recognizing the different emphasis of these two sources, Trevaskis argues that H identifies sexual relations with a menstruant as an abominable foreign custom (Lev. 18:19) and, for this reason, H prescribes the כרת-penalty for those who transgress this taboo, while P merely imposes a seven-day quarantine. Leigh M. Trevaskis, 'Dangerous Liaisons:

female's nakedness attracts the כרת-penalty, but not the death penalty. This observation can be explained from a mimetic perspective. The death penalty is reserved as a means of venting excessive mimetic rivalry between fathers and sons, when one has uncovered the other's nakedness, or when a male commits נאף with a fellow ingroup member's wife (Lev. 20:10-12). But, the divinely mediated כרת-penalty is prescribed when a man uncovers a close female relative's nakedness and there is no close male to engage in rivalry. Because no rivalry is generated through these offences the כרת-penalty is sufficient to separate the offender from the community. This separation allows the ingroup to faithfully reflect the divine image.

Leviticus 20:20-21 states that a man who uncovers his uncle's or brother's nakedness, by engaging in sexual intercourse with his wife, will die childless (ערירי). Jonathan Burnside argues that the female relatives considered in these verses are either divorced or widowed. Burnside supports this reading by noting that, unlike sexual relations with a neighbour's wife, these offences are not labelled as נאף, but rather are described with the innocuous verb שכב. Furthermore, Burnside states that 'it makes no sense to claim that relations with the wife of your (living) neighbour is capital (20.10) but that relations with the wife of your living uncle is non-capital'.[64] However, I would argue that the lack of נאף in vv. 11-21 can be accounted for by the shift in focus from נאף with a non-family member in v. 10 to sexual relations with family members. As Ziskind notes, the audience of Leviticus 20 may not have considered the offences listed in vv. 11-21 as נאף.[65] Moreover, while vv. 17-19 address the

Sex with the Menstruating Woman in Leviticus', in Landy, Trevaskis, and Bibb, eds, *Text, Time, and Temple*, 150–2. The different treatment of the offender, who has sexual relations with a menstruant, prescribed in Lev. 15:24 and Lev. 20:18 can be further explained from a mimetic perspective. As argued above, Lev. 18:24-30 portrays a potential mimetic crisis through natural-disaster imagery, for which the offenders listed in this chapter are blamed. Leviticus 18:29 and Lev. 20:18 command that these offenders receive the כרת-penalty to protect the community from the threatened mimetic crisis. Through this act a distinction between the ingroup and outgroup is made, which allows mimetic rivalry to be focused and vented upon particular scapegoats. The identification of Girard's scapegoat mechanism in Lev. 18 supports this reading of Lev. 18:19 and 20:18. However, the scapegoat mechanism is not present in Lev. 15, which lacks any of Girard's scapegoat stereotypes. From a mimetic perspective, the harsh treatment of those who engage in sexual relations with a menstruant in Lev. 18:29 and 20:18 can be accounted for by presence of the scapegoat mechanism in these verses.

64. Burnside, 'Strange Flesh', 400–401.
65. Ziskind, 'The Missing Daughter in Leviticus XVIII'.

uncovering of a female's nakedness, suggesting their unmarried status, the offences of vv. 20 and 21 uncover the nakedness of a male relative, which suggests that these females are married. No other instance of uncovering a dead person's nakedness can be found within the Pentateuch. Although Burnside's assertion that the males whose nakedness is uncovered in Lev. 20:20-21 are deceased is plausible, it remains uncertain. Yet, if Burnside's reading of this text is correct, it explains why the lesser ערירי penalty is prescribed instead of human immolation. If the wives of Lev. 20:20-21 are indeed widows, there is no male to engage in rivalry with the other male, who partakes in sexual intercourse with these widows.

Another plausible reading of Lev. 20:20-21 is presented by Raymond Westbrook, who argues that the uncles and brothers mentioned in these verses are alive and remain married to their wives. Westbrook argues that the offences considered in Lev. 20:20-21 are not technically adultery, but rather a form of assisted reproduction and, for this reason, the unique ערירי penalty is prescribed:

> It is not adultery in the strict legal sense. The paramour agrees to sleep with his companion's wife with the consent of the husband, evidently in order to provide 'seed', i.e., offspring for a childless couple. There is therefore no prospect of legal proceedings by the husband, or indeed of the matter ever coming to light.[66]

If Lev. 20:20-21 addresses a similar practice, then this observation may also explain why the death penalty is not prescribed here. The offence addressed in Lev. 20:20-21 follows the logic of Levirate marriage, a practice which assumes that legitimate descendants can be conceived through one's brother (Deut. 25:5-10), and extends this concept to include securing descendants through one's nephew. Unlike Levirate marriage, however, in Lev. 20:20-21 the male relative is still alive and remains married to his wife.[67] Despite the presence of two male family members and a female spouse in this scenario, there is no betrayal, deceit, or rivalry because all parties have agreed to work together to achieve conception. Moreover, uncles and brothers are another step removed from the pure patrilineal uncovering of nakedness addressed in vv. 11 and 12. This step places a greater distance between the subject, model, and object, both relationally and spatially, which results in less potential for rivalry than the offences described in Lev. 20:11-12. For these reasons, the ערירי

---

66. Raymond Westbrook, 'Adultery in Ancient Near Eastern Law', *Revue Biblique* (1990): 568.

67. Bigger, 'The Family Laws of Leviticus 18 in Their Setting', 199.

penalty is deemed a sufficient consequence for those who attempt to conceive offspring by uncovering the nakedness of their uncle or brother. Because this offence does not generate mimetic rivalry, immolation is not required. Whether Burnside's or Westbrook's reading of this text is adopted, the offences committed in Lev. 20:20-21 do not generate mimetic rivalry between male community members. The lack of rivalry conceived through this offence is key to a mimetic interpretation of why human immolation is not prescribed in Lev. 20:20-21.

Surprisingly, Leviticus 18 and 20 contains no prohibition of sexual relations between a father and daughter. Various explanations have been offered for this omission. For example, Guillaume Cardascia argues that absence of this taboo reflects the community's values at the time.[68] Alternatively, Eve Levavi Feinstein claims the omission is purely accidental.[69] Others, including Karl Elliger and Jonathan Ziskind, point to stylistic reasons for the taboo's exclusion, while Baruch Levine and Susan Rattray both argue that the prohibition is implied by v. 6, which forbids sexual relations between close relatives.[70] Still others have suggested that a prohibition against father–daughter sex would have been unnecessary because other factors ensure this act is not performed.[71] Although space does not allow an in-depth discussion and evaluation of these explanations here, I suggest that the mimetic approach also provides a compelling explanation for the silence concerning father–daughter sex in Leviticus 18 and 20. According to this approach, Leviticus 18 and 20 are chiefly concerned with managing mimetic rivalry. In contrast to the sex acts prohibited in Leviticus 18 and 20, sex between a father and his daughter, who is neither married nor betrothed, generates no rivalry because the daughter's sexuality was considered her father's property. This observation may explain

---

68. Guillaume Cardascia, 'Egalité et Inégalité des Sexes en Matière d'atteinte aux Moeurs dans le Proche-Orient Ancien', *Die Welt des Orients* 11 (1980): 8–10.

69. Feinstein, *Sexual Pollution in the Hebrew Bible*, 172–3.

70. Karl Elliger, 'Das Gesetz Leviticus 18', *Zeitschrift für die Alttestamentliche Wissenschaft* 67, no. 1 (1955): 1–7; Ziskind, 'The Missing Daughter in Leviticus XVIII', 129–30; Levine, *Leviticus*, 120; Susan Rattray, *Marriage Rules, Kinship Terms and Family Structure in the Bible* (Atlanta: Scholars Press, 1987), 542.

71. Henry T. C. Sun argues that the reduction in bride price incurred by having sex with one's daughter would have ensured this taboo was not practiced, while Tikvah Frymer-Kensky suggests that Israel's patriarchal society inhibited father–daughter sex. Henry Sun, 'An Investigation into the Compositional Integrity of the So-Called Holiness Code (Leviticus 17–26)' (Claremont Graduate School, 1990), 159; Tikvah Frymer-Kensky, 'Law and Philosophy: The Case of Sex in the Bible', in *Studies in Bible and Feminist Criticism* (Philadelphia: Jewish Publication Society, 2005), 94.

the omission of the father–daughter taboo if, as I have argued above, the primary concern of Leviticus 18 and 20 is the management of mimetic rivalry within the community.

In sum, the mimetic approach presented above identifies many of the taboos listed in Lev. 20:10-21 as a means of controlling mimetic rivalry within the community and its familial units. Because the potential for desire and mimetic rivalry are inversely proportionate to the distance between the subject, model, and object, family units have the potential to harbour fierce rivalries between kin who engage in mimetic rivalry over a desired female relative. This potential is reflected in the consequences prescribed for each offense. Those who uncover the nakedness of their closest male relatives must be immolated to vent the excessive mimetic rivalry generated by this offence. Conversely, those who attempt to conceive offspring by uncovering the nakedness of their (dead) uncle or brother only receive the ערירי penalty. In this scenario, no rivalry is generated between male community members. Likewise, the absence of a male rival means that those who illegitimately uncover the nakedness of a close, unmarried female receive the כרת-penalty instead of the death penalty. Through these prescriptions, the Pentateuch attempts to manage the mimetic rivalry generated within the community through illegitimate sexual relations.

2.4. *Female Rivalry in Leviticus 18:17-18 and 20:14*

Leviticus 18:17-18 and 20:14 invert the model of two males competing for a common female, to consider cases in which two close female family members struggle over the same man. The mother–daughter relationship addressed in 18:17 and 20:14 represents the female equivalent of the father–son relationship addressed in 20:11-12. Just as the father and son of 20:11-12 may easily become doubles of each other, so too a fierce rivalry may be kindled between the mother and daughter of 18:17. Likewise, two sisters (18:18) could also become doubles. From a mimetic perspective, 18:17-18 prohibits males from marrying females, who are closely related and may become doubles, to minimize mimetic rivalry within the family unit. In what follows, I support this interpretation by presenting a narrative reading of 18:17-18. Next, a mimetic approach is applied to a narrative reading of 20:14 to interpret the burning of these offenders as a means of venting mimetic rivalry.

Leviticus 18:18 prohibits a man from marrying 'a woman as a rival wife to her sister'. As Feinstein notes, this familial arrangement would produce 'an inappropriate rivalry between' the two sisters.[72] In this situation, two

---

72. Feinstein, *Sexual Pollution in the Hebrew Bible*, 112.

sisters struggle for the affection of one male who represents their common object of desire. The narrative approach recognizes that excessive mimetic rivalry between female doubles permeates Genesis 29–35. This passage narrates the bitter rivalry between two sisters, Rachael and Leah, who are simultaneously married to Jacob. In their struggle for Jacob's affection, the two sisters strive to produce the most offspring, even recruiting their female slaves to bear children as surrogates. Out of this rivalry Jacob's sons, the patriarchs of Israel, are conceived. Rivalry also flourishes between Jacob's sons, which ultimately leads to the expulsion of Joseph (Gen. 37). Mimetic theorists have noted that Joseph's expulsion fits the pattern of the communal scapegoat.[73] As the Genesis narrative suggests, the fierce rivalry between sisters who struggle against each other for the affection of a single man can spread to their offspring and generate discord throughout the family unit. Prohibitions such as Lev. 18:18 attempt to prevent the kindling of such rivalries between potential doubles.[74]

Leviticus 20:14 prescribes the unique consequence of burning in cases where a man marries both a woman and her mother.[75] In this union, a mother and daughter struggle together over the coveted object: the affection of their husband.[76] This struggle generates a bitter rivalry between the two women, similar to that addressed in Lev. 18:18 (cf. Lev. 18:17). Leviticus 18:17 and 20:14 communicate the destructive potential of this offence by labelling it זמה. Apart from Lev. 18:17 and 20:14, this term appears only once within the Pentateuch. Leviticus 19:29 commands the people, 'Do not profane your daughter by making her a prostitute, lest the Land fall into prostitution and the Land become full of זמה'. In this verse, the destructive potential of זמה is emphasized by the warning that the prostitution of one's daughter may incite imitation throughout the

---

73. Williams, *The Bible, Violence, and the Sacred*, 54–9; Sandor Goodhart, *The Prophetic Law: Essays in Judaism, Girardianism, Literary Studies, and the Ethical* (East Lansing: Michigan State University Press, 2014), 10–19; René Girard, *I See Satan Fall Like Lightning*, trans. James G. Williams (Leominster: Gracewing, 2001), 107–12.

74. Tirzah Meacham, 'The Missing Daughter: Leviticus 18 and 20', *Zeitschrift für die Alttestamentliche Wissenschaft* 109, no. 2 (1997): 258.

75. Although the Rabbinic sources debate whether this verse describes the burning of all three parties (R. Akiva), or just the man and the second wife (R. Ishmael), the phrase אתו ואתהן suggests that the man and both his wives are burned. Shaul Bar, 'The Punishment of Burning in the Hebrew Bible', *Old Testament Essays* 25, no. 1 (2012): 28.

76. Bigger notes that such a union would cause a 'bitter tension within the domestic sphere'. Bigger, 'The Family Laws of Leviticus 18 in Their Setting', 201.

Land. As the narrative approach acknowledges, the mimetic process of filling the Land (ארץ + מלא) with זמה through prostitution in Lev. 19:29 describes a similar process to the rampant cycle of blood vengeance, which fills the Land (ארץ + מלא) with murderous violence in Gen. 6:11.[77] The use of זמה in Lev. 18:17 and 20:14 also describes the destructive potential of the intense rivalry between mothers and daughters, who struggle against each other over the same man, as this rivalry is imitated by their offspring.

The mimetic approach also helps explain why these offenders receive the unique sentence of execution by burning, as opposed to communal stoning. In contrast to the rivalries between fellow kinsmen discussed above, the rivalry addressed in Lev. 20:14 takes place within a marriage. Because this rivalry is contained within the marital unit, it does not generate rivalry across the community like the offences addressed in Lev. 20:10-12. This containment means that at the communal level there is no rivalry to be vented through communal stoning and, therefore, the community's active participation in the offender's execution is unnecessary and unfruitful. Although the potential rivalry generated when a man marries both a woman and her mother remains confined to the marital unit, this rivalry must be vanquished before it spreads outside the marital unit. As discussed above, the rivalry between two close female relatives who marry the same man may spread beyond the marital unit when their offspring become enemy brothers and engage in mimetic rivalry with each other. To prevent the generation of a powerful rivalry between enemy brothers, Lev. 20:14 prescribes the unique consequence of burning, which also engages the community's sense of smell. The odour of charred flesh, combined with the heat and sight of the flames, may also remind the community of the cathartic nature of this action, as these sensory stimuli are similar to those generated through burnt animal sacrifices.

Scholars have argued that, like animal sacrifices, the immolation of the offenders through burning in Lev. 20:14 cleanses the impurity associated with this offence.[78] The narrative approach acknowledges the dual role of fire within the Hebrew Bible as an agent of purification and destruction.[79] For example, in the Pentateuch celestial fire brings destruction upon

---

77. The use of these common terms satisfies Hayes' second criteria for biblical echoes.

78. John E. Hartley, *Leviticus*, WBC 4 (Waco: Word, 1992), 339, 349; Erhard S. Gerstenberger, *Leviticus: A Commentary* (Louisville: Westminster John Knox, 1996), 296–7; David Hoffmann, *Das Buch Leviticus, vol. 2* (Berlin: Poppelauer, 1906), 71–2. Lorerbaum, *In God's Image*, 103–4; Burnside, *God, Justice, and Society*, 366.

79. Burnside, *The Signs of Sin*, 124–5.

Israel's outgroup rivals, the city of Sodom (Gen. 19:24) and the Land of Egypt (Exod. 9:23-24). Meanwhile, YHWH's beneficent presence among his people, Israel, is also portrayed through the imagery of fire (e.g. Exod. 3:2-5; 13:21-22; Num. 14:14).[80] But, this benevolent presence can turn lethal if YHWH is approached in an inappropriate fashion (cf. Num. 16:35). YHWH's beneficent yet lethal presence among the Israelites is perfectly illustrated in Lev. 9:1–10:3. After Aaron correctly performs his cultic duties, YHWH's blessing and glory is manifested to all Israel, as the burnt offering is consumed by celestial fire (Lev. 9:1-24).[81] However, in the following verses, the same fire consumes Nadab and Abihu, who fail to correctly carry out their cultic duties (10:1-3). In this way, Leviticus juxtaposes YHWH's glory and his blessing of the faithful ingroup with the destruction of outgroup members. When read within this context, the fire's destruction of the offenders in Lev. 20:14 also purifies the community from a dangerous union that threatens to unleash mimetic violence.[82] Through this purification the community experiences YHWH's blessing and glory.

In sum, Lev. 18:17-18 address the potential rivalry which may arise between female doubles. To this end, Lev. 18:17-18 prohibits unions in which two females struggle against each other for the affection of a single male. If allowed to spread, the rivalry conceived through these unions could undermine the familial and social order. Furthermore, in cases where a man marries a woman and her daughter Lev. 20:14 prescribes the immolation of all of these parties through burning. This form of execution purges the mimetic rivalry conceived through such unions, while graphically communicating the catharsis of the community.

---

80. Stuart, *Exodus*, 327–8; Janzen, *Exodus*, 175–6; John I. Durham, *Exodus*, Word Biblical Commentary 3 (Waco: Word, 1987), 185; Sarna, *Exodus*, 70.

81. Levine, *Leviticus*, 58.

82. Shaul Bar cites Eccl. 12:7 to argue that the destruction of the body through burning also denies offenders a proper burial, without which they cannot find rest with their ancestors in the afterlife. Yet, this interpretation has a number of difficulties. First, as Milgrom has noted, execution through burning does not necessarily deny the possibility of burial. Second, the return of a person's רוח to God at death in Eccl. 12:7 does not refer to an immortal soul, but rather to the 'decomposition of the living being' (Fox). This reading is further supported by doubt concerning an afterlife expressed in Eccl. 3:20-21. Third, although Bar attempts to bolster his interpretation by citing Gen. 40:19 and 1 Sam. 17:44, these verses are irrelevant to the discussion because they do not mention the afterlife. Bar, 'The Punishment of Burning in the Hebrew Bible'; Hartley, *Leviticus*, 339; Milgrom, *Leviticus 17–22*, 1751; Michael V. Fox, *The JPS Bible Commentary: Ecclesiastes* (Philadelphia: Jewish Publication Society, 2004), 82.

2.5. *Homosexual Coitus and Bestiality (Leviticus 20:13, 15-16)*

This section argues that mimetic theory may also be applied to help explain the execution of those engaged in homosexual coitus and bestiality prescribed in Lev. 20:13, 15-16, in a way that other approaches cannot. I have already demonstrated this method's unique explanatory power with reference to the treatment of Molech worshippers in Lev. 20:2-4. Yet, Jacob Milgrom claims that approaches such as mine, which view incest prohibitions as a means of maintaining peace and harmony within the family unit, fail to explain the taboos addressing 'private matters', such as Molech worship, homosexual coitus, bestiality, and sex with a menstruant.[83] Milgrom attempts to explain the prohibition of these offences on the grounds that they 'would produce no seed'. This explanation stems from Milgrom's problematic structuralist approach to Israelite religion, which presupposes that the production and maintenance of life lies behind all prohibitions, cultic rituals, and purity regulations.[84] Milgrom's schema seems rather arbitrary, outdated, and finds little support within the text itself. In what follows, I offer a more plausible and robust explanation of why Leviticus prescribes the execution of those who engage in homosexual coitus and bestiality (Lev. 20:13, 15-16).

Leviticus 18:22 prohibits homosexual coitus between two males.[85] Although some have argued that the use of the term תועבה in Lev. 18:22 and 20:13 suggests that this offence may have been part of foreign idolatrous rituals, this reading cannot be demonstrated conclusively.[86] Yet, some insights regarding this practice may be gleaned from a closer

---

83. Milgrom, *Leviticus 17–22*, 1530.

84. Cf. Milgrom, *Leviticus 1–16*, 718. Also drawing upon the work of Mary Douglas, Athalya Brenner presents a structuralist analysis of the incest laws in Lev. 18 and 20 to argue that these laws attempt to establish and maintain communal boundaries. Athalya Brenner, 'On Incest', in *The Feminist Companion to Exodus to Deuteronomy*, ed. Athalya Brenner (Sheffield: Sheffield Academic, 1994), 113–38. For a critique of structuralist approaches to biblical ritual and purity regulations, see Lemos, 'Where There Is Dirt, Is There System?' 266–80.

85. Leviticus 18:22 and 20:13 appear to specifically address homosexual, anal coitus. See Péter-Contesse and Ellington, *A Handbook on Leviticus*, 279; Saul M. Olyan, '"And with a Male You Shall Not Lie the Lying Down of a Woman": On the Meaning and Significance of Leviticus 18:22 and 20:13', *Journal of the History of Sexuality* 5, no. 2 (1994): 185–6. Yet, Eva Levavi Feinstein argues that this phrase may include other sex acts. Feinstein, *Sexual Pollution in the Hebrew Bible*, 175.

86. John Boswell, *Christianity, Social Tolerance, and Homosexuality: Gay People in Western Europe from the Beginning of the Christian Era to the Fourteenth Century* (Chicago: University of Chicago Press, 1980), 100–101; Levine, *Leviticus*, 123; Olyan, '"And with a Male You Shall Not Lie the Lying Down of a Woman,"' 199.

reading of 18:22 and 20:13. For example, in these verses, the term תועבה communicates disgust and stigmatizes men who engage in homosexual coitus.[87] Furthermore, according to Lev. 18:22, homosexual coitus generates an impurity, one which threatens the wellbeing of the Israelite community (cf. 18:24-30).[88] Also, the blanket prohibition of this practice in 18:22 and 20:13 is unique among other ancient Near Eastern texts.[89] This observation emphasises the foreign nature of homosexual coitus. While the offence addressed in 18:22 and 20:13 may or may not have been part of a foreign idolatrous ritual, this crime is portrayed as a dangerous, impure, foreign custom. In this way, 18:22 and 20:13 identify men who partake in homosexual coitus as outgroup members who threaten the community's ability to reflect the divine image.

Others have taken a structuralist approach to Lev. 18:22 and 20:13 to argue that sexual coitus between two men is prohibited because it blurs socially defined sexual categories.[90] However, this explanation seems

---

87. See for this use of תועבה, see Bartor, *Reading Law as Narrative*, 80–1; Kazen, 'The Role of Disgust in Priestly Purity Law', 9; Feinstein, *Sexual Pollution in the Hebrew Bible*, 20–1.

88. Olyan, '"And with a Male You Shall Not Lie the Lying Down of a Woman,"' 189–90. Although a full discussion of this impurity goes beyond the scope of the present chapter, various explanations of how this act generates impurity have been suggested. For example, Olyan has suggested that the mixing of faeces with sperm may have a defiling effect. Others have suggested that homosexual coitus is defiling because it represents a waste of sperm, in which conception is impossible (Biale, Milgrom, Eilberg Schwartz). Alternatively, Thomas M. Thurston argues that homosexual coitus defiles because the receptive male does not fulfil the normal role of a male in sexual intercourse, while others have suggested that Lev. 18:22 and 20:13 refer to a foreign cultic ritual, which involved homosexual coitus with male cult prostitutes (Boswell and Snaith). Thomas M. Thurston, 'Leviticus 18:22 and the Prohibition of Homosexual Acts', in *Homophobia and the Judaeo-Christian Tradition*, ed. M. L. Stemmeler and J. M. Clark (Dallas: Monument, 1990), 7–23; David Biale, *Eros and the Jews: From Biblical Israel to Contemporary America* (Berkeley: University of California Press, 1992), 28–9; Milgrom, *Leviticus 17–22*, 1567–8; Howard Eilberg-Schwartz, *The Savage in Judaism: An Anthropology of Israelite Religion and Ancient Judaism* (Bloomington: Indiana University Press, 1990), 183; Boswell, *Christianity, Social Tolerance, and Homosexuality*, 100–101; Norman Henry Snaith, *Leviticus and Numbers* (Nashville: Nelson, 1967), 126.

89. Milgrom, *Leviticus 17–22*, 1566; Olyan, '"And with a Male You Shall Not Lie the Lying Down of a Woman,"' 190–5.

90. Olyan, '"And with a Male You Shall Not Lie the Lying Down of a Woman,"' 204–6; Thurston, 'Leviticus 18:22 and the Prohibition of Homosexual Acts', 15–16; Frymer-Kensky, 'Law and Philosophy', 247–8.

problematic in light of the Pentateuch's silence concerning lesbian sex, which also represents a confusion of sexual categories. Some attempt to explain this silence by focusing on the different mechanics of these two sex acts, such as the lack of penile insertion, deposit of semen, and risk of pregnancy involved with lesbian sex.[91] But, these explanations tend to rely upon either a structuralist framework or the assumption that the laws of Leviticus 18 and 20 are solely concerned with patriarchal descent. A more adequate explanation is offered by Ken Stone, who argues that throughout the ancient Near East homosexual coitus degraded the receptive partner's masculinity and social standing:

> Within a culture marked by rigid gender differentiation and hierarchy, a man who assumes the role allotted by convention to a woman is moving, socially, *downward*. If this role is forced upon him by another male, as is the case in homosexual rape, then the effect is both a challenge to his masculinity and a challenge to his honor. The subject of the rape, the man who does the forcing, is thereby making a statement about the inability of the male object to emulate a certain socially inscribed model of masculinity.[92]

Stone's claim that the chief concern with homosexual coitus is the receptive partner's failure to fulfil the 'socially inscribed model of masculinity' resonates with the prohibition of this act in Lev. 18:22 and 20:13.[93] The phrase ישכבאת־זכר משכבי אשה in these verses emphasizes the receptive male's feminization. Through this act the insertive partner seeks to degrade and gain power over another man.[94] From a mimetic perspective, these men struggle against each other for possession of the desired object: power and social status. This struggle can generate a powerful rivalry between the men involved.[95] In cases of homosexual coitus between two men, this rivalry must be vented through human immolation (Lev. 20:13). Stone's observations also help explain why this act is prohibited, while lesbian sex is not. Although homosexual coitus between two males

---

91. Ellens, *Women in the Sex Texts*, 76–7; Milgrom, *Leviticus 17–22*, 1787; Frymer-Kensky, 'Law and Philosophy', 248.

92. Italics in original quote. Stone, *Sex, Honor and Power in the Deuteronomistic History*, 79.

93. See also Olyan, '"And with a Male You Shall Not Lie the Lying Down of a Woman,"' 193–4.

94. Stone, *Sex, Honor and Power in the Deuteronomistic History*, 84.

95. Girard argues that intense mimetic rivalry may generate homosexual desire as the subject's fascination with their rival translates into sexual attraction. Girard, Oughourlian, and Lefort, *Things Hidden*, 343–6.

degrades the receptive partner's social standing downwards, lesbian sex does not degrade anyone's social standing.[96] For these reasons, the Pentateuch prohibits homosexual coitus between men, but remains silent on lesbian sex.

The concern for the degradation of community member's social status may also explain the blanket prohibition of bestiality in ancient Israel. Other ancient Near Eastern peoples appear to have accepted at least some forms of bestiality.[97] However, the Pentateuch describes this offence as תבל, that is, an inappropriate mixing (Lev. 18:23).[98] Through this mixing, the human who engages in bestiality is degraded, as he or she becomes like an animal. As the narrative approach acknowledges, in Gen. 2:16-25 Eve is created for Adam because none of the animals were deemed suitable sexual partners for him.[99] This observation suggests that Israel, as Adam's descendants, must abstain from bestiality to reflect the divine image. Bestiality is incompatible with the community's vocation as divine imagebearers, who exercise dominion over the animal kingdom (Gen. 1:26, 28).[100] Because both male and female ingroup members bear the divine image (1:27), bestiality attracts the death penalty regardless of the offender's gender (Lev. 20:15-16). Through the offender's immolation, the ingroup restore their correct relation to the animal kingdom and purge the impurity associated with bestiality (Lev. 18:23). In this way, the ingroup vents their collective rivalries as peace and order are restored within the community.

---

96. Stone, *Sex, Honor and Power in the Deuteronomistic History*, 78.

97. The only condemnation of bestiality in the ancient Near East outside of Israel is found in the Hittite Laws. Although the Hittite Laws prescribe the death penalty for a man who has sex with a cow, sheep, or pig (§187, 188, 199), sex with a horse or mule is permitted (§200a). Sarna, *Exodus*, 136; James C. Moyer, 'Hittite and Israelite Cultic Practices: A Selected Comparison', in *Scripture in Context II: More Essays on the Comparative Method*, ed. William W. Hallo, James C. Moyer, and Leo G. Perdue (Winona Lake: Eisenbrauns, 1983), 25–7; Harry A. Hoffner, 'Incest, Sodomy and Bestiality in the Ancient Near East', in *Orient and Occident: Essays Presented to Cyrus H. Gordon on the Occasion of His Sixty-Fifth Birthday*, ed. Harry A. Hoffner (Neukirchen-Vluyn: Neukirchener Verlag, 1973), 82–3; A van Selms, *Marriage & Family Life in Ugaritic Literature* (London: Luzac, 1954), 81–2.

98. Yet, it should be noted that this term is also used to describe other sexual taboos, such as relations with one's daughter-in-law (Lev. 20:12). Bigger, 'The Family Laws of Leviticus 18 in Their Setting', 203; Feinstein, *Sexual Pollution in the Hebrew Bible*, 118.

99. Tigay, *Deuteronomy*, 256.

100. Merrill, *Deuteronomy*, 350.

But why must the animal be executed in cases of bestiality? One possible solution to this question is that the beast is considered morally culpable and must, therefore, be punished for its part in the sex act. This view is presented by Baruch Levine, who argues that Gen. 6:7 and 9:5 regard animals as morally responsible agents.[101] However, the narrative approach recognizes that the prohibition and punishment of bestiality in Lev. 18:23 and 20:13 is not concerned with morality but purity.[102] As discussed above, the chief concerns of Leviticus 18 and 20 are holiness, purity, and the danger associated with this impurity being contracted by the Land.[103] According to Lev. 18:23, those who engage in bestiality defile (טמא) themselves. This observation suggests that the answer to the question posed above lies in the contagious nature of impurity. Perhaps bestiality renders both the animal and human perpetrator unclean. Within this framework, the animal's impurity is not a moral failing on the beast's part, but rather a necessity on account of the impurity it bears, which threatens to bring a mimetic crisis upon the community (Lev. 18:24-30). For this reason, mimetic rivalry must be vented from the community by executing both the offending human and the animal.

In sum, the Pentateuch prohibits male homosexual coitus because this offence degrades the social status of the receptive partner, who is feminized (Lev. 18:22), and generates a powerful rivalry which must be vented through human immolation. Bestiality is also prohibited because this act generates impurity and degrades the human involved, as he or she becomes like an animal (Lev. 18:23). The degraded social status of these offenders inhibits the community's ability to reflect the divine image. For this reason, those who engage in bestiality must be executed. Through this act, peace and order are restored as mimetic rivalry is purged from the community.

---

101. Levine, *Leviticus*, 138. See also Milgrom, *Leviticus 17–22*, 1752.

102. *Sanhedrin* 7:4 does not hold animals morally responsible for acts of bestiality: 'He who has sexual relations with a male [Lev. 20:13, 15-16], or a cow, and the woman who brings an ox on top of herself – if the human being has committed a sin, what sin has the beast committed? But because a human being has offended through it, therefore the Scripture has said, *Let it be stoned.*' Translation cited in Jacob Neusner, *The Mishnah* (New Haven: Yale University Press, 1988), 596.

103. Feinstein, *Sexual Pollution in the Hebrew Bible*, 122; Milgrom, *Leviticus 17–22*, 1579; Bigger, 'The Family Laws of Leviticus 18 in Their Setting', 202.

3. Conclusion

This chapter has explored the immolation of outgroup members, who transgress the taboos of Leviticus 18 and 20. Leviticus 18 threatens a communal crisis by claiming that certain taboos, and those who partake in them, defile the Land, which threatens the ingroup's expulsion from the Land. Furthermore, Leviticus 20 claims that these offenses threaten the community's sacred status and, for this reason, offenders must be immolated. By abstaining from certain taboos and immolating those who do not, the ingroup maintain their sanctity and secure their wellbeing in the Land. In this way, Leviticus 18 and 20 encourage the scapegoating of certain individuals who do not observe communal norms. Through these acts the community aim to minimize mimetic rivalry between community members and avoid mimetic crises. The next chapter examines Deut. 22:13-29, which also presents guidance on how to manage the mimetic rivalry generated through certain sexual offences.

Chapter 8

SEXUAL OFFENCES AND MIMETIC RIVALRY IN DEUTERONOMY 22:13-29

This chapter examines the prescription of immolation for various sexual offences in Deut. 22:13-27. Although this text employs different language and concepts to those used in Leviticus 18 and 20, Deut. 22:13-21 also aims to vent the dangerous rivalry generated through the transgression of sexual taboos. The first section of this chapter examines the case of the suspected Unchaste Bride in Deut. 22:13-21. This text provides guidance on how to diffuse the rivalry generated through a husband's claim that his wife's alleged sexual impropriety was dishonestly concealed by her father. The second section examines Deut. 22:22-29, which outlines how to manage the rivalry generated when a man engages in sexual relations with another man's wife or fiancée. As I shall argue, the legislation of Deut. 22:13-27 is primarily concerned with limiting rivalry between male members of community. This observation provides further support for the hypothesis that human immolation functions as a means of managing mimetic rivalry within the Pentateuch.

1. *Deuteronomy 22:13-21*

[13] 'If any man takes a wife	כִּי־יִקַּח אִישׁ אִשָּׁה
and goes in to her and then hates her	וּבָא אֵלֶיהָ וּשְׂנֵאָהּ:
[14] and accuses her of sexual misconduct	וְשָׂם לָהּ עֲלִילֹת דְּבָרִים
and brings a bad name upon her,	וְהוֹצִיא עָלֶיהָ שֵׁם רָע
saying, "I took this woman,	וְאָמַר אֶת־הָאִשָּׁה הַזֹּאת לָקַחְתִּי
and when I came near her, I did not find her	וָאֶקְרַב אֵלֶיהָ וְלֹא־מָצָאתִי לָהּ
bĕtûlîm,"[1]	בְּתוּלִים:

1. I have left the noun בתולים untranslated here because its meaning, which is disputed, has little bearing on my argument in this chapter. While Wenham argues that

¹⁵ then the young woman's mother and father shall take	וְלָקַח אֲבִי הַנַּעֲרָ וְאִמָּהּ
and bring out the young woman's *bĕtûlîm*	וְהוֹצִיאוּ אֶת־בְּתוּלֵי הַנַּעֲרָ
to the elders of the city in the gate.	אֶל־זִקְנֵי הָעִיר הַשָּׁעְרָה׃
¹⁶ And the young woman's father shall say to the elders,	וְאָמַר אֲבִי הַנַּעֲרָ אֶל־הַזְּקֵנִים
"I gave my daughter to this man to marry,	אֶת־בִּתִּי נָתַתִּי לָאִישׁ הַזֶּה לְאִשָּׁה
and he hates her;	וַיִּשְׂנָאֶהָ׃
¹⁷ and behold, he has accused her of misconduct,	וְהִנֵּה־הוּא שָׂם עֲלִילֹת דְּבָרִים
saying, 'I could not find your daughter's *bĕtûlîm*'.	לֵאמֹר לֹא־מָצָאתִי לְבִתְּךָ בְּתוּלִים
And yet this is my daughter's *bĕtûlîm*."	וְאֵלֶּה בְּתוּלֵי בִתִּי
And they shall spread the cloak before the elders of the city.	וּפָרְשׂוּ הַשִּׂמְלָה לִפְנֵי זִקְנֵי הָעִיר׃
¹⁸ Then the elders of that city shall take the man	וְלָקְחוּ זִקְנֵי הָעִיר־הַהִוא אֶת־הָאִישׁ
and whip him,	וְיִסְּרוּ אֹתוֹ׃
¹⁹ and they shall fine him a hundred shekels of silver	וְעָנְשׁוּ אֹתוֹ מֵאָה כֶסֶף
and give them to the father of the young woman,	וְנָתְנוּ לַאֲבִי הַנַּעֲרָה
because he has brought a bad name upon a virgin of Israel.	כִּי הוֹצִיא שֵׁם רָע עַל בְּתוּלַת יִשְׂרָאֵל
And she shall be his wife.	וְלוֹ־תִהְיֶה לְאִשָּׁה
He may not divorce her all his days.	לֹא־יוּכַל לְשַׁלְּחָהּ כָּל־יָמָיו׃
²⁰ But if the thing is true,	וְאִם־אֱמֶת הָיָה הַדָּבָר הַזֶּה
that the young woman's *bĕtûlîm* could not be found,	לֹא־נִמְצְאוּ בְתוּלִים לַנַּעֲרָ׃
²¹ then they shall bring out the young woman	וְהוֹצִיאוּ אֶת־הַנַּעֲרָ
to the door of her father's house,	אֶל־פֶּתַח בֵּית־אָבִיהָ
and the men of her city shall stone her to death with stones,	וּסְקָלוּהָ אַנְשֵׁי עִירָהּ בָּאֲבָנִים וָמֵתָה
because she has committed folly in Israel	כִּי־עָשְׂתָה נְבָלָה בְּיִשְׂרָאֵל
by fornicating in her father's house.	לִזְנוֹת בֵּית אָבִיהָ
So you shall purge the evil from your midst.	וּבִעַרְתָּ הָרָע מִקִּרְבֶּךָ׃

this term refers to a young girl of marriageable age, others suggest that within a legal context the term בתולים refers to the young girl's virginity (Pressler, Locher, Ellens). Alternatively, Burnside argues that the בתולים were the bride's pre-marital garments, recently stained with menstrual blood, which proved that she was not pregnant at the time of marriage. For Burnside, the issue is not virginity, but the assurance that any offspring birthed by the bride belong to the husband. Gordon J. Wenham, 'Betûlāh "a Girl of Marriageable Age"', *Vetus Testamentum* 22, no. 3 (1972): 330–6; Carolyn Pressler, *The View of Women Found in the Deuteronomic Family Laws* (Berlin: de Gruyter, 1993), 25–31; Clemens Locher, *Die Ehre Einer Frau in Israel: Exegetische und Rechtsvergleichende Studien zu Deuteronomium 22, 13-21*, vol. 70 (Göttingen: Vandenhoeck & Ruprecht, 1986), 192; Ellens, *Women in the Sex Texts*, 207–9; Burnside, *The Signs of* Sin, 136–54.

In what follows I offer a mimetic reading of Deut. 22:13-21, which interprets this text as an attempt to manage mimetic rivalry within the community. Deuteronomy 22:13-21 discusses the management of a case, in which a husband accuses his new bride of sexual misconduct. Yet, in this text the bride fades into the background. She remains silent, while the bride's father and her husband engage in mimetic rivalry. This rivalry is highlighted by the imitation between the husband and father in this text. For example, the husband's words, 'I took this woman, and when I came near to her I did not find her בתולים'(v. 14), are mirrored in the father's reply, 'I gave my daughter to this man…and behold, he has said "I did not find your daughter's בתולים"' (vv. 16-17). The husband expresses his contempt for the bride by referring to her as 'this woman'. The father, however, counters the husband's speech with a rhetoric of his own, in which he utters a slightly altered version of the husband's words. In so doing, the father simultaneously expresses his contempt for the husband, who he refers to as 'this man', and his intimate relationship to the bride when he refers to her as his daughter.[2] In this way, the mimetic verbal exchange between the father and the husband in this text portrays a bitter rivalry.

In Deut. 22:13-21, the husband and father engage in rivalry over social standing, not the bride. Unfortunately, neither the father nor the husband wants the alleged Unchaste Bride. In this way, the rivalry described in Deut. 22:13-21 is very different to those addressed in Leviticus 18 and 20. The laws of Leviticus 18 and 20 aim to manage the rivalry generated between two people who struggle against each other over a common object: the desired lover. In Deut. 22:13-21, however, the coveted object over which the father and husband struggle is not a lover, but social status.[3] The father's social standing is attacked through the husband's allegation, because in ancient Israel a father assumed responsibility for his daughter's sexuality until marriage.[4] The father rebuts the husband's allegations and defends his social status by presenting his daughter's בתולים (vv. 13-17). Although the meaning of this term is disputed, the presentation of בתולים somehow proves the husband's accusation to be false. In this way, the father defends the social status and integrity of both himself and his

2. Bartor, *Reading Law as Narrative*, 103.
3. Daube, *The Culture of Deuteronomy*, 30–1.
4. Willis, *The Elders of the City*, 225–7; Burnside, *The Signs of Sin*, 149–50; Caryn A. Reeder, *The Enemy in the Household: Family Violence in Deuteronomy and Beyond* (Grand Rapids: Baker, 2012), 46–7; Joseph Fleishman, 'The Delinquent Daughter and Legal Innovation in Deuteronomy XXII 20-21', *Vetus Testamentum* 58, no. 2 (2008): 197; Stone, *Sex, Honor and Power in the Deuteronomistic History*, 44; David R. Mace, *Hebrew Marriage* (New York: Philosophical Library, 1987), 227.

daughter. This process controls mimetic rivalry by restraining the husband and father from seeking vengeance upon each other.

If the בתולים presented by the father is deemed sufficient, the husband is then publicly flogged, fined, and forbidden from divorcing his wife (vv. 18-19). The public nature of these proceedings ensures that the father's social standing is restored, as he is vindicated in the presence of the community. Furthermore, the rivalry between the husband and father is quenched in three ways. First, the public flogging of the husband fulfils the father's desire for vengeance. Second, the fine compensates the father for the false accusation levelled against him and his daughter.[5] Third, the husband cannot divorce the wife he wrongly accused. This consequence ensures the father that his daughter will be kept and protected by her husband for life.[6] Through these stipulations, Deut. 22:18-19 attempts to dispel any ill feelings that the father might harbour towards the husband.

In contrast to the father, who is publicly vindicated and restored, the husband responsible for the false allegation is shamed through public flogging.[7] Deuteronomy 22:18-19 relies upon this act of public shaming to motivate the husband's submission to his father-in-law, and discourage any future acts of reprisal.[8] The shame of the public flogging also degrades the husband's social standing below that of his father-in-law.[9] From a mimetic perspective, this shaming places greater social distance between the husband and his father-in-law. Because rivalry dissipates as the distance between rivals increases, the increased social distance between the husband and his father-in-law diffuses the rivalry between them.[10] In this way, the humiliation of the husband coupled with the father's vindication maintains peace and order within the community.

---

5. Merrill, *Deuteronomy*, 303.
6. Pressler, *The View of Women*, 29.
7. The shaming potential of public flogging is noted in Deut. 25:3. This text states that forty is the maximum number of blows permitted in a public flogging, 'lest, if one should go on to beat him with more stripes than these, your brother be degraded in your sight'.
8. As others have noted, shame is a powerful form of social control, which is employed throughout Deuteronomy. Bechtel, 'Shame as a Sanction of Social Control in Biblical Israel', 56; Daube, *The Culture of Deuteronomy*.
9. As Bechtel notes, 'shame decreases honor and lowers status'. Bechtel, 'Shame as a Sanction of Social Control in Biblical Israel', 53. See also Johanna Stiebert, *The Construction of Shame in the Hebrew Bible: The Prophetic Contribution* (Edinburgh: A. & C. Black, 2002), 20, 82.
10. As Girard notes, the intensity of mimetic rivalry decreases as the distance between the subject and model increases. Girard, *Deceit, Desire, and the Novel*, 84–5.

Although some have suggested that the consequences prescribed in Deut. 22:18-19 reflect the *lex talionis* principle, this interpretation requires some additional explanation in light of the definition of *lex talionis* provided in Deut. 19:15-21.[11] According to this passage, the *lex talionis* principle demands that a false witness receives whatever penalty he attempted to bring upon 'his brother' through spurious accusations (v. 19). This act satisfies the *lex talionis* principle, as it was explained in Chapter 4, because it achieves reparation for the false allegation. At first glance, when Deut. 22:13-21 is read in light of 19:15-21, one might expect the husband, who falsely accuses his wife of sexual misconduct, to be executed in the same manner as the Unchaste Bride (22:20-21). However, the dishonest husband is not executed. The apparent inconsistency between Deut. 19:19 and 22:13-19 can be resolved through a closer mimetic reading of these texts. As discussed above, in Deut. 22:13-21 the husband does not engage in rivalry with his wife, but his father-in-law. When this rivalry is viewed through the lens of Deut. 19:19, the father-in-law represents the husband's 'brother', upon whom he attempts the inflict harm through his false allegations. This observation suggests that, according to the *lex talionis* principle as it is expressed in Deut. 19:19, the consequence imposed upon a husband, who falsely accuses his wife of sexual misconduct, should be commensurate with the harm he intended to bring upon his father-in-law through his false allegations. Because the father of the Unchaste Wife is not sentenced to death, neither is the dishonest husband in Deut. 22:13-19.

In accordance with Deut. 19:15-21, the consequences imposed upon the dishonest husband in Deut. 22:13-19 reflect the *lex talionis* principle. Through his accusations the husband presumably seeks to terminate his marriage contract, receive his dowry back, and bring shame upon his father-in-law. Consequences similar to these are imposed upon the husband, who falsely accuses his wife of sexual misconduct. First, the dishonest husband suffers the financial loss that he attempted to bring upon his father-in-law, as he pays a second dowry, instead of receiving a refund of his initial dowry.[12] Second, the husband suffers social shame,

---

11. For example, Merrill writes that the *lex talionis* legal principle is 'implicit in the husband's inability ever to free himself of his wife. He had tried to rid himself of her by duplicity but now must forever remain in union with her.' Merrill, *Deuteronomy*, 303. See also John D. Currid, *A Study Commentary on Deuteronomy* (Darlington: Evangelical, 2006), 369.

12. According to Gordon McConville, the fine imposed upon the husband in this text is double the amount that he would have originally paid as a dowry. Double pecuniary restitution is often applied in biblical applications of the *lex talionis* legal

much like he intended to bring upon his father-in-law, while his father-in-law is vindicated. Third, although the husband attempted to transfer his responsibility for the unwanted bride back to her father, he must now assume responsibility for her for life. These consequences could be considered an adequate application of the *lex talionis* principle, as it is defined in Deut. 19:15-21.

If the bride's בתולים cannot be presented, she is stoned at the door of her father's house (v. 21).[13] Her guilt separates her from the ingroup, who alone bears the divine image, and identifies her as an outgroup member. The bride's outgroup status is determined by the elders of the city, before whom the father is unable to produce his daughter's בתולים. Following this failure, the father separates himself from his daughter, and hands her over for immolation.[14] The daughter's execution is interesting, given that in ancient Israel a father was considered responsible for his daughter's sexuality. Although one might expect that the father of the Unchaste Bride might be executed for his negligence, the daughter is forced to take full responsibility for her father's transgression. The Unchaste Bride fulfils the role of the scapegoat, as she bears the sin of her father's negligence. Through her death the rivalry between her husband and her father is vented.[15] This interpretation is supported by the presence of three of Girard's scapegoat stereotypes in Deut. 22:13-21.

Girard's first stereotype can be observed in the description of the Unchaste Bride's conduct as נבלה (v. 21). The term נבלה describes an

---

principle (Exod. 22:3-8). J. Gordon McConville, *Deuteronomy*, Apollos Old Testament Commentary (Downers Grove: IVP, 2002), 340.

13. The location of the stoning at the door of the father's house, as opposed to the city gate (cf. Deut. 22:24), appears to confirm that the restoration of the father's social status is the focus of this rite. Willis, *The Elders of the City*, 226; Reeder, *The Enemy in the Household*, 49. Alternatively, this action could serve to solidify the father's shame. Burnside argues that the father is guilty and shamed because he made his daughter work as a prostitute. According to Burnside, her grave, which is positioned at the entrance to the family home, may also serve as a perpetual reminder of this shame. Burnside, *The Signs of Sin*, 153–4.

14. Fleishman argues that the girl's execution outside the family home 'publicly proclaims her uprooting formally and finally from that house... [This act] is the first step necessary for the rehabilitation of the father's house that was damaged as a result of the girl's behaviour.' Fleishman, 'The Delinquent Daughter', 205.

15. As Willis notes, 'the punishments are intended to forestall any future hostilities. The father will do nothing more against an offending son-in-law, because his daughter is a permanent member of the latter's house (her husband can never divorce her). The husband will do nothing against an offending father-in-law, because he has already been humiliated before the community.' Willis, *The Elders of the City*, 228.

impious disregard for communal norms, which brings disaster and shame.[16] The potential of נבלה for causing a mimetic crisis is illustrated in Genesis 34. In this text Shechem, the son of Hamor, sees Jacob's daughter, Dinah, 'takes her, lies with her, and humbles her' (v. 2).[17] When Jacob's sons hear about these events they become 'indignant and very angry', because through his actions Shechem has committed נבלה by treating Dinah like a זֹנָה (34:7, 31). In response two of Jacob's sons, Simeon and Levi, take up their swords, kill all the men of Shechem's city, and plunder it (34:25-29). In this narrative an act of נבלה generates an intense rivalry between Shechem and Jacob's sons, which ultimately destroys Shechem's city. Deuteronomy 22:13-21 echoes Genesis 34 through the employment of the terms נבלה and זנה within the shared context of sexual misconduct and heightened rivalry.[18] Through this echo, Deut. 22:13-21 suggests that, like Shechem's actions, the Unchaste Bride's נבלה generates an intense rivalry between her husband and her father, which may place the community in danger of a mimetic crisis. In this way, Deut. 22:13-21 fulfils Girard's first and second stereotype when it blames the Unchaste Bride's נבלה and זנה for a potential mimetic crisis (Deut. 22:21).

Although Girard's third stereotype is not discernible, his fourth stereotype is present as 'the men of her city' stone the Unchaste Bride (v. 21). This phrase suggests that all the men of the city band together to immolate the Unchaste Bride as a communal scapegoat. In so doing, the men of the city, including the Unchaste Bride's husband and father, vent their

---

16. Louis Göldberg, 'נְבָלָה', in *Theological Wordbook of the Old Testament*, ed. Robert Laird Harris, Gleason Leonard Archer, and Bruce K. Waltke (Chicago: Moody, 1980), 547; M. Sæbø, 'נָבָל', in *Theological Lexicon of the Old Testament*, ed. Ernst Jenni and Claus Westermann (Peabody: Hendrickson, 1997), 712; Phillips, *Essays on Biblical Law*, 239–44.

17. While some argue that Shechem rapes Dinah (Blyth, Shemesh), other suggest that the sex act described in Gen. 34:2 was more or less consensual (Betchel, Joseph). However, as Pressler notes, this argument is moot because only a father can legitimately give consent to sex acts involving his unmarried and unbetrothed daughter. Caroline Blyth, *The Narrative of Rape in Genesis 34: Interpreting Dinah's Silence* (Oxford: Oxford University Press, 2010), 48–92; Yael Shemesh, 'Rape Is Rape Is Rape: The Story of Dinah and Shechem (Genesis 34)', *Zeitschrift für die Alttestamentliche Wissenschaft* 119, no. 1 (2007): 2–21; Lyn M. Bechtel, 'What if Dinah Is Not Raped? (Genesis 34)', *Journal for the Study of the Old Testament*, no. 62 (1994): 19–36; Alison L. Joseph, 'Understanding Genesis 34:2: *'Innâ*', *Vetus Testamentum* 66, no. 4 (2016): 663–68; Carolyn Pressler, 'Sexual Violence and Deuteronomic Law', in Brenner, ed., *A Feminist Companion to Exodus to Deuteronomy*, 111.

18. This echo strongly satisfies Hayes' second criterion.

mimetic rivalry, as each man actively participates in the Unchaste Bride's communal stoning. The cathartic effect of this act is communicated with the phrase 'so you shall purge the evil from your midst' (v. 21). With this purgation peace and order are restored to the community. In this way, the execution of the Unchaste Bride in Deut. 22:13-21 fulfils Girard's fourth stereotype. The presence of Girard's first, second, and fourth stereotypes confirms the presence of the scapegoat mechanism within this text, and supports the reading of Deut. 22:13-21 presented above.

In sum, Deut. 22:13-21 provides instruction on how to deal with a case in which a husband accuses his wife of sexual misconduct. In so doing, the husband engages in rivalry with his father-in-law, who was responsible for his daughter's sexuality until marriage. If the husband's allegations are found to be spurious, in addition to paying a fine to his father-in-law the husband is shamed through public flogging and forbidden from divorcing his wife. By these means, reparation is made for the social and financial injury incurred by the father, and the rivalry between the two men is stifled. However, if the husband's accusations are true, the rivalry between the two men is vented through the immolation of the Unchaste Bride, who acts as a scapegoat.

2. *Deuteronomy 22:22-29*

Deuteronomy 22:22-29 addresses various examples of illicit sex between a man and a woman. Verses 22 states that those who engage in adultery must be immolated (cf. Lev. 20:10). Next, the consequences for engaging in sex with an unmarried but betrothed young woman are addressed (vv. 23-27). If this offence is committed in a field, only the male offender is executed (vv. 25-27). But if the sex act is performed in the city, both parties must be immolated (vv. 23-24). Finally, vv. 28-29 stipulate that a male who engages in sexual relations with a woman who is neither married nor betrothed must pay a dowry and marry the girl with no provision for divorce. In each of these laws, the young woman's marital status, rather than the sex act itself, determines the consequence prescribed.[19] In what follows, I offer a mimetic reading of Deut. 22:22-29 that interprets each of the consequences prescribed in this text as an attempt to manage mimetic rivalry between males.

Immolation is prescribed in vv. 22-27 for those who engage in sexual intercourse with a woman who is either married or betrothed to another man. In each case the woman involved, or at least her sexuality, is

---

19. Ellens, *Women in the Sex Texts*, 227–33.

considered the property of her husband or fiancé.[20] In these verses, the male offender attempts to wrest the woman's sexuality from her husband or fiancé by engaging in sexual intercourse with the woman. This act may generate a powerful rivalry between the woman's paramour and her husband or fiancé, who struggle against each other for possession of the women's sexuality. In the case of the married woman, this rivalry is vented through the execution of both the woman and the male offender (v. 22; cf. Lev. 20:10). The phrase 'you shall purge the evil from Israel' confirms the cathartic effect of this event. As explained in the previous section, the Unchaste Bride functions as a scapegoat. Through her death, the mimetic rivalry between her husband and father is vented (22:13-21). The same dynamic is noted in vv. 22 and 24 when this formula is applied to describe the immolation of women who participate in illicit sex acts. As I shall argue below, each of these executions aims to vent rivalry, and the purge formula describes the catharsis achieved by this act.

The purge formula is also applied to the punishment of false witnesses (19:19), which follows the statement that two or three witnesses are required to prove someone's guilt in v. 15. But how might a witness' veracity be determined? The only measure of a witness' veracity available to the community, a judge, or an elder would be the presence or absence of other witnesses, who corroborate their allegation. From a mimetic perspective, the presence of multiple witnesses does not necessarily prove the guilt of the accused. A person who makes a false accusation may be imitated by another, and another, which satisfies the law's requirement for two or three witnesses. Therefore, a false witness is simply someone who brings an accusation that is not imitated by subsequent witnesses. Unfortunately for this individual, someone within the community accuses them of bearing false testimony. This accusation is then imitated by others, who also testify against the alleged false witness. In this way, even the Pentateuchal law against false witnesses empowers the community to band together against a single scapegoat, who they identify as a false witness.

According to Deut. 19:18-21, the false witness must be recompensed with the same punishment which he attempted to bring upon 'his brother' (vv. 18-21). This text addresses the case of two males who are locked in a rivalry with one another, similar to that observed in the previous section between the husband, who accuses his wife of sexual misconduct, and his father-in-law (Deut. 22:13-21). In both cases, the dispute between the two male rivals is brought before a panel of authority figures for

20. Ibid., 210–11.

adjudication.[21] The quotation of the talion in Deut. 19:21 suggests that the goal of this process is to achieve reparation for the damage incurred through false allegations. This reparation pacifies the man who has been falsely accused by his fellow Israelite and, in this way, the excessive rivalry between these two men is vented. The purge formula in Deut. 19:19 appears to describe the peace and order achieved through this act.

In Deut. 13:5 and 17:7 the purge formula is applied to the execution of false prophets and adherents of non-Yahwistic religious practices, because these people support and participate in groups which stand in rivalry against the Deuteronomic religious schema and its prophets. These cases are not dissimilar to the case of Molech worshippers (Lev. 20:2-5), discussed in Chapter 7, who must also be immolated to vent the excessive rivalry between the Molech priesthood and the Aaronic priests. Like Molech worshippers, false prophets and adherents of non-Yahwistic religious practices represent monstrous doubles of the Deuteronomic religious scheme and its adherents. In contrast to the Deuteronomic prophets, false prophets teach rebellion against YHWH (Deut. 13:5), which portrays them as monstrous doubles of YHWH's prophets. False prophets and those who worship YHWH's monstrous doubles, the 'other gods' (17:3-7), must be immolated to vent the mimetic rivalry between the Deuteronomic religious entities and other religious groups. The peace and order resulting from these executions is expressed by the purge formula (13:5; 17:7). Therefore, in Deut. 13:5 and 17:7 the purge formula describes the catharsis achieved through the immolation of monstrous doubles.

As discussed in the next chapter, Deut. 21:21 employs the purge formula to describe the venting of mimetic rivalry achieved through the execution of the Rebellious Son. The final use of the purge formula in Deuteronomy is applied to the execution of the kidnapper (24:7), who is portrayed as a dangerous outgroup member. This offender attempts to enslave 'one of his brothers of the people of Israel'. In so doing, the kidnapper repeats the actions of Pharaoh, who enslaves the entire nation of Israel (Exod. 1:8-14). Through this repetition the kidnapper is identified as a dangerous rival to the Israelite ingroup. For this reason, the kidnapper must be executed, which vents excessive rivalry within the community and ensures that peace and order is restored, as described by the purge formula (Deut. 24:7). From a mimetic perspective, as this brief survey

---

21. In Deut. 22:17 the elders of the city determine the outcome of the case by examining the בתולים, while the priests and judges 'inquire diligently…if the witness is a false witness and has accused his brother falsely' in 19:17-18.

has highlighted, the use of the purge formula throughout Deuteronomy denotes the effective venting of excessive mimetic rivalry from the community.

Significantly, the purge formula is only applied in Deuteronomy 22 when a female is executed.[22] Central to explaining this observation is the realization that the execution of females in Deuteronomy 22 functions to vent excessive rivalry between male community members.[23] The purge formula describes the peace and order achieve through this process. This interpretation of the purge formula in Deuteronomy 22 accounts for the social role of women, or at least their sexuality, as property which always belongs to particular man within the Deuteronomic framework. Furthermore, this interpretation also explains how the female's execution achieves a resolution to the rivalry between males in each case. Within this framework, it is not surprising that v. 22, which prescribes the execution of a wife and her paramour, offers no consideration of the woman's guilt or innocence.[24] The chief concern of this law is the resolution of male rivalry, which is achieved through the execution of the wife and her paramour. Yet, in cases involving an unmarried betrothed woman who becomes involved in an illicit sex act, her perceived guilt or innocence determines her fate (vv. 23-27).

The narrative approach recognizes that the betrothed woman, who is raped outside the city is not executed because she is considered an innocent victim. Significantly, the attack took place in the field (שדה), and when she 'cried (צעק) for help there was no one to rescue her' (vv. 25-27). As the narrative approach acknowledges, these details echo Cain's slaying of Abel, which also took place in a שדה (Gen. 4:8). Because no one is present to intervene Cain slays his brother and Abel's blood צעק to YHWH from the ground (v. 10). By utilizing this same imagery, Deut. 22:25-27 identifies the woman with Abel, which proclaims her innocence, while her attacker is identified with Cain and, thereby, portrayed as a dangerous outgroup member.[25] Verse 26 strengthens this association when it states that 'this case is like that of a man attacking and murdering his

22. Ellens, *Women in the Sex Texts*, 204.

23. Ellens argues that in Deut. 22 this formula provides 'instructional advice, warning the addressee to rid... the community of behavior that undermines... property rights'. Ibid., 204–5.

24. The married woman in v. 22 is executed regardless of the circumstances surrounding the sex act. Ibid., 228–9; Pressler, 'Sexual Violence and Deuteronomic Law', 107.

25. Both these texts employ the terms שָׂדֶה and צעק within a shared context of rivalry. These observations satisfy Hayes' second criterion.

neighbour'. In so doing, Deut. 22:26 suggests that this offence generates powerful mimetic rivalry between fellow community members, which is comparable to that generated through murder.[26] From a mimetic perspective, this comment suggests that raping a betrothed woman may initiate a cycle of mimetic violence that could culminate in a mimetic crisis.

To prevent a mimetic crisis this rivalry must be vented through the immolation of the woman's attacker as a communal scapegoat (Deut. 22:25). The presence of Girard's first, second, and fourth stereotype in Deut. 22:25-27 confirms this interpretation. Girard's first stereotype is fulfilled through the threat of a mimetic crisis in this text. The potential for this act to generate a dangerous cycle of mimetic rivalry is noted by the comment, 'this case is like that of a man attacking and murdering his neighbour'. Through this comment, Deut. 22:25-27 also blames the rapist for the mimetic crisis, which satisfies Girard's second stereotype. Finally, the execution of the rapist fulfils Girard's fourth stereotype (Deut. 22:25). Therefore, in Deut. 22:25-27 the rapist becomes a communal scapegoat, as his immolation prevents a mimetic crisis by venting the intense rivalry generated through his actions.

A betrothed woman who engages in sexual relations with a man other than her fiancé, within the city, must be immolated along with her paramour (vv. 23-24). In contrast to the woman described in vv. 25-27, the actions of the woman in vv. 23-24 do not echo those of the innocent victim, Abel, because 'she did not צעק for help though she was in the city'. The betrothed woman, who engages in illicit sex within the city, is assumed to be a willing participant.[27] For this reason, she must be immolated. Her male paramour must also be executed because he 'humbled (ענה) his neighbour's woman' (v. 24). Notice that the text focuses upon the fiancé's ownership of the woman's sexuality, rather than the woman herself. Through this woman's ענה, her fiancé's social status is

26. The echo of Gen. 4 in this text further strengthens this interpretation. Burnside discerns a parallel between literally 'throwing down a man and killing him (= murder) and the social "throwing down" of the husband by debasing the betrothed woman (= rape)'. Burnside, *God, Justice, and Society*, 374–5.

27. Ellens, *Women in the Sex Texts*, 229–32. The location of the offense may indicate the young woman's guilt or innocence. As Currid notes, 'it is also common in ancient Near-Eastern texts to draw a distinction on the basis of the locale in which a seduction has taken place. In Hittite law, for example, the following statute appears: "If a man seizes a woman in the mountains, it is the man's crime and he will be killed. But if he seizes her in [her] house, it is the woman's crime and the woman shall be killed. If the husband finds them, he may kill them; there shall be no punishment for him."' Currid, *Deuteronomy*, 372.

diminished.[28] Perhaps this offence represents a stronger attack upon the fiancé's social status than the offence addressed in vv. 25-27, because the woman would be perceived as a willing participant in the sex act. The community's perception of the woman as sexually promiscuous further diminishes her fiancé's social standing. Moreover, this act is more visible because it takes place in the city, in contrast to the sex act performed in vv. 25-27, which occurs in a שָׂדֶה. These factors may add to the fiancé's humiliation, generating greater social shame than the other offences addressed in Deuteronomy 22. To achieve adequate reparation for this humiliation, the community band together to stone not only the woman but also her paramour. Through these executions, mimetic rivalry is purged from the community, as noted by the purge formula (v. 24).

Significantly, the man who rapes an unbetrothed and unmarried woman is not executed, but rather welcomed into the family.[29] Although the rapist has diminished the social standing of his victim, as indicated by the term ענה (v. 29), the father's social standing is not challenged. Unlike the husband who directly challenges his father-in-law's social status in vv. 13-17, and who must be publicly flogged and humiliated to reinforce his inferior social status, the rapist of vv. 28-29 merely steals the young woman's virginity from her father. In this case, no flogging is necessary because the rapist of vv. 28-29 does not engage in direct rivalry with the woman's father. Yet, the rapist must still provide adequate reparation for his theft by paying a dowry and the marrying his victim with no

---

28. Ibid., 213.

29. I have followed the majority of scholars by labelling the offence described in Deut. 22:28 as 'rape', on account of the woman's role as an almost passive sexual object throughout Deut. 22:13-29 and the father's ownership of his daughter's sexuality. Within this framework, which differs significantly from our modern Western concept of personal sexual autonomy, only the father can give legitimately give consent for sex acts. As Carolyn Pressler notes, 'the girl's consent is not a material factor in the case'. However, it should be noted that Weinfeld focuses on the women's lack of protest and the different verbs employed in Deut. 22:28-29 to argue that this sex act is more of a 'seduction' than a rape. Moshe Weinfeld, *Deuteronomy and the Deuteronomic School* (Winona Lake: Eisenbrauns, 1992), 286–7. For others who interpret the sex act of Deut. 22:28 as rape, meaning the female is an unwilling participant in this act, see Tigay, *Deuteronomy*, 208; David Halivni Weiss, 'A Note on אשר לא ארשה', *Journal of Biblical Literature* 81, no. 1 (1962): 67; Ellens, *Women in the Sex Texts*, 200–204; Pressler, *The View of Women*, 37–8; Alexander Rofé, 'Family and Sex Laws in Deuteronomy and the Book of Covenant', *Henoch* 9, no. 2 (1987): 133–4; Gerhard von Rad, *Deuteronomy: A Commentary* (Louisville: Westminster John Knox, 1966), 142–3.

possibility for divorce (Deut. 22:28-29). The treatment of the rapist in this text highlights that Deut. 22:22-29 is primarily concerned with the rights and responsibilities of males regarding female sexuality:

> A man has rights to the exclusive use of the sexuality of his wife. It belongs only to him. A father has rights to the money and honor the virginity of his daughter brings him. While the money and honor from her virginity is preserved if she marries the rapist, the 'exclusivity' of the adulteress has been for ever damaged because another man has entered where only one man may go. One man has irrevocably stolen from another man. He cannot ever give back or compensate for what he took....
>
> A man's right to exclusive use of his wife's sexuality or his right to the money and honor from his daughter's virginity is the primary concern of the law. When those rights are abrogated such that no 'fix' can occur – death is the penalty.[30]

In sum, vv. 22-29 prescribe the management of various situations in which a man's right of ownership over his wife or fiancée is violated. In vv. 22-27 the rivalry generated through these violations is vented through the execution of the woman's paramour and in some cases the woman is also immolated (vv. 22-24). The intense jealousy generated through these offences produces a fierce rivalry between the two males, who become fixated upon one another.[31] Rivalries of this intensity may only be vented through human immolation. Yet, execution is not prescribed when a woman who is neither betrothed nor married is raped (vv. 28-29). Although the loss of the woman's virginity in this case potentially represents a financial loss to her father, the rapist provides reparation for this loss by marrying the woman and paying a dowry to her father.[32] In this case, execution is unnecessary because, unlike the fixated rivalries addressed in vv. 22-27, the rivalry between the father and his daughter's rapist is more focused upon the common desired object: the daughter's virginity and the financial and social value ascribed to this object. For this reason, the rapist can pacify the father by offering him reparation for his daughter's virginity. In this way, any potential rivalry between the father and his daughter's rapist is stifled.

---

30. Ellens, *Women in the Sex Texts*, 213.
31. Girard notes the intricate relationship between jealousy and mimetic rivalry. Girard, *Deceit, Desire, and the Novel*, 12–14.
32. Pressler, 'Sexual Violence and Deuteronomic Law', 104–5.

3. Conclusion

This chapter argued that the legislation of Deut. 22:13-29 aims to manage the mimetic rivalry generated through various forms of sexual misconduct. Deuteronomy 22:13-21 addresses the case of a husband who accuses his wife of sexual misconduct. If these accusations are found to be spurious, the wife's father is appeased through the humiliation of his son-in-law, pecuniary compensation, and the promise that his son-in-law will protect and provide for his wife for life. Through these means, the rivalry between the husband and father is diffused. Yet, if the husband's accusations are true, the rivalry between the husband and his father-in-law is vented through the wife's execution. In this way, the Unchaste Wife fulfils the role of the scapegoat. In a similar manner, those who engage in illicit sex with another man's wife or fiancée must also be executed. These observations highlight that Deut. 22:13-29 is primarily concerned with managing the mimetic rivalry generated through the alleged violation of marriage rights and responsibilities. The next chapter discusses the execution of the Rebellious Son in Deut. 21:18-21 as another means of venting excessive rivalry.

Chapter 9

THE REBELLIOUS SON OF DEUTERONOMY 21:18-21*

Previous chapters have revealed the scapegoat mechanism in various texts which prescribe and describe human immolation throughout the Pentateuch. This observation suggests that human immolation within the Pentateuch restores peace and order to the community by venting excessive mimetic rivalry. As demonstrated in the previous chapter, Deut. 22:21 describes this process as purging evil from the community. The present chapter reveals the role of the scapegoat mechanism in the execution of the Rebellious Son of 21:18-21. Again, the catharsis achieved through this process is described as purging evil from the community (21:21). However, in contrast to the examples surveyed in previous chapters, which charge the scapegoat with a particular offence, 21:18-21 broadly describes the Rebellious Son as a 'glutton and a drunkard', who disregards his parent's instruction. Deuteronomy links obedience to blessing, while disobedience is tied to disaster (28:1-68). When read within this framework, the narrative approach acknowledges that the Rebellious Son's disobedience places the community in danger.

In this chapter I argue that, according to Deut. 21:18-21, rebellious offspring must be immolated as communal scapegoats. This argument is explained and defended over two sections. The first section reviews previous interpretations of the Rebellious Son's death in 21:18-21. A mimetic reading of this text is then offered and defended in the second section by identifying three of Girard's scapegoat stereotypes in 21:18-21. By employing the narrative approach, I argue that the Rebellious Son's behaviour in 21:18-21 mirrors that of the rebellious wilderness generation. In this way rebellious offspring, who spurn their parent's instruction, threaten the

---

* This chapter is based on a previously published article: Simon Skidmore, 'A Mimetic Reading of Deuteronomy 21:18-21', *Heythrop Journal – Quarterly Review of Philosophy and Theology* 61, no. 6 (2020): 913–23.

wellbeing of the community. Just as the rebellious wilderness generation died before reaching the Promised Land, so rebellious offspring must be immolated and denied any inheritance in the Land. In so doing, the ingroup encourage Torah observance by removing rebellious offspring, who may serve as undesirable models within the community. The immolation of rebellious offspring also allows the community to vent their mimetic rivalries.

1. *Interpreting Deuteronomy 21:18-21*

[18] If a man has a stubborn and rebellious son	כִּי־יִהְיֶה לְאִישׁ בֵּן סוֹרֵר וּמוֹרֶה
who will not obey the voice of his father	אֵינֶנּוּ שֹׁמֵעַ בְּקוֹל אָבִיו
or the voice of his mother	וּבְקוֹל אִמּוֹ
and, though they instruct him, will not listen to them,	וְיִסְּרוּ אֹתוֹ וְלֹא יִשְׁמַע אֲלֵיהֶם:
[19] then his father and his mother shall take hold of him	וְתָפְשׂוּ בוֹ אָבִיו וְאִמּוֹ
and bring him out to the elders of his city	וְהוֹצִיאוּ אֹתוֹ אֶל־זִקְנֵי עִירוֹ
at the gate of the place where he lives,	וְאֶל־שַׁעַר מְקֹמוֹ:
[20] and they shall say to the elders of his city,	וְאָמְרוּ אֶל־זִקְנֵי עִירוֹ
'This our son is stubborn and rebellious;	בְּנֵנוּ זֶה סוֹרֵר וּמֹרֶה
he will not obey our voice;	אֵינֶנּוּ שֹׁמֵעַ בְּקֹלֵנוּ
he is a glutton and a drunkard'.	זוֹלֵל וְסֹבֵא:
[21] Then all the men of the city shall stone him	וּרְגָמֻהוּ כָּל־אַנְשֵׁי עִירוֹ
to death with stones.	בָאֲבָנִים וָמֵת
So you shall purge the evil from your midst,	וּבִעַרְתָּ הָרָע מִקִּרְבֶּךָ
and all Israel shall hear, and fear.	וְכָל־יִשְׂרָאֵל יִשְׁמְעוּ וְיִרָאוּ:

In what follows, I review and critique previous interpretations of Deut. 21:18-21 in preparation for the next section, which applies Girard's four scapegoat stereotypes to a narrative reading of this text.

The Rebellious Son violates the fifth commandment of the Decalogue when he fails to honour his parents.[1] This statement is supported by the chiastic structure of Deut. 21:1-23:[2]

A: vv. 1-9 – The management of dead bodies, which defile the land
    B: vv. 10-13 – Captive female slave girl honours her parents through mourning
        C: vv. 14 – Unloved slave girl emancipated
        C[1]: vv. 15-17 – Unloved firstborn son receives inheritance
    B[1]: vv. 18-21 – Rebellious Son fails to honour his parent's instruction
A[1]: vv. 22-23 – The management of dead bodies, which defile the land

---

1. Burnside, *The Signs of Sin*, 59–61.
2. Gordon J. Wenham and J. Gordon McConville, 'Drafting Techniques in Some Deuteronomic Laws', *Vetus Testamentum* 30, no. 2 (1980): 251.

Deuteronomy 21:1-9 and 22-23, which both address the defiling effect of corpses upon the land, form the bookends of this chiasm. The centre of the chiasm, vv. 14 and 15-17, deals with unloved slave girls and firstborn sons, respectively. Within the chiastic structure the execution of the Rebellious Son in vv. 18-21 parallels the provision for captive slave girls to mourn for their parents (vv. 10-13), which suggests that both these texts are concerned with correctly honouring one's parents.³ The Rebellious Son dishonours his parents by ignoring their instruction and adopting a destructive lifestyle which echoes the behaviour of Israel in the wilderness.⁴

This reading is supported by the description of the Rebellious Son as סורר ומורה in Deut. 21:18-21, which recalls the same imagery that was applied to Israel's wilderness generation. To gain an understanding of this extremely rare phrase and the סורר ומורה word pair, examples outside the Pentateuch must be considered. However, these examples still represent very strong echoes, which others have also noted. For example, the סורר ומורה word pair is employed in Ps. 78:8 to describe Israel's unfaithful behaviour in the wilderness.⁵ Just as the סורר ומורה wilderness generation persistently rebelled against YHWH, so too the סורר ומורה son in Deut. 21:18-21 perpetually rebels against his parents' instruction (vv. 18, 20).⁶ This son is also described as זולל וסבא in v. 20. The wise father uses this same word pair to instruct his son in the book of Proverbs:

---

3. Ibid. Stephen A. Kaufman, who argues that the structure of the Deut. 12:1–24:7 follows the Decalogue, suggests that Deut. 21:18-21 was misplaced from its original place in this corpus. According to Kaufman's schema, Deut. 21:18-21 should be placed among other passages which deal with disregard for authority, namely, Deut. 16:18–18:22. Stephen A Kaufman, 'The Structure of the Deuteronomic Law', *MAARAV* 1, no. 2 (1979): 114.

4. Burnside, *The Signs of Sin*, 59–77.

5. As a Deuteronomistic insert, which stems from the same tradition as rebele lion motif within the Pentateuch, vv. 5-8 of Ps. 78 apply this same word pair to describe Israel's rebellion against YHWH in the wilderness period. George W. Coats, *Rebellion in the Wilderness: The Murmuring Motif in the Wilderness, Traditions of the Old Testament* (Nashville: Abingdon, 1968), 199–214. Although this echo goes beyond the Pentateuch, it stems from the Deuteronomic tradition, which assumes Deuteronomy and, in this way, satisfies Hayes' first, fourth, fifth, and sixth criteria. Furthermore, this echo also satisfies Hayes' second criterion because it uses the rare word pair, סורר ומורה, in the shared context of a parent–child relationship.

6. Elizabeth Bellefontaine, 'Deuteronomy 21:18-21: Reviewing the Case of the Rebellious Son', *Journal for the Study of the Old Testament* 13 (1979): 19; Burnside, *The Signs of Sin*, 50–1.

> Hear (שמע), my son, and be wise, and direct your heart in the way.
> Be not among drunkards (סבא) or among gluttonous eaters of meat (זלל),
> for the drunkard (סבא) and the glutton (זלל) will come to poverty,
> and slumber will clothe them with rags. (Prov. 23:19-21)

Echoing Deut. 21:18-21, Prov. 23:19-21 argues that drunkenness and gluttony lead to poverty.[7] This idea resonates with Deuteronomy's insistence that Torah observance, viz. adherence to YHWH's 'statutes and rules', leads to prosperity, while rebellion against YHWH and his Torah leads to destruction (e.g. Deut. 28:1-68).[8] The זולל וסבא word pair also communicates an immoral lifestyle, which goes beyond excessive eating and drinking 'to include more destructive forms of behaviour'.[9] For example, Isaiah describes those who excessively eat and drink as ignoring YHWH's works (5:11-12), and accuses those who are 'heroes at drinking wine, and valiant men in mixing strong drink' of corruption (5:22-23).[10] In the ancient world social, political, and religious relationships were expressed through the appropriate consumption of food and drink. Drunkenness and gluttony signalled a breakdown of these relationships.[11] In this way, the Rebellious Son of Deut. 21:18-21 is portrayed as a dangerous, immoral outgroup member whose behaviour threatens the established social order.

Elizabeth Bellefontaine argues that this person is portrayed as part of a 'bad lot':

> His excessive eating and drinking ran counter to accepted social norms; this is implied in the accusation itself. Further, these particular vices suggest that he was a non-productive, non-contributing parasite in the community. Being undisciplined and unpredictable, he would be untrustworthy in time of crises such as war. At any time, his unrestrained behaviour could have offended others and strained inter-family or inter-clan relationships risking retaliation or feud against himself, his family and his community. Then there was the peril of the divine wrath which might fall upon all the people because of the presence of the evil-doer in their midst. Thus, the son's deviant

---

7. The shared use of rare terms used, again, within the context of a parent–child exchange satisfies Hayes' second criterion. Hayes' sixth criterion is also satisfied by Burnside's acknowledgment of this echo. As Burnside notes, 'a clearer tip of the hat to Deut. 21.18-21 is hard to imagine'. Burnside, *The Signs of Sin*, 54.

8. Proverbs, itself, perpetuates the Deuteronomistic ideal of obedient children adhering to their parents teaching. The Rebellious Son is analogous to the 'fool' character referred to throughout Proverbs. Reeder, *The Enemy in the Household*, 54–6.

9. Burnside, *The Signs of Sin*, 54.

10. See also Isa. 56:10-12 and Amos 4:1.

11. Burnside, *The Signs of Sin*, 66–7.

behaviour not only corrupted himself but may have meant serious negative consequences for his neighbours. He was indeed an undesirable member of society and he at last attained the state of the 'finally intolerable'. It is understandable that the elders of the place where he lived would condemn such a man to death.[12]

Bellefontaine rightly observes that the Rebellious Son's refusal to respect Torah threatens the community's wellbeing.[13] Her statement that 'the son's deviant behaviour...may have meant serious negative consequences for his neighbours' is consistent with Deuteronomy's assertion that Israel's welfare depends upon Torah observance. Yet, Bellefontaine also suggests that the Rebellious Son's lack of contribution in daily life and unreliability during warfare necessitate his execution. While there may be some truth to this suggestion, the current chapter offers a slightly different perspective upon the Rebellious Son's execution, which pays careful attention to the specific concerns expressed within Deut. 21:18-21. This text primarily stresses the Rebellious Son's refusal to obey his parent's instructions. As I shall argue below, when read within the context of Deuteronomy, this refusal could threaten the wellbeing of the entire community, especially if others imitate the Rebellious Son.[14] From a mimetic perspective, this imitation could lead to a collapse of the social order and hierarchy as Torah is abandoned. Without this social order, mimetic rivalry flourishes, and a mimetic crisis may precipitate. The mimetic approach employed in the present chapter suggests that the Rebellious Son must be executed because his actions threaten to bring a mimetic crisis upon the community.

Anselm C. Hagedorn has argued that the immolation of the Rebellious Son in Deut. 21:18-21 does not promote the execution of rebellious children, but rather encourages parents to diligently teach Torah to their children.[15] According to Hagedorn, this text affirms the value of 'family honour, a status that can be displayed by having a wise son that listens to his father's discipline'.[16] However, there are a few difficulties with

---

12. Bellefontaine, 'Deuteronomy 21:18-21', 21–2.
13. Bellefontaine's argument is weakened by its reliance upon anthropological observations drawn from African tribes, as opposed to ancient Near Eastern peoples. Furthermore, Bellefontaine fails to prove her hypothesis that the Rebellious Son of Deut. 21:18-21 is part of a 'bad lot'. Joseph Fleishman, 'Legal Innovation in Deuteronomy XXI 18-20', *Vetus Testamentum* 53, no. 3 (2003): 321.
14. As Willis writes, the Rebellious Son's behaviour 'could influence others of his generation to pursue an equally disruptive course'. Willis, *The Elders of the City*, 179.
15. Hagedorn, 'Guarding the Parents' Honour'.
16. Ibid., 115.

this reading. First, the mode of immolation, communal stoning, suggests that the offender's actions affect the whole community and not just the parent's honour.[17] Second, v. 21 confirms that the Rebellious Son's immolation positively impacts the whole community as they 'purge the evil' from their midst. Moreover, the shift to the second-person imperative, 'you shall purge the evil from among you', in v. 21 directly commands the Israelite community to execute rebellious offspring.[18] Third, in Deut. 21:18-21 the parents faithfully instruct their son in Torah, but he refuses to listen. Deuteronomy 21:18-21, therefore, focuses upon the responsibility of offspring to listen to their parents' instruction, rather than the parents' responsibility to teach their offspring. This reading is confirmed by the result clause of v. 21, which also focuses upon the responsibility of offspring to heed their parents' instruction: 'all Israel shall hear and fear'. Meanwhile, family honour is not mentioned. For these reasons, the present study lays aside Hagedorn's reading of 21:18-21.

Keith Whitelam argues that, as a result of urbanization, the legislation of Deut. 21:18-21 limits the power of the *paterfamilias* by transferring the responsibility for a rebellious child's immolation to the city elders.[19] However, this theory assumes that urbanization accounts for a supposed change in communal power structures, and that parents who execute their offspring without consulting the city elders would be prosecuted.[20] These assumptions cannot be proven.[21] Although Whitelam cites Laban's condemnation of Jacob in Genesis 31, and Judah's condemnation of Tamar in Genesis 38 in support of his theory, neither of these texts support the

17. Bellefontaine, 'Deuteronomy 21:18-21', 21; Reeder, *The Enemy in the Household*, 42.

18. By directly addressing its audience the second person imperative strongly compels the Israelite community to obey this command. For the rhetorical function of the second person imperative see James W. Watts, *Reading Law: The Rhetorical Shaping of the Pentateuch* (Edinburgh: A. & C. Black, 1999), 64.

19. Keith W. Whitelam, *The Just King: Monarchical Judicial Authority in Ancient Israel* (Sheffield: JSOT, 1979), 42. See also Hans Jochen Boecker, *Law and the Administration of Justice in the Old Testament and Ancient East*, trans. Jeremy Moiser (London: Society for Promoting Christian Knowledge, 1980), 28–30; John M. Salmon, 'Judicial Authority in Early Israel: An Historical Investigation of Old Testament Institutions' (PhD diss., Princeton Theological Seminary, 1969), 24–35. Similarly, Louis Stulman argues that several Deuteronomic passages, including Deut. 21:18-21, remove the *paterfamilias'* absolute power to execute members of their family. The criticisms raised here against Whitelam's work could also be applied to Stulman's thesis.

20. Willis, *The Elders of the City*, 175–6.

21. Pressler, *The View of Women*, 18–19.

validity of his assumptions.²² Contra Whitelam, Laban's claim that he has power to harm Jacob (31:29) is most likely an empty threat of violence, and not a statement of Laban's political power as the *paterfamilias*. This reading is supported by Laban's obligation to prove his allegation of theft (v. 32) before harming Jacob, which further demonstrates that his position as *paterfamilias* does not afford him unfettered authority. Laban's inability to prove his allegations before his kin renders him powerless before Jacob.²³ Whitelam's citation of this text to support his claim that the *paterfamilias* once wielded absolute power over his household seems unconvincing, because in Gen. 31:25-32 Laban is accountable to his kinsmen for his actions.²⁴

The second text that Whitelam references to support his argument is Judah's condemnation of Tamar in Gen. 38:24. However, far from depicting an older form of clan justice, in which the *paterfamilias* had absolute power to immolate his clan members, Judah's command to burn Tamar is considered a later Priestly gloss.²⁵ Furthermore, this text follows the same pattern as that of the Rebellious Son in Deut. 21:18-21. In both cases an offending family member is presented for immolation by a parental figure. Moreover, Judah is consulted on how to deal with Tamar on account of his position as the clan head.²⁶ This pattern mirrors the consultation of Moses in texts such as Lev. 24:10-23 and Num. 15:32-36. Although Judah appears to have ultimate power over Tamar's fate in Gen. 38:24, this power is on account of his position as the head of the clan, and not as Tamar's *paterfamilias*. Judah cannot be considered Tamar's *paterfamilias* as she is only betrothed to Judah's son, Shelah, and not yet living in Judah's house.²⁷ Judah's role in this passage mirrors that of the elders in Deut. 21:18-21 and, therefore, should not be interpreted as an older function of the *paterfamilias*. For these reasons, the present study lays aside Whitelam's interpretation of Deut. 21:18-21.

---

22. Whitelam, *The Just King*, 40.

23. Charles Mabee, 'Jacob and Laban: The Structure of Judicial Proceedings (Genesis XXXI 25-42)', *Vetus Testamentum* 30, no. 2 (1980): 196, 200–203.

24. Even though Laban claims that 'everything belongs to him, he cannot do anything about it'. In light of his impotence Laban lays aside his empty threat of violence, and proposes a 'treaty of nonaggression'. Roop, *Genesis*, 204.

25. Driver and Miles, *The Babylonian Laws*, 495–6.

26. Among semi-nomadic groups, the head of the clan was responsible for ensuring all offenders were punished appropriately. Ze'ev Wilhelm Falk, *Hebrew Law in Biblical Times: An Introduction* (Jerusalem: Books, 1964), 35–7.

27. Westbrook, 'Adultery in Ancient Near Eastern Law', 546; Anthony Phillips, 'Another Example of Family Law', *Vetus Testamentum* 30, no. 2 (1980): 243.

An alternative reading of Deut. 21:18-21 is offered by Timothy M. Willis, who argues that the Rebellious Son threatens the community's wellbeing when he fails to keep the fifth commandment:[28]

> The commandment to honor one's parents is a part of Israel's foundational religious tenets. The 'stubborn and rebellious' son is blatantly contemptuous toward that commandment. This betrays a contempt for Yahweh himself. Such a person threatens to bring divine wrath down on the entire community. To avert that, the community must see to it that that person is removed from their midst...
>
> The elders represent the community and probably have been among those pressuring the parents to 'do something' about their son. But they do not circumvent the parents to punish the son. They honor the parents (even though the son does not) by waiting for them to hand over the rebellious son to the community... By allowing them to hand him over the elders signal the community's acceptance of the rest of the family.[29]

Willis correctly recognizes the danger inherent in the Rebellious Son's actions. Within ancient Israel, honouring one's parents was viewed as crucial to the community's wellbeing and underpinned the social, economic, and theological structure of communal life.[30] The call to honour, fear, and revere parents, which the fifth commandment encourages, may also contribute to a healthy respect for other authority figures, such as judges, kings, and priests.[31] Furthermore, the Deuteronomic ideal of parents passing on their faith tradition to their children relies upon filial adherence to the fifth commandment.[32] By

---

28. In a similar vein, Joseph Fleishman argues that the Rebellious Son of Deut. 21:18-21 violates the prohibition of Exod. 21:17, which he interprets as forbidding children from dishonouring and belittling their parents. Fleishman, 'Legal Innovation in Deuteronomy XXI 18-20', 315–19.

29. Willis, *The Elders of the City*, 180.

30. Burnside, *The Signs of Sin*, 61–4; Willis, *The Elders of the City*, 179; Stulman, 'Sex and Familial Crimes in the D Code', 53; Christopher J. H. Wright, 'The Israelite Household and the Decalogue: The Social Background and Significance of Some Commandments', *Tyndale Bulletin* 30 (1979): 104.

31. Hence Deuteronomy's expansion of the fifth commandment to include honour for these figures (16:18–18:22). Patrick D. Miller Jr, 'The Place of the Decalogue in the Old Testament and Its Law', *Union Seminary Review* 43, no. 3 (1989): 238–9.

32. Reeder, *The Enemy in the Household*, 40; Phillips, *Ancient Israel's Criminal Law*, 81; Peter C. Craigie, *The Book of Deuteronomy* (Grand Rapids: Eerdmans, 1976), 157–8.

refusing to keep the fifth commandment, the Rebellious Son's actions threaten the stability of the nation as much as more heinous crimes, such as apostasy or idolatry.[33]

In light of the threat posed by his actions, the community pressures the Rebellious Son's parents to present their son for immolation.[34] Deuteronomy 21:18-21 urges the reluctant parents to yield to this petition for the wellbeing of the community.[35] The parents present their son for immolation with the words 'this son of ours', which express their estrangement from him and confirm his guilt (vv. 19-20).[36] As they do so, the parents set themselves apart from their offspring and declare their allegiance to the ingroup. The same dynamic can be observed in Deut. 22:20-21, as the father of the Unchaste Bride confirms his allegiance to the ingroup by presenting his daughter for immolation as a scapegoat.[37] Likewise, the Rebellious Son of Deut. 21:18-21 is presented as a scapegoat to the elders of the city, who subsequently approve his immolation by communal stoning. As the community immolate the offender, mimetic rivalry is purged from the community and peace and order maintained (Deut. 21:21). This reading may be confirmed by applying Girard's scapegoat stereotypes to a narrative reading of Deut. 21:18-21.

---

33. Wright, 'The Israelite Household and the Decalogue', 114; Stulman, 'Sex and Familial Crimes in the D Code', 55; McConville, *Deuteronomy*, 331.

34. Willis, *The Elders of the City*, 179; Reeder, *The Enemy in the Household*, 42. Dion argues that the additional description of the Rebellious Son as a 'glutton and a drunkard' in v. 20 denotes the public nature of his actions. Paul E. Dion, 'La Procedure d'elimination des fils Rebelle (Deut 21:18-21): Sens Littéral et Signes de Développement Juridique', in *Biblische theologie und Gesellschaftlicher Wandel*, ed. G. Braulik (Freiburg: Herder, 1993), 78–9.

35. This reading is consistent of Hagedorn's assertion that 'Mediterranean people would never carry their internal affairs voluntarily into the public [domain], for that would imply running the risk of gossip and shame'. Hagedorn, 'Guarding the Parents' Honour', 115.

36. As Asnat Bartor notes, these parents' statement in vv. 19-20 'reflects a negative attitude or scorn toward the person referenced, it is clear that its use here expresses the parents' estrangement from and revulsion towards their son... The daunting image they project aims, and succeeds, at alienating the tribunal from the rebellious son, persuading them to remove him from the community. It removes all doubt from the heart of the judges (and of the readers) regarding the necessity of the death penalty.' Bartor, *Reading Law as Narrative*, 100–101.

37. See Chapter 8.

2. Mimesis in Deuteronomy 21:18-21

In what follows, I employ the narrative approach and build upon the insights gleaned in the previous section to argue that the Rebellious Son's behaviour in Deut. 21:18-21 mirrors that of unfaithful Israel in the wilderness. Just as the unfaithful Israelite generation failed to inherit the Promised Land of Canaan, so rebellious offspring, who refuse to follow Torah, will lose their inheritance in the Promised Land. The Rebellious Son's behaviour threatens the wellbeing of the community, as he disobeys Torah and serves as a potential model for others to imitate. From a mimetic perspective, I argue that the Rebellious Son must be immolated to stop others from imitating his behaviour and to provide a channel through which the community can vent their mimetic rivalries. This process draws the community together and reaffirms Torah observance as a core communal value. Through these means, the immolation of rebellious offspring maintains peace and order within the community, and facilitates the community's reflection of the divine image through Torah observance. The application of Girard's four stereotypes to Deut. 21:18-21 confirm this reading.

2.1. *A Narrative Reading of Deuteronomy 21:18-21*

As noted above, Deut. 21:18-21 focuses upon the Rebellious Son's failure to 'obey the voice' of his parents as they instruct him in YHWH's Torah. According to Deuteronomy, following YHWH's statutes and rules ensures the community's wellbeing in the Land:

> Now this is the commandment – the statutes and the rules – that the YHWH your God commanded me to teach you, that you may do them in the land to which you are going over to possess it, that you may fear YHWH your God, you and your son and your son's son, by keeping all his statutes and his commandments, which I command you, all the days of your life, and that your days may be long. Hear (שמע), therefore, O Israel and be careful to do them, that it may go well with you, and that you may multiply greatly, as YHWH, the God of your fathers, has promised you, in a land flowing with milk and honey... And these words that I command you today shall be on your heart. You shall teach them diligently to your children... (Deut. 6:1-3, 6-7)

This text emphasizes the importance of observing Torah, and teaching one's progeny to do likewise, for the wellbeing of the community. For this reason, the Israelites are commanded to diligently teach 'these words' to their children (vv. 5-6). Failure to do so threatens the very fabric of the community and Israel's existence in the land.[38] As the narrative approach recognizes, this threat is highlighted by the example of the wilderness generation in the Exodus narrative.

According to Deuteronomy, Israel's wilderness generation perpetually rebelled against YHWH in the wilderness. Israel 'rebelled (מרה) against the command of YHWH' when they refused to attack the Canaanites (1:26-28; 9:23) and, again, when they 'presumptuously went up into the hill country' (9:7). In response to this rebellion, YHWH states that 'not one of these men of this evil generation shall see the good Land that I swore to give to your fathers', with the exception of Caleb and Joshua because they were faithful to YHWH and not rebellious (1:35-38). The wilderness generation failed to enter the Land of Canaan on account of their rebellion. In this way, Deuteronomy warns the people about the dangers of rebelling against YHWH. The narrative approach recognizes that just as the wilderness generation's rebellion against YHWH prevents them from entering Canaan, so too Deuteronomy warns subsequent generations that rebelling against YHWH's Torah will endanger Israel's inheritance of the Promised Land.

Torah protects the community from excessive mimetic rivalry. If someone rebels against the rules of Torah, he or she could become a model for someone else to imitate. With the repetition of this process, the community as a whole may abandon Torah, and imitate one another instead. With no rules to limit mimetic rivalry, everyone imitates everybody else, which generates excessive rivalry within the community. This rivalry may culminate in a mimetic crisis. The legal material of Deut. 21:18-21 aims to stop this process before a mimetic crisis precipitates by immolating rebellious offspring. The immolation of these offenders also vents mimetic rivalry and, in this way, prevents mimetic crises. Furthermore, as community members participate in this act they simultaneously reaffirm their status as ingroup members, who reflect the divine image through Torah observance, and denounce the Rebellious Son, who does not. This reading is confirmed by the presence of Girard's first, second, and fourth stereotypes within Deut. 21:18-21.

2.2. *Girard's Four Stereotypes*
In what follows, I reveal the scapegoat mechanism in Deut. 21:18-21 by applying Girard's four scapegoat stereotypes to this text. Girard's first stereotype is that of the mimetic crisis. Although Deut. 21:18-21 does

---

38. Merrill, *Deuteronomy*, 161; Ronald E. Clements, *Deuteronomy* (Sheffield: Sheffield Academic, 1997), 44–5.

not explicitly describe a mimetic crisis, the fear of a communal crisis lingers in the background of this text. The description of the Rebellious Son as 'stubborn and rebellious' recalls Israel's behaviour during their wilderness wanderings.[39] Furthermore, the Rebellious Son's refusal to listen (שמע) to his parent's voice (קול) and heed their instruction (v. 18) contravenes the command of Deut. 6:1-3, 6-7. This blatant rebellion against the Deuteronomic ideal also mirrors Israel's refusal to listen (שמע) to YHWH's voice (קול) in the wilderness, which caused the death of that generation (8:20).[40] According to Deuteronomy, if subsequent generations also fail to שמע YHWH's קול, the community will suffer dire consequences (28:15-68). The narrative approach interprets Deut. 21:18-21 within the context of this threat to perceive the Rebellious Son's behaviour as jeopardizing Israel's existence within Canaan. If the Rebellious Son's behaviour is imitated throughout the community, a communal crisis may ensue which places Girard's first stereotype in the background of this text.

While one may not discern Girard's third stereotype within Deut. 21:18-21, his second and fourth stereotypes are present in this text. The Rebellious Son is brought to the city elders, who approve his immolation on the basis of his parents' testimony (vv. 19-20). As Willis notes, the parents of the Rebellious Son succumb to the community's insistence regarding their son's conduct.[41] The community have already identified the Rebellious Son as a dangerous outgroup member whose behaviour threatens to bring a mimetic crisis upon the community. The role of the parents in condemning their son demonstrates that the community unanimously blames the Rebellious Son for the potential mimetic crisis. In this way, Girard's second stereotype is fulfilled. Girard's fourth stereotype is satisfied when the Rebellious Son is immolated by communal stoning (v. 21). Through this act, the community purge their mimetic rivalry, preventing the mimetic crisis threatened by the Rebellious Son's actions. The cathartic nature of this event is confirmed by the use of the purge formula (v. 21).[42] The presence of Girard's first, second, and fourth stereotypes confirms the presence of the scapegoat mechanism within this text, which supports the reading of Deut. 21:18-21 presented above.

---

39. Burnside, *The Signs of Sin*, 47–50.
40. The echo of these words within the context of rebellion and death satisfies Hayes' second criterion.
41. Willis, *The Elders of the City*, 180.
42. As discussed in Chapter 8, the purge formula describes the effective purgation of mimetic rivalry from the community.

3. Conclusion

This chapter has argued the Rebellious Son of Deut. 21:18-21 must be immolated on account of his disregard for Torah, which threatens Israel's wellbeing within the Land. Torah observance limits mimetic rivalry within the community. If members of the community disregard Torah, then excessive rivalry may result, culminating in a mimetic crisis. The law of Deut. 21:18-21 aims to prevent these crises by immolating offspring who refuse to follow Torah. Once these offenders are removed from the community they cannot serve as models for others to imitate. The Rebellious Son's death facilitates Torah observance and, in so doing, facilitates the ingroup's reflection of the divine image. In this way, the Rebellious Son of Deut. 21:18-21 functions as a communal scapegoat, upon whom the community vent their mimetic rivalries to prevent the outbreak of a mimetic crisis. The absence of a specific allegation in Deut. 21:18-21 highlights the arbitrary nature of the scapegoat mechanism. In the midst of a mimetic crisis, scapegoats are arbitrarily selected, which renders their guilt ultimately irrelevant. More important than just punishment for certain offences is the purgation of mimetic rivalry upon a communal scapegoat. The case of the Rebellious Son of Deut. in 21:18-21 reminds us of this chilling fact.

Chapter 10

CONCLUDING COMMENTS

This book has presented a synchronic reading of key texts concerned with human immolation within the Pentateuch. By applying mimetic theory to this reading I have argued that within the Pentateuch human immolation functions to vent mimetic rivalry. In the midst of a mimetic crisis, this process restores peace and order, and saves the community from self-destruction. In this way, the current study makes a valuable and unique contribution to the literature on human immolation within the Pentateuch. While others have attempted to explain such cases of human immolation as either a necessary enforcement of divine judgment or purgation of impurity, this study considered human immolation as a means of establishing and maintaining social order within the world of the Pentateuch.[1] The present chapter reviews the key findings of this study, explains the theoretical implications of these findings, and suggests some avenues for future research.

1. *Key Findings*

Chapter 2 examined the concept of *imago dei* within the context of the rivalry that flourishes throughout the Pentateuch. Through this examination, I argued that the Pentateuch presents a dichotomy between the Israelite ingroup and their outgroup rivals. Foreign outgroups, such as the Egyptians and Canaanites, compromise Israel's ability to reflect the divine image through Torah observance. By observing Torah, the ingroup fulfil their vocation as the children of YHWH. In this way, the concept of

---

1. For other approaches that explain capital punishment within the Pentateuch as either the visitation of divine justice or purgation of impurity, see Harland, *The Value of Human Life*, 28–44; Frymer-Kensky, 407–8; Klawans, *Impurity and Sin in Ancient Judaism*, 58.

imago dei within the Pentateuch functions to identify the people of Israel as YHWH's blessed children, and sets them apart from other peoples. This interpretation allows the concept of *imago dei* to be read synchronically with other Pentateuchal texts, which pronounce curses upon Israel's enemies (e.g. Gen. 9:25). Furthermore, this reading also explains the citation of *imago dei* in Gen. 9:6 in a way that other approaches cannot. Israelites who commit offences including murder, Sabbath desecration, and blasphemy threaten the ingroup's ability to reflect the divine image. To fulfil their vocation as YHWH's image-bearing children, the ingroup must execute these offenders.

Chapter 3 explained the method employed throughout this study, namely, the application of mimetic theory to produce a fresh reading of key texts concerned with human immolation in the Pentateuch. This approach paid careful attention to the fierce rivalry between the Israelite ingroup and their outgroup rivals. By identifying Girard's scapegoat stereotypes in key texts, the present study revealed the presence of the scapegoat mechanism in each of these passages. Through this approach, I argued that human immolation, as it is prescribed within the Pentateuch, maintains and restores peace and order within the community. When rivalry among community members reaches excessive levels, a mimetic crisis may ensue. Unless this rivalry is vented upon an external party, the entire community could potentially be destroyed. Alternatively, the scapegoat mechanism may prompt the community to band together and vent their collective rivalry upon a scapegoat. By these means, community-wide peace and order is restored. When compared with other approaches to biblical human immolation, this model provides a more satisfying and robust explanation of communal execution within the Pentateuch.

Through the application of this method, Chapter 4 identified the scapegoat mechanism in Lev. 24:10-23. This text narrates the communal stoning of a man who fought with an unidentified Israelite and 'blasphemed the Name'. In this way, the Blasphemer threatens the Israelite ingroup's ability to reflect the divine image. To fulfil their vocation as YHWH's children, the community vent their collective rivalries upon the Blasphemer through communal stoning (v. 23). In his death, the Blasphemer fulfils his role as the communal scapegoat. A similar process was observed in Chapter 5, which examined the stoning of a man who threatened the ingroup's identity by desecrating the Sabbath in Num. 15:32-36. By applying Girard's stereotypes I argued that this man is also executed as a communal scapegoat. The identification of the scapegoat mechanism in Lev. 24:10-23 and Num. 15:32-36 confirmed that these texts narrate the purgation of the community's collective rivalries through communal stoning. The application of mimetic theory to these texts produced a unique explanation of why the apparently victimless crimes of blasphemy and Sabbath desecration receive the death penalty in the Pentateuch.

Chapter 6 considered the Pentateuch's prescription of the death penalty in cases of murder. Killing another person in ancient Israel could spark a dangerous blood feud. These blood feuds may generate mimetic crises, as murderous violence is imitated by each subsequent avenger of blood who arises to avenge the death of their kin. To prevent these crises, the Pentateuch appoints Asylum Cities, in which accused murderers may find sanctuary from the avenger of blood (Num. 35:6-15; Deut. 19:1-10). However, if the accused is considered guilty of illegitimate bloodshed, he or she must be handed over to the avenger of blood for immolation (Num. 35:16-21; Deut. 19:11-13). Having studied the key Pentateuchal texts which address murder (Exod. 21:12-14; Num. 35:30-34; Deut. 19:11-13), I argued that these passages specifically address the murder of those who belong to the Israelite ingroup. This offence attracts the death penalty because it threatens to involve the ingroup in a dangerous blood feud. Such feuds are avoided through the execution of murderers upon whom the community vent their mimetic violence. The unique strength of this reading is its ability to provide a consistent explanation of how human immolation diffuses the potential damage incurred through murder, even though the Pentateuchal texts themselves present competing aetiologies (e.g. Num. 35:30-34 vs. Deut. 19:1-10).

The prescription of human immolation for various offences in Leviticus 20 was addressed in Chapter 7. In this chapter, the double penalty of execution plus the כרת-penalty is prescribed for Molech worshippers and their families (Lev. 20:2-5). I argued that this offence was considered particularly dangerous because it engaged the services of a rival priesthood. To vent the rivalry between the Molech and Aaronic priesthoods, those who partake in Molech worship must be executed. Furthermore, the enforcement of the כרת-penalty removes the families of Molech worshippers from the community to avoid the imitation of this practice. This reading provides a unique explanation of why Lev. 20:2-5 prescribes the double penalty in cases of Molech worship. Other taboos listed in Leviticus 18 and 20 address sexual relations with the wives of near kinsmen. Offences such as these could lead to a fierce rivalry between potential doubles, which must be vented through the immolation of offenders who become communal scapegoats. These chapters also express anxiety over potential rivalries which may arise between two sisters, or a mother and her daughter, who marry the same man (Lev. 18:17-18; 20:14). The potential for these unions to generate mimetic rivalry, which may spread to the community through the perpetrators' rival offspring, is nullified through the offenders' execution. Rivalry may also be vented by executing males who partake in homosexual coitus (Lev. 20:13), those who curse their parents (v. 9), or people who engage in sexual intercourse with animals (vv. 15-16). While other commentators have attempted to explain the various sexual taboos listed in Leviticus 18 and 20 with reference to disgust or structuralist systems, my method considers their role in maintaining communal peace and order. A major advantage of this method is its ability to also explain the execution of offenders who transgress taboos which generate rivalry between close relatives (Lev. 20:10-14).

In Chapter 8 I argued that the chief focus of Deut. 22:13-29 was the management of mimetic rivalry between males. The rivalry between a man and his son-in-law, who accuses his wife of sexual misconduct, is addressed in Deut. 22:13-21. If the accusations are false, the rivalry between these two men can be diffused through pecuniary means, the husband's public shaming, and the promise that he will never divorce the wife he accused (22:13-19). In this way, the father is compensated for the false allegations. However, if the allegations are true, the rivalry between these men must be vented through the immolation of the Unchaste Bride, who fulfils the role of a scapegoat (vv. 20-21). Acts which violate a man's exclusive access to his wife or fiancée also demand execution (vv. 20-27), because of the intense rivalry generated through these acts. This rivalry cannot be stifled through other means because the males in these cases become fixated upon one another, instead of the female as the common object of desire. While some commentators have bemoaned this female's objectification, others have argued that these texts are actually concerned with her welfare. However, these discussions become moot once male rivalry is appreciated as the focus of Deut. 22:13-29. Because this text focuses on resolving rivalry between males, it does not address the thoughts and desires of the woman involved.

The final text considered in this study was the legislation concerning the Rebellious Son in Deut. 21:18-21. This passage is particularly interesting because, unlike the other texts considered in the current book, Deut. 21:18-21 does not accuse the Rebellious Son of any specific crime. The Rebellious Son is merely described as 'stubborn and rebellious' because he does not obey his parent's instruction. In Chapter 9 I argued that this text, when read within the context of Deuteronomy, suggests that the Rebellious Son's behaviour places the community in danger of a mimetic crisis. To prevent this crisis, the community must purge their mimetic rivalries by stoning the Rebellious Son. In this way, the Rebellious Son of Deut. 21:18-21 serves as a communal scapegoat for the Israelite ingroup.

When viewed from this perspective, an exact description of the Rebellious Son's offence would be counterproductive. The non-descript accusation levelled at the Rebellious Son makes Deut. 21:18-21 incredibly versatile, as it allows the scapegoating of any individual who is accused of rebelling against their parent's instruction in some way. The community's unanimous condemnation, including the offender's parents, determines the offender's guilt. According to Deut. 21:18-21, the offender's execution restores Torah observance within the community as all Israel 'hear and fear' (v. 21). As the community observe Torah, they fulfil their vocation as YHWH's divine image-bearing children. The Rebellious Son's execution, therefore, fulfils the dual role of venting mimetic rivalry and restoring the structures which prevent mimetic rivalry in the first place.

2. Theoretical Implications

Having outlined the major findings of this study, I shall now discuss some of the implications of these findings. In what follows, I address the question of why the Pentateuch prescribes human immolation for particular offences. Next, I recount some of the pro-capital punishment arguments presented by Hebrew Bible scholars that cite passages and concepts discussed in the current study. These arguments are then assessed in light of the current study's findings.

2.1. Why the Pentateuch Prescribes Human Immolation

The present study revealed the presence of the scapegoat mechanism in major texts concerning human immolation within the Pentateuch. These findings suggest that human immolation within the Pentateuch is driven by excessive mimetic rivalry. In Chapters 4 and 5 I argued that Lev. 24:10-23 and Num. 15:32-36 both describe a mimetic crisis that threatens to destroy the community. In response to these crises, the scapegoat mechanism prompts the community to band together, and search for a scapegoat to blame. The community then present their scapegoat to Moses, who in turn receives the divine instruction to execute these malefactors through communal stoning (Lev. 24:11-16; Num. 15:33-35). From a mimetic perspective, the divine instruction to execute these malefactors describes the scapegoat mechanism, as it drives the community band together against their scapegoat. Having executed the scapegoat, peace and order is restored to the community, which legitimates and justifies the community's violence. Convinced of YHWH's hand in these events, the Pentateuchal writers then portray them as incidents of divinely sanctioned killing, which save the Israelite community from annihilation in the midst of mimetic crises.

Within the Pentateuch, offences that have the potential to generate fierce rivalry and precipitate a mimetic crisis attract the death penalty. For example, Chapter 6 examined the death penalty in cases of murder and concluded that the execution of murderers, when exercised in conjunction with Asylum Cities, protects the community from mimetic crises by stalling dangerous cycles of blood vengeance. As noted in Chapter 7, mimetic crises are also avoided through the execution of males who engage in sexual relations with the wife of their father or son (Lev. 20:11-12). In this way, the fierce rivalry between these close kinsmen is vented. In a similar manner, as explained in Chapter 8, the fierce rivalry between the husband of an alleged unchaste wife and his father-in-law is vented through the unchaste wife's execution (Deut. 22:13-21). Furthermore, Chapter 9 argued that the Pentateuch's call to execute rebels, who refuse to follow Torah, aims to purge rivalry from the community (Deut. 21:18-21). In each of these cases a powerful rivalry is generated, one which threatens to bring a mimetic crisis upon the community. Human immolation within the Pentateuch vents this rivalry and thereby protects the community from mimetic crises.

Other capital offences may not directly generate mimetic rivalry, but still attract the death penalty because they pose a serious challenge to the community's core identity as YHWH's image-bearing children. In so doing, these offences threaten to spark a mimetic crisis because they undermine the distinction between Israel and the other nations. For example, as discussed in Chapter 5, desecrating the Sabbath undermines Israel's freedom and liberation from Egypt (Deut. 5:15)—the central narrative of the Pentateuch, upon which Israel's unique identity as YHWH's people is built.[2] Furthermore, the Sabbath rhythm pervades the priestly creation account (Gen. 1:1–2:3), which states that האדם was formed in the divine image. As argued in Chapter 2, האדם refers to the Israelite ingroup who bear the divine image as they continue YHWH's creative work. According to Exod. 31:16-17, while carrying out this vocation the Sabbath rhythm must be observed. A synchronic reading of the Pentateuch suggests that the Sabbath rhythm is intimately connected to Israel's vocation as divine image-bearers. This observation suggests

---

2. A similar explanation could be offered for human immolation in cases of idolatry, a crime that also threatens the community's identity as YHWH's people. Raymond Schwager has argued that idolatry represents an imitation of foreign cults and rituals. This imitation would generate conflict between Israel and the nations they imitate, as they become doubles of each other. Schwager, *Must There Be Scapegoats?*, 76–81. Unfortunately, space has not permitted an examination of the Pentateuch's command to execute idolaters in the present study.

that Israelites who refuse to observe the Sabbath threaten the ingroup's ability to reflect the divine image, which is characterized by dominion over the animal kingdom (Gen. 1:26, 28). The ingroup's reflection of the divine image is also threatened by those who become like animals as they engage in bestiality (Lev. 18:23). The ingroup must, therefore, execute those who commit bestiality or desecrate the Sabbath, even though these offences do not appear to generate any mimetic rivalry. In so doing, the community remove negative models from their midst, ones who might otherwise inspire others to imitate their conduct.

In sum, the Pentateuch's prescription of human immolation may be explained as a means of venting mimetic rivalry upon a scapegoat. This process restores peace and order to the community, which serves Torah's ultimate function of protecting the community from mimetic violence. Some capital offences, such as murder and incest, threaten the community through the excessive rivalry they generate. These rivalries, and the threats they pose, are described within the Pentateuch through the language of bloodguilt (Deut. 19:11-13) and impurity (Lev. 18:24-30; Num. 35:30-34). Other capital offences, such as Sabbath desecration and bestiality, do not appear to generate mimetic rivalry. Yet, these offences still attract the death penalty because they undermine the community's core identity. Within the Pentateuch all capital offenders are set apart from the faithful ingroup and identified as outgroup rivals. The execution of these rivals is necessary for the community to fulfil their unique vocation of reflecting the divine image.

2.2. *The Pentateuch and Capital Punishment in the United States of America*

While most Western countries have abolished capital punishment, this practice is still performed in some states of the USA. Some Christians cite texts from the Pentateuch to support this practice.[3] These arguments are often complicated by a desire to remain faithful to the both the Hebrew Scriptures and the Christian tradition's abandonment of Levitical Law. According to the Christian tradition, the church abandoned Levitical Law very early in its history (Acts 15). At the Jerusalem Council, church leaders decided not to ask Gentile Christian converts to adhere to the Mosaic Law (Acts 15:19-20). The following comments made by Mark F. Rooker, concerning the prescription of human immolation in Leviticus 20, are typical of the Christian response to the Levitical Law:

---

3. Robert L. Young, 'Religious Orientation, Race and Support for the Death Penalty', *Journal for the Scientific Study of Religion* (1992): 76–7.

As moral laws the sexual offenses are still applicable during the age of the church, though like the crime of cursing of parents the capital punishments for these offenses were limited to the time when God's people constituted a redeemed theocratic nation (John 8:1-11). Thus the capital punishments for these sexual offenses were not intended to be executed beyond Israel.[4]

Yet, some American Christians cite texts outside of Leviticus, such as Gen. 9:6 and Exodus 20–21, to support capital punishment in cases of murder.[5] These arguments commonly draw upon biblical principles and concepts including *imago dei, lex talionis,* and the belief that murder defiles and pollutes the land. In what follows, I cite some Hebrew Bible scholars who have used these concepts to support the modern practice of executing murderers. I shall then assess the validity of these arguments in light of the current study's findings. Having done so, I argue that simply citing theological concepts, such as *imago dei, lex talionis,* and the defiling effect of murder to support modern capital punishment anachronistically collapses the differences between the social world of the Pentateuch and our modern world. The purpose of this exercise is not to oppose or support capital punishment, but rather to expose the illegitimate use of the biblical texts within this debate.

Peter J. Harland argues that all murderers must receive the death penalty:

> The protection given to man is grounded in the divine image. An attack on the image is an assault on God's rightful dominion: murder confronts God, and is a revolt against him. The story singles out murder from all the sins of the Decalogue as being particularly wicked, emphasizing that God will exercise the ultimate sanction in this matter. This is not just a command for Israel, but is binding on all peoples wherever they may be…[6]

---

4. Rooker, *Leviticus*, 271.
5. Randall Styers, 'Slaughter and Innocence: The Rhetoric of Sacrifice in Contemporary Arguments Supporting the Death Penalty', in Finsterbusch, Lange, and Römheld, eds, *Human Sacrifice in Jewish and Christian Tradition*, 321–51; Charles W. Colson, 'Capital Punishment: A Personal Statement (Chuck Colson)', http://www.freerepublic.com/focus/f-religion/1274579/posts; Randy Alcorn, 'Capital Punishment: Right or Wrong?', https://www.epm.org/resources/1987/Aug/1/capital-punishment-right-or-wrong/; Solange Strong Hertz, 'The Death Penalty', https://www.remnantnewspaper.com/Archives/archive-death%20penalty.htm; Dudley Sharp, 'Death Penalty Paper', http://www.prodeathpenalty.com/dp.html#F.Christianity.
6. Harland, *The Value of Human Life*, 162–3.

In this passage, Harland argues that Gen. 9:6 is binding for all peoples and cultures, without exception, because all humans bear the divine image. However, the findings of the present study challenge Harland's assumption that all humans bear the divine image and that this text may be applied across all cultures and people groups. As noted in Chapter 2, Gen. 9:1-7 is addressed specifically to Noah and his sons, who are commissioned to repopulate the Land as the new humanity. Within this context, האדם in v. 6 must be interpreted as Noah and his sons, who bear the divine image. This text cannot, therefore, be interpreted as 'binding for all cultures and eras', as Harland argues, because it specifically addresses the murder of those who bear the divine image at the hands of another who does not. As I have argued, according to the Pentateuch, faithful Israel inherit the divine image from Noah through his son, Shem. This observation suggests that האדם in v. 6 may be extrapolated to include the faithful Israelite ingroup, but not to others outside of this group who do not bear the divine image. For this reason, Harland's application of Gen. 9:6 to 'all peoples wherever they may be' is problematic.

According to Baruch A. Levine, texts such as Num. 35:30-34 justify capital punishment as a means of purifying the Land from bloodshed:

> The land must be cleansed of the blood of the slain that flows into the earth. This is a passive reflex of the notion that the land demands retribution for the loss of life. But, 'the land will not be granted expiation' (*welā'āreṣ lō' yekuppar*) unless murder is avenged by the shedding of the murderer's own blood. Idiomatic *šāpak dām* 'to shed blood' figures prominently in priestly statements on life such as Genesis 9:6: *šōpēk dam hā'ādām, bā'ādām dāmô yiššāpēk* 'Whoever sheds the blood of man, by man shall his blood be shed'. This pronouncement authorizes duly constituted courts to take the life of the premeditated murderer, to shed his blood.[7]

In addition to Num. 35:30-34, the defiling effect of bloodshed can be observed in the flood narrative of Genesis 6–9. In this narrative, YHWH purifies the land from murderous violence by killing everything that breathes.[8] As argued in Chapter 6, the excessive violence described in Gen. 6:11 depicts a mimetic crisis fuelled by blood vengeance, which almost wipes out everyone living on the land. A synchronic reading of the Pentateuch suggests that this violence spreads from Cain, who was exiled but never executed for killing his brother (Gen. 4:1-24). These events serve as a warning against allowing murderers to live. In light of

---

7. Levine, *Numbers 21–36*; see also Harland, *The Value of Human Life*, 168–9.
8. Harland, *The Value of Human Life*, 28–44.

this warning, Num. 35:30-34 and Deut. 19:11-13 call for the execution of murderers. Both of these texts recognize the potential for blood vengeance to precipitate a mimetic crisis and prescribe the execution of murderers as a means of venting mimetic violence in ancient Israel.

However, citing the defiling potential of bloodshed in ancient Israel to support capital punishment in modern USA is problematic, because of the many differences between these two settings. Although murder in ancient Israel threatened to spark a mimetic crisis fuelled by blood vengeance, this threat is much less in modern American society. As Girard argues, modern legal systems are the most effective means of managing mimetic rivalry because they constrain violence.[9] These systems enable many Western countries to effectively manage mimetic rivalry, and prevent mimetic crises, without capital punishment. While human immolation may have been necessary to halt mimetic crises within ancient Israel, which did not have access to modern legal processes, the same cannot be said for modern capital punishment in the USA. Furthermore, within the Pentateuch the Israelite community vent their mimetic rivalries by actively participating in communal stoning.[10] By contrast, modern capital punishment in the USA is highly medicalized, ritualized, and almost completely private.[11]

---

9. Girard, *Violence and the Sacred*, 20–1.

10. As Foucault writes, in pre-modern Europe, the crowd also played an important role in capital punishment: 'People were summoned as spectators: they were assembled to observe public exhibitions… Not only must people know, they must see with their own eyes. Because they must be made to be afraid; but also because they must be the witnesses, the guarantors, of the punishment, and because they must to a certain extent take part in it. The right to be witnesses was one that they possessed and claimed; a hidden execution was a privileged execution, and in such cases it was often suspected that it had not taken place with all its customary severity… The people also had a right to take part. The condemned man, carried in procession, exhibited, humiliated, with the horror of his crime recalled in innumerable ways, was offered to the insults, sometimes to the attacks of the spectators. The vengeance of the people was called upon to become an unobtrusive part of the vengeance of the sovereign… [M]ud and other refuse, though no stone or anything injurious, could be thrown at their faces… In calling on the crowd to manifest its power, the sovereign tolerated for a moment acts of violence, which he accepted as a sign of allegiance.' Michel Foucault, *Discipline and Punish: The Birth of the Prison*, trans. A. Sheridan (New York: Vintage, 1979), 58–9.

11. Participation in modern capital punishment is limited to the 'ritual specialists and a small group of carefully chosen witnesses (usually excluding the prisoner's family and friends, and the family members of the victims). Crowds of politically active supporters and opponents of the death penalty may gather outside the prison,

The hidden aspect of modern capital punishment, coupled with a complete lack of public participation, casts doubt upon the ability of this act to effectively purge mimetic rivalry from the community.[12]

Moreover, the modern Western world has a unique sympathy for victims, which also impacts the effectiveness of capital punishment as a means of purging mimetic rivalry from the community.[13] In some ways, this sympathy increases the scapegoat mechanism's ability to incite a community to vent their collective rivalries upon a single scapegoat. The more violent and heinous the crime committed by the scapegoat, the greater the concern for the victim, which is expressed as a desire to exact revenge upon the offender. In contrast to their victims, violent offenders are villainized and dehumanized through the application of labels such as 'scum', 'monsters', 'mad dogs', and 'animals'.[14] These labels identify certain offenders as dangerous outgroup members, functioning in a similar manner to terms such as תועבת and תבל within the Pentateuch.[15] The identification of the offender as a dangerous outgroup member, when combined with the victim's perceived innocence, helps rally the community against their scapegoat.

But capital punishment can transform offenders into victims of state-sanctioned violence, which also appeals to our modern sympathy for victims.[16] The unprecedented ability of capital offenders to elicit this sympathy makes unanimously uniting the community against a capital

but, as Johnson notes, "they have no real awareness of what is going on," and they certainly are not allowed any "meaningful involvement in the execution Process"…' Smith, 'Capital Punishment and Human Sacrifice', 9.

12. Scott Cowdell also notes the inability of modern capital punishment to purge mimetic rivalry. Cowdell, *René Girard and Secular Modernity*, 140–1.

13. 'Examine the ancient sources', Girard writes, 'inquire everywhere, dig up the corners of the planet, and you will not find anything anywhere that even remotely resembles our modern concern for victims'. Girard, *I See Satan Fall Like Lightning*, 161.

14. Smith, 'Capital Punishment and Human Sacrifice', 13–14. These terms also dehumanize offenders, which encourages their persecution. For modern studies which have documented this effect, see Lasana T. Harris and Susan T. Fiske, 'Social Neuroscience Evidence for Dehumanised Perception', *European Review of Social Psychology* 20, no. 1 (2009): 192–231; 'Dehumanizing the Lowest of the Low Neuroimaging Responses to Extreme out-Groups', *Psychological Science* 17, no. 10 (2006): 847–53; Hanah A. Chapman and Adam K. Anderson, 'Things Rank and Gross in Nature: A Review and Synthesis of Moral Disgust', *Psychological Bulletin* 139, no. 2 (2013): 315.

15. See Chapter 7 for the use of these terms in Lev. 18 and 20.

16. Bailie, *Violence Unveiled*, 81–2.

offender extremely difficult. This difficulty undermines the effective venting of mimetic rivalry through capital punishment, and precipitates the execution of more capital offenders in a desperate attempt to achieve catharsis.[17] In this way, the modern sympathy for victims perpetuates the practice of capital punishment in the USA, while simultaneously rendering it unable to establish and maintain peace and order within the community. For these reasons, I argue that it is anachronistic to assume that killing murderers in modern USA achieves a similar catharsis to that described in connection with human immolation within the Pentateuch.

Some claim that the *lex talionis* legal principle demands the modern execution of murderers.[18] Yet, as I shall argue, this application of the *lex talionis* legal principle is problematic. According to Kenneth A. Mathews, the command to execute murderers in Gen. 9:6 constitutes a necessary application of the *lex talionis* legal principle:

> The severity of the punishment is required because of the heinous nature of the crime. This long-standing principle of jurisprudence, known as *lex talionis* (i.e., 'an eye for an eye'), insures that the punishment is commensurate with the weight of the crime... In accordance with the principle of *lex talionis*, Israelite law recognizes, as did ancient law in general, that particular circumstances, such as involuntary manslaughter (Exod 21:20-21; Deut 19; Num 35), mitigate the consequences of lesser degrees of homicide.[19]

However, even if the execution of murderers in the Pentateuch constitutes an application of the *lex talionis* principle, it does not necessarily follow that modern capital punishment also satisfies the *lex talionis* principle.[20] As most scholars agree, the *lex talionis* principle does not describe the literal reciprocation of physical harm, but rather the provision of adequate reparation for victims which was commonly, but not always, achieved

---

17. As Bailie notes, when the scapegoat mechanism fails an 'unquenched appetite for violence lingers', which leads to the repetition of violent acts aimed at achieving catharsis. Ibid., 90–1.
18. Colson, 'Capital Punishment'; Eckman, *Biblical Ethics*, 68.
19. Mathews, *Genesis 1–11: 26*, 404–5.
20. The execution of murderers within the world of the Pentateuch could possibly be considered an expression of *lex talionis*, as it achieves compensation for the victims in the form of blood vengeance. In this way, mimetic rivalry is vented in a similar manner to the case of the Blasphemer discussed in Chapter 4, which is also described as an act of *lex talionis* (Lev. 24:10-23). Yet, it should be noted that the execution of murderers is never described as an expression of the *lex talionis* legal principle within the Pentateuch.

through pecuniary means.[21] In the quote above, Mathews applies a different reading of *lex talionis* which focuses upon the enforcement of appropriate punishment, and not the provision of reparation. The *lex talionis* legal principle's concern with achieving reparation can be seen in stoning of the Blasphemer, which is also framed as an expression of this concept (Lev. 24:10-23). At first glance, the death penalty administered in this case appears excessive. Yet, as argued in Chapter 4, the Blasphemer's stoning satisfies the *lex talionis* legal principle because it achieves reparation by venting mimetic rivalry from the community. For modern capital punishment to be considered a legitimate expression of the *lex talionis* legal principle, this practice must achieve adequate reparation for the crime committed by purging the mimetic rivalry generated by this offence. But, as argued above, the effective purgation of mimetic rivalry is rarely achieved through modern capital punishment. Because of this lack of purgation, modern capital punishment cannot be considered a valid expression of the *lex talionis* legal principle.

In sum, many advocates of capital punishment in the USA cite various Pentateuchal texts to support their case. However, the findings of the present book challenge the way these texts are employed. For example, although Gen. 9:6 is often cited to support the execution of murderers, this text only prescribes the execution of those who kill members of the Israelite ingroup. Furthermore, the argument that murder pollutes the land and that capital punishment purges this pollution (cf. Num. 35:30-34; Deut. 19:11-13) is anachronistic. Finally, this study also challenges the claim that the legal principle of *lex talionis* demands capital punishment in all cases of murder. The present study, therefore, calls into the question the practice of quoting those Pentateuchal texts that prescribe and describe human immolation to support the state-sanctioned execution of murderers in the USA.

3. *Suggestions for Future Research*

The current project has argued that throughout the Pentateuch purging mimetic rivalry through human immolation restores peace and order to the community. In what follows, I suggest some avenues for future research that build upon the insights gleaned from this study. First, although space has not permitted a full examination of the execution of idolaters

---

21. Kim, 'Lex Talionis in Exod 21:22–25', 4–5; Westbrook, 'Lex Talionis and Exodus 21, 22-25'; Schwienhorst-Schönberger, *Bundesbuch (Ex 20,22-23,33)*, 100–105.

within the Pentateuch, the method employed throughout the current book could also be applied to this end. Second, as noted in Chapter 4, within the Pentateuch human immolation is practiced when Israel lacks an external national rival. For example, the stoning of the Blasphemer (Lev. 24:10-23) and the Sabbath Gatherer (Num. 15:32-36) both take place during Israel's wilderness wanderings. Furthermore, the laws that prescribe human immolation within the Pentateuch are also birthed in the wilderness period, and are intended to be implemented in Canaan at a time when Israel has vanquished its foreign rivals. As the current study has argued, these executions vent mimetic rivalry upon a scapegoat in the absence of a national enemy. The need for a scapegoat diminishes when rivalry can be directed outwards toward an external party. This observation suggests that rivalry and war with other nations may draw the Israelite community together, and provide another means for venting mimetic rivalry. If so, a mimetic approach like the one employed in the current book may contribute to our understanding of the social import of war within the Pentateuch.[22]

My third suggestion for future research concerns the role of mimesis in Israelite culture and sacrifice. Despite the limitations of Girard's double substitution theory, a mimetic approach may still contribute to our understanding of how animal sacrifice functions within the Pentateuch. For example, the שלם offering may stifle mimetic rivalry between rivals as they reconcile and share a sacred meal together (Deut. 27:7). The Passover meal may serve a similar function as families set aside their rivalries to partake in the annual festivities. This event also reinforces the community's identity by commemorating their liberation from slavery in Egypt (Exod. 12:1-28; Deut. 16:1-8).[23] In this way, the Passover draws the community together and focuses their collective rivalries upon the Egyptians. Observations such as these would serve as a good starting point for a mimetic approach to sacrificial texts within the Hebrew Bible. Texts should be carefully searched for mimetic features to avoid anachronistically imposing a mimetic hermeneutic upon it. To this end, the current project employed Girard's scapegoat stereotypes. A sound mimetic approach should also be developed in close conversation with the work of Hebrew Bible scholars, as this book has demonstrated.

---

22. Susan Niditch has noted that a mimetic approach may shed some light on the dynamics of war including the concept of the ban (e.g. Deut. 20:16-18). Susan Niditch, *War in the Hebrew Bible: A Study in the Ethics of Violence* (Oxford: Oxford University Press, 1995), 25, 60–1.

23. Sarna, *Exodus*, 57; Stuart, *Exodus*, 282; Clements, *Deuteronomy*, 62–3.

A mimetic approach similar to that employed in the current study may also help generate a new theory concerning the origins of the Israelite priesthood. As argued in Chapter 4, the עָוֹן/חטא + נשא formula, when applied to capital offenders, identifies their role as the community's scapegoat. Significantly, the עָוֹן/חטא + נשא formula is also applied to the Priests and Levites (Lev. 10:17; Num. 18:1), which may suggest that these groups were originally scapegoats (cf. Lev. 10:1-3) who eventually rose to religious prominence by executing others in their stead.[24] The Levites inaugurate their priesthood by repeating the same offence as Cain when each of them kills 'their brother' (Exod. 32:25-29).[25] Like Cain, these scapegoats survive the mimetic crisis by killing others in their stead.[26] Although this speculation is impossible to verify, applying mimetic theory to examine the use of the עָוֹן/חטא + נשא formula in connection with the Priests and Levites may help generate an interesting theory concerning the genesis of the Israelite priesthood and cult.

4. Closing Remarks

The prescription of human immolation within the Pentateuch has presented a conundrum for both the Jewish and Christian faith traditions. Throughout their history, these traditions have grappled with how to reconcile human immolation with the doctrine of *imago dei* and the high value the Jewish and Christian worldviews place upon human life. As the opening chapter of this book noted, to date, no single theory has been able to explain all of the Pentateuch's prescriptions of human immolation. The commands to execute blasphemers (Lev. 24:10-23) and those who desecrate the Sabbath (Num. 15:32-36) have proved particularly problematic. The present book addressed this gap in the current literature by examining human immolation within the Pentateuch through the lens of mimetic theory. This study provides a novel and robust explanation of human immolation within the Pentateuch, which also accounts for the execution of those who commit apparently victimless crimes.

---

24. Williams, *The Bible, Violence, and the Sacred*, 124.
25. Interestingly, Joseph's brothers also consider killing him, but settle for selling him (Gen. 37:18-28). There appears to be a link between the scapegoating and killing of brothers in the Pentateuch.
26. Bailie, *Violence Unveiled*, 147–8.

Bibliography

Alcorn, Randy. 'Capital Punishment: Right or Wrong?' https://www.epm.org/resources/1987/Aug/1/capital-punishment-right-or-wrong/.
Alexander, T. Desmond. *From Paradise to the Promised Land: An Introduction to the Pentateuch*. Grand Rapids: Baker, 2012.
Alison, James, Wolfgang Palaver, Trevor Cribben Merrill, and Sheelah Treflé Hidden. 'General Introduction'. In *The Palgrave Handbook of Mimetic Theory and Religion*, edited by James Alison, Wolfgang Palaver, Trevor Cribben Merrill and Sheelah Treflé Hidden, 1–7. New York: Palgrave Macmillan, 2017.
Alter, Robert. *Art of Biblical Narrative*, 2nd edn. New York: Basic, 2011.
Amit, Yairah. 'Who Decided to Open the Torah with the Creation of the Sabbath?' Translated by Betty Sigler Rozen. In *In Praise of Editing in the Hebrew Bible*, edited by Yairah Amit, 1–23. Sheffield: Sheffield Phoenix, 2012.
The Ante-Nicene Fathers, Volume 1: The Apostolic Fathers-Justin Martyr-Irenaeus. Grand Rapids: Eerdmans, 1956.
Bailie, Gil. *Violence Unveiled: Humanity at the Crossroads*. New York: Crossroad, 1995.
Bar, Shaul. 'The Punishment of Burning in the Hebrew Bible'. *Old Testament Essays* 25, no. 1 (2012): 27–39.
Barmash, Pamela. *Homicide in the Biblical World*. Cambridge: Cambridge University Press, 2005.
Barr, James. 'Man and Nature – the Ecological Controversy and the Old Testament'. *Bulletin of the John Rylands Library of the University of Manchester* 55 (1972): 9–32.
Barth, Karl. *Church Dogmatics: Volume III: The Doctrine of Creation: Part One*. Translated by Harold Knight, A. Hart Edwards and Oscar Bussey. London: T & T Clark, 1958.
Bartor, Assnat. *Reading Law as Narrative: A Study in the Casuistic Laws of the Pentateuch*. Atlanta: Society of Biblical Literature, 2010.
Bassett, Frederick W. 'Noah's Nakedness and the Curse of Canaan a Case of Incest?' *Vetus Testamentum* 21, no. 2 (1971): 232–7.
Bechtel, Lyn M. 'Shame as a Sanction of Social Control in Biblical Israel: Judicial, Political, and Social Shaming'. *Journal for the Study of the Old Testament* 49 (1991): 47–76.
Bechtel, Lyn M. 'What f Dinah Is Not Raped? (Genesis 34)'. *Journal for the Study of the Old Testament* 62 (1994): 19–36.
Bellefontaine, Elizabeth. 'Deuteronomy 21:18-21: Reviewing the Case of the Rebellious Son'. *Journal for the Study of the Old Testament* 13 (1979): 13–31.
Benjamin, Don C. *Deuteronomy and City Life: A Form Criticism of Texts with the Word City ('Ir) in Deuteronomy 4: 41–26: 19*. Lanham: University Press of America, 1983.

Bernat, David A., and Jonathan Klawans. *Religion and Violence: The Biblical Heritage*. Sheffield: Sheffield Phoenix, 2007.
Biale, David. *Eros and the Jews: From Biblical Israel to Contemporary America*. Berkeley: University of California Press, 1992.
Bibb, Bryan D. *Ritual Words and Narrative Worlds in the Book of Leviticus*. New York: Bloomsbury, 2009.
Bigger, Stephen F. 'The Family Laws of Leviticus 18 in Their Setting'. *Journal of Biblical Literature* 98, no. 2 (1979): 187–203.
Bird, Phyllis A. '"Male and Female He Created Them": Gen 1: 27b in the Context of the Priestly Account of Creation'. *Harvard Theological Review* 74, no. 2 (1981): 129–60.
Blyth, Caroline. *The Narrative of Rape in Genesis 34 Interpreting Dinah's Silence*. Oxford: Oxford University Press, 2010.
Boecker, Hans Jochen. *Law and the Administration of Justice in the Old Testament and Ancient East*. Translated by Jeremy Moiser. London: Society for Promoting Christian Knowledge, 1980.
Boswell, John. *Christianity, Social Tolerance, and Homosexuality: Gay People in Western Europe from the Beginning of the Christian Era to the Fourteenth Century*. Chicago: University of Chicago Press, 1980.
Brenner, Athalya. 'On Incest'. In *The Feminist Companion to Exodus to Deuteronomy*, edited by Athalya Brenner, 113–38. Sheffield: Sheffield Academic, 1994.
Brueggemann, Walter. *Genesis: A Bible Commentary for Teaching and Preaching*. Westminster: John Knox, 1982.
Buber, M. *Werke: Vol. 2: Schriften Zur Bibel*. Munich: Köselverlag, 1964.
Burke, Kenneth. *Permanence and Change: An Anatomy of Purpose*. 3rd edn. Berkeley: University of California Press, 1984.
Burke, Kenneth. *The Rhetoric of Religion: Studies in Logology*. Berkeley: University of California Press, 1970.
Burnside, Jonathan. *God, Justice, and Society: Aspects of Law and Legality in the Bible*. Oxford: Oxford University Press, 2010.
Burnside, Jonathan. '"What Shall We Do with the Sabbath-Gatherer?": A Narrative Approach to a "Hard Case" in Biblical Law (Numbers 15:32-36)'. *Vetus Testamentum* 60, no. 1 (2010): 45–62.
Burnside, Jonathan. *The Signs of Sin: Seriousness of Offence in Biblical Law*. Sheffield: Sheffield Academic, 2003.
Burnside, Jonathan. 'Strange Flesh: Sex, Semiotics and the Construction of Deviancy in Biblical Law'. *Journal for the Study of the Old Testament* 30, no. 4 (2006): 387–420.
Burnside, Jonathan. 'The Medium and the Message: Necromancy and the Literary Context of Leviticus 20'. In *Leviticus in Its Contexts: Method, Rhetoric and Theology*, edited by Francis Landy, Leigh M. Trevaskis and Bryan D. Bibb, 41–62. Sheffield: Sheffield Phoenix, 2010.
Calasso, Roberto. *Ardor*. New York: Macmillan, 2014.
Cardascia, Guillaume. 'Egalité et Inégalité des Sexes en Matière d'atteinte aux Moeurs dans le Proche-Orient Ancien'. *Die Welt des Orients* 11 (1980): 7–16.
Cassuto, Umberto. *A Commentary on the Book of Exodus*. Jerusalem: Magnes, 1967.
Chapman, Hanah A., and Adam K. Anderson. 'Things Rank and Gross in Nature: A Review and Synthesis of Moral Disgust'. *Psychological bulletin* 139, no. 2 (2013): 300–327.
Cherry, Shai. *Torah through Time: Understanding Bible Commentary from the Rabbinic Period to Modern Times*. Philadelphia: Jewish Publication Society, 2010.

Chilton, Bruce. *Abraham's Curse: The Roots of Violence in Judaism, Christianity, and Islam*. New York: Doubleday, 2008.
Chilton, Bruce. 'René Girard, James Williams, and the Genesis of Violence'. *Bulletin for Biblical Research* 3 (1993): 17–29.
Clements, Ronald Ernest. *Deuteronomy*. Sheffield: Sheffield Academic, 1997.
Clines, David J. A. 'The Image of God in Man'. *Tyndale Bulletin* 19 (1968): 53–103.
Coats, George W. *Genesis, with an Introduction to Narrative Literature. Vol. 1*. Grand Rapids: Eerdmans, 1983.
Coats, George W. *Rebellion in the Wilderness: The Murmuring Motif in the Wilderness, Traditions of the Old Testament*. Nashville: Abingdon, 1968.
Cohen, Shaye J. D. 'Was Timothy Jewish (Acts 16:1-3)? Patristic Exegesis, Rabbinic Law, and Matrilineal Descent'. *Journal of Biblical Literature* (1986): 251–68.
Cohn, Robert Greer. 'Desire: Direct and Imitative'. *Philosophy Today* 33, no. 4 (1989): 318–29.
Collins, Brian. 'The Eastern Revolution: From the Vedas to Buddhism, Jainism, and the Upanishads'. In *The Palgrave Handbook of Mimetic Theory and Religion*, edited by James Alison, Wolfgang Palaver, Trevor Cribben Merrill and Sheelah Treflé Hidden, 111–17. New York: Palgrave Macmillan, 2017.
Colson, Charles W. 'Capital Punishment: A Personal Statement (Chuck Colson)'. http://www.freerepublic.com/focus/f-religion/1274579/posts.
Cowdell, Scott. *René Girard and Secular Modernity: Christ, Culture, and Crisis*. Notre Dame: University of Notre Dame Press, 2013.
Craigie, Peter C. *The Book of Deuteronomy*. Grand Rapids: Eerdmans, 1976.
Crouch, Carly L. 'Genesis 1:26-27 as a Statement of Humanity's Divine Parentage'. *Journal of Theological Studies* 61, no. 1 (2010): 1–15.
Crüsemann, Frank. *Torah: Theology and Social History of Old Testament Law*. London: Bloomsbury, 1996.
Currid, John D. *A Study Commentary on Deuteronomy*. Darlington: Evangelical Press, 2006.
Daube, David. *The Culture of Deuteronomy*. Ibadan: University of Ibadan Press, 1969.
Day, John. *Molech: A God of Human Sacrifice in the Old Testament*. Cambridge: Cambridge University Press, 1989.
De Heusch, Luc. *Sacrifice in Africa: A Structuralist Approach*. Manchester: Manchester University Press, 1985.
Dion, Paul E. 'La Procedure d'elimination des fils Rebelle (Deut 21:18-21): Sens Littéral et Signes de développement Juridique'. In *Biblische the-Ologie Und Gesellschaftlicher Wandel*, edited by G. Braulik, 73–82. Freiburg: Herder, 1993.
Dorff, Elliot N. *For the Love of God and People: A Philosophy of Jewish Law*. Philadelphia: Jewish Publication Society, 2007.
Douglas, Mary. 'Atonement in Leviticus'. *Jewish Studies Quarterly* 1, no. 2 (1993): 109–30.
Driver, Samuel Rolles, and John C. Miles. *The Babylonian Laws. Vol. 1*. Oxford: Clarendon, 1952.
Driver, Samuel Rolles. *A Critical and Exegetical Commentary on Deuteronomy*. London: T & T Clark, 1902.
Durham, John I. *Exodus*. Word Biblical Commentary 3. Waco: Word, 1987.
Eckman, James P. *Biblical Ethics*. Wheaton: Crossway, 2004.
Edenburg, Cynthia. 'How (Not) to Murder a King: Variations on a Theme in 1 Sam 24; 26'. *Scandinavian Journal of the Old Testament* 12, no. 1 (1998): 64–85.

Ehrlich, Arnold B. *Randglossen zur Hebräischen Bibel: Textkritisches, Sprachliches und Sachliches. Vol. 2.* Leipzig: J. C. Hinrichs, 1909.

Eilberg-Schwartz, Howard. *The Savage in Judaism: An Anthropology of Israelite Religion and Ancient Judaism.* Bloomington: Indiana University Press, 1990.

Eissfeldt, Otto. *Molk als Opferbegriff im Punischen und Hebraischen und das Ende des Gottes Moloch.* Halle: Max Niemeyer, 1935.

Ellens, Deborah L. *Women in the Sex Texts of Leviticus and Deuteronomy: A Comparative Conceptual Analysis.* London: T&T Clark, 2008.

Elliger, Karl. 'Das Gesetz Leviticus 18'. *Zeitschrift für die Alttestamentliche Wissenschaft* 67, no. 1 (1955): 1–25.

Erickson, Millard J. *Christian Theology.* 2nd edn. Grand Rapids: Baker Academic, 1998.

Falk, Ze'ev Wilhelm. *Hebrew Law in Biblical Times: An Introduction.* Jerusalem: Wahrmann, 1964.

Feinberg, John S., and Paul D. Feinberg. *Ethics for a Brave New World: Updated and Expanded.* Wheaton: Crossway, 2010.

Feinstein, Eve Levavi. *Sexual Pollution in the Hebrew Bible.* Oxford: Oxford University Press, 2014.

Finkelstein, Jacob J. 'The Ox That Gored'. *Transactions of the American philosophical society* 71, no. 2 (1981): 1–89.

Fleishman, Joseph. 'The Delinquent Daughter and Legal Innovation in Deuteronomy XXII 20-21'. *Vetus Testamentum* 58, no. 2 (2008): 191–210.

Fleishman, Joseph. 'Legal Innovation in Deuteronomy XXI 18-20'. *Vetus Testamentum* 53, no. 3 (2003): 311–27.

Flemming, Chris. *René Girard: Violence and Mimesis.* Cambridge: Polity, 2004.

Foucault, Michel. *Discipline and Punish: The Birth of the Prison.* Translated by A. Sheridan. New York: Vintage, 1979.

Fox, Michael V. *The JPS Torah Commentary: Ecclesiastes.* Philadelphia: Jewish Publication Society, 2004.

Fox, Michael V. 'The Sign of the Covenant: Circumcision in the Light of the Priestly 'Ot Etiologies'. *Revue Biblique* 81, no. 4 (1974): 557–96.

Frymer-Kensky, Tikvah. 'Pollution, Purification, and Purgation in Biblical Israel'. In *The Word of the Lord Shall Go Forth: Essays in Honor of David Noel Freedman in Celebration of His Sixtieth Birthday*, edited by Carol L. Meyers, 3–16. Winona Lake: Eisenbrauns, 1983.

Frymer-Kensky, Tikvah. 'Law and Philosophy: The Case of Sex in the Bible'. In *Studies in Bible and Feminist Criticism*, edited by Tikvah Frymer-Kensky, 241–57. Philadelphia: Jewish Publication Society, 2005.

Gane, Roy. *Cult and Character: Purification Offerings, Day of Atonement, and Theodicy.* Winona Lake: Eisenbrauns, 2005.

Garr, W. Randall. *In His Own Image and Likeness: Humanity, Divinity, and Monotheism.* Leiden: Brill, 2003.

Gerstenberger, Erhard S. *Leviticus: A Commentary.* Louisville: Westminster John Knox, 1996.

Gilders, William K. *Blood Ritual in the Hebrew Bible: Meaning and Power.* Baltimore: Johns Hopkins University Press, 2004.

Girard, René. *Deceit, Desire, and the Novel.* Translated by Yvonne Freccero. Baltimore: Johns Hopkins University Press, 1965.

Girard, René. 'Generative Scapegoating'. In *Violent Origins: Walter Burkert, René Girard, and Jonathan Z. Smith on Ritual Killing and Cultural Formation*, edited by Robert G. Hamerton-Kelly, 73–145. Stanford: Stanford University Press, 1987.
Girard, René. *I See Satan Fall Like Lightning*. Translated by James G Williams. Leominster: Gracewing, 2001.
Girard, René. *Job, the Victim of His People*. London: Athlone, 1987.
Girard, René. *The Scapegoat*. Translated by Yvonne Freccero. Baltimore: Johns Hopkins University Press, 1989.
Girard, René. *A Theatre of Envy: William Shakespeare*. Leominster: Gracewing, 2000.
Girard, René. *Violence and the Sacred*. Translated by Patrick Gregory. Baltimore: Johns Hopkins University Press, 1977.
Girard, René. *Sacrifice*. Translated by Matthew Pattillo and David Dawson. East Lansing: Michigan State University Press, 2011.
Girard, René, Jean-Michel Oughourlian, and Guy Lefort. *Things Hidden since the Foundation of the World*. Translated by Stephen Bann and Michael Metteer. Stanford: Stanford University Press, 1987.
Girard, René, and Raymund Schwager. *René Girard and Raymund Schwager Correspondence 1974–1991*. Translated by Chris Fleming and Sheelah Treflé Hidden. London: Bloomsbury Academic, 2016.
Göldberg, Louis. 'נְבֵלָה'. In *Theological Wordbook of the Old Testament*, edited by Robert Laird Harris, Gleason Leonard Archer and Bruce K. Waltke. Chicago: Moody, 1980.
Golsan, Richard. 'Girard's Critics and the Girardians'. In *Rene Girard and Myth: An Introduction*, 107–28. London: Routledge, 2014.
Good, Robert McClive. *The Sheep of His Pasture: A Study of the Hebrew Noun 'am(m) and Its Semitic Cognates*. Atlanta: Scholars Press, 1983.
Goodhart, Sandor. *The Prophetic Law: Essays in Judaism, Girardianism, Literary Studies, and the Ethical*. East Lansing: Michigan State University Press, 2014.
Gorman, Frank H. *The Ideology of Ritual: Space, Time and Status in the Priestly Theology*. Edinburgh: A. & C. Black, 1990.
Greenberg, Moshe. 'The Biblical Conception of Asylum'. *Journal of Biblical Literature* (1959): 125–32.
Greenberg, Moshe. *Studies in the Bible and Jewish Thought*. Philadelphia: Jewish Publication Society, 1995.
Greifenhagen, Franz V. *Egypt on the Pentateuch's Ideological Map: Constructing Biblical Israel's Identity*. London: Bloomsbury, 2003.
Grenz, Stanley J. *The Social God and the Relational Self: A Trinitarian Theology of the Imago Dei*. Louisville: Westminster John Knox, 2001.
Guillaume, Philippe. *Land and Calendar: The Priestly Document from Genesis 1 to Joshua 18*. Edinburgh: A. & C. Black, 2009.
Hagedorn, Anselm C. 'Guarding the Parents' Honour – Deuteronomy 21.18-21'. *Journal for the Study of the Old Testament* 25, no. 88 (2000): 101–21.
Hamilton, Victor P. *The Book of Genesis: Chapters 1–17*. Grand Rapids: Eerdmans, 1990.
Harding, Roberta M. 'Capital Punishment as Human Sacrifice: A Societal Ritual as Depicted in George Eliot's Adam Bede'. *Buffalo Law Review* 48 (2000): 175–297.
Harland, Peter J. *The Value of Human Life: A Study of the Story of the Flood (Genesis 6–9)*. Leiden: Brill, 1996.
Harris, Lasana T., and Susan T. Fiske. 'Dehumanizing the Lowest of the Low: Neuroimaging Responses to Extreme Out-Groups'. *Psychological Science* 17, no. 10 (2006): 847–53.

Harris, Lasana T., and Susan T. Fiske. 'Social Neuroscience Evidence for Dehumanised Perception'. *European Review of Social Psychology* 20, no. 1 (2009): 192–231.

Hartley, John E. *Leviticus*. Word Biblical Commentary 4. Waco: Word, 1992.

Hartung, John. 'Love Thy Neighbor'. *Skeptic* 3, no. 4 (1995): 86–99.

Hasel, G. F. 'Karat'. In *Theological Dictionary of the Old Testament*, edited by G Johannes Botterweck, Helmer Ringgren and Heinz-Josef Fabry, 339–52. Grand Rapids: Eerdmans, 2006.

Hasel, G. F. 'The Sabbath in the Pentateuch'. In *The Sabbath in Scripture and History*, edited by Kenneth Albert Strand, 21–43. Washington: Review & Herald, 1982.

Haven, Cynthia L. *Evolution of Desire: A Life of René Girard*. East Lansing: Michigan State University Press, 2018.

Hayes, Richard B. *Echoes of Scripture in the Letters of Paul*. New Haven: Yale University Press, 1989.

Heider, George C. *The Cult of Molek: A Reassessment*. Sheffield: JSOT, 1985.

Hendrix, Ralph E. 'A Literary Structural Overview of Exod 25–40'. *Andrews University Seminary Studies* 30, no. 2 (1992): 1.

Hens-Piazza, Gina. 'A Theology of Ecology: God's Image and the Natural World'. *Biblical Theology Bulletin* 13 (1982): 107–10.

Hertz, Solange Strong. 'The Death Penalty'. https://www.remnantnewspaper.com/Archives/archive-death%20penalty.htm.

Hieke, Thomas. 'Das Alte Testament und die Todesstrafe'. *Biblica* 85 (2004): 349–74.

Hoffmann, David. *Das Buch Leviticus, Vol. 1*. Berlin: Poppelauer, 1905.

Hoffmann, David. *Das Buch Leviticus, Vol. 2*. Berlin: Poppelauer, 1906.

Hoffner, Harry A. 'Incest, Sodomy and Bestiality in the Ancient Near East'. In *Orient and Occident. Essays Presented to Cyrus H. Gordon on the Occasion of His Sixty-Fifth Birthday*, edited by Harry A. Hoffner, 81–90. Neukirchen-Vluyn: Neukirchener Verlag, 1973.

Hooke, S. H. 'The Theory and Practice of Substitution'. *Vetus Testamentum* 2, no. 1 (1952): 2–17.

Houston, Walter. *Purity and Monotheism Clean and Unclean Animals in Biblical Law*. Sheffield: JSOT, 1993.

Hutton, Rodney R. 'The Case of the Blasphemer Revisited (Lev. XXIV 10-23)'. *Vetus Testamentum* 49, no. 4 (1999): 532–41.

Hutton, Rodney R. 'Narrative in Leviticus: The Case of the Blaspheming Son (Lev 24, 10-23)'. *Zeitschrift für Altorientalische und Biblische Rechtsgeschichte* 3 (1997): 145–63.

Jackson, Bernard S. 'Modelling Biblical Law: The Covenant Code'. *Chicago-Kent Law Review* 70 (1994): 1745–827.

Janowski, Bernd. *Sühne als Heilsgeschehen: Studien zur Sühnetheologie der Priesterschrift und zur Wurzel Kpr im Alten Orient und im Alten Testament*. Neukirchen-Vluyn: Neukirchener Verlag, 1982.

Janzen, Waldemar. *Believers Church Bible Commentary: Exodus*. Independence: Herald, 2000.

Jenson, Philip Peter. *Graded Holiness: A Key to the Priestly Conception of the World*. Edinburgh: A. & C. Black, 1992.

Joosten, Jan. *People and Land in the Holiness Code: An Exegetical Study of the Ideational Framework of the Law in Leviticus 17–26*. Leiden: Brill, 1996.

Joseph, Alison L. 'Understanding Genesis 34:2: *'Innâ'*. *Vetus Testamentum* 66, no. 4 (2016): 663–8.

Kaminsky, Joel S. *Yet I Loved Jacob: Reclaiming the Biblical Concept of Election*. Nashville: Abingdon, 2007.

Kaufman, Stephen A. 'The Structure of the Deuteronomic Law'. *MAARAV* 1, no. 2 (1979): 105–58.

Kazen, Thomas. 'Dirt and Disgust: Body and Morality in Biblical Purity Laws'. In *Perspectives on Purity and Purification in the Bible*, edited by Baruch J. Schwartz, David P. Wright, Jeffrey Stackert and Naphtali S. Meshel, 43–64. London: T & T Clark, 2008.

Kazen, Thomas. 'The Role of Disgust in Priestly Purity Law'. *Journal of Law, Religion and State* 3, no. 1 (2014): 62–92.

Keil, Carl Friedrich, and Franz Delitzsch. *Biblical Commentary on the Old Testament*. London: T. & T. Clark, 1870.

Kim, Yung Suk. 'Lex Talionis in Exod 21:22–25: Its Origin and Context'. *Journal of Hebrew Scriptures* 6 (2009).

Kiuchi, Nobuyoshi. *The Purification Offering in the Priestly Literature: Its Meaning and Function*. Edinburgh: A. & C. Black, 1987.

Klawans, Jonathan. *Impurity and Sin in Ancient Judaism*. Oxford: Oxford University Press 2000.

Klawans, Jonathan. *Purity, Sacrifice, and the Temple: Symbolism and Supersessionism in the Study of Ancient Judaism*. Oxford: Oxford University Press, 2006.

Kline, Meredith G. *Treaty of the Great King: The Covenant Structure of Deuteronomy: Studies and Commentary*. Eugene: Wipf & Stock, 2012.

Knohl, Israel. *The Sanctuary of Silence: The Priestly Torah and the Holiness School*. Winona Lake: Eisenbrauns, 2007.

Koch, Klaus. 'Sühne und Sündenvergebung um die Wende von der Exilischen zur Nachexilischen Zeit'. *Evangelische Theologie* 26, no. 5 (1966): 217–39.

Koch, Klaus. 'עָוֹן'. In *Theological Dictionary of the Old Testament*, edited by G. Johannes Botterweck, Helmer Ringgren and Heinz-Josef Fabry, 546–62. Grand Rapids: Eerdmans, 2004.

Köhler, Ludwig. *Old Testament Theology*. Translated by A. Stewart Todd. Louisville: Westminster, 1957.

Kraemer, David. *The Meanings of Death in Rabbinic Judaism*. New York: Routledge, 2002.

Labuschagne, C. J. 'The Meaning of Beyad Rama in the Old Testament'. In *Von Kanaan Bis Kerala: Festschrift für J. P. M. Van Der Ploeg*, edited by W. C. Delsman. Leiden: Brill, 1982.

LaCocque, Andre. *The Trial of Innocence: Adam, Eve, and the Yahwist*. Eugene: Wipf & Stock, 2006.

Landy, Joshua. 'Deceit, Desire, and the Literature Professor: Why Girardians Exist'. *Republics of Letters* 3 (2012): 1–21.

Lemos, Tracy M. 'Where There Is Dirt, Is There System? Revisiting Biblical Purity Constructions'. *Journal for the Study of the Old Testament* 37, no. 3 (2013): 265–94.

Levenson, Jon D. *Creation and the Persistence of Evil*. Princeton: Princeton University Press, 1988.

Levenson, Jon D. *The Death and Resurrection of the Beloved Son: The Transformation of Child Sacrifice in Judaism and Christianity*. New Haven: Yale University Press, 1995.

Levenson, Jon D. 'The Temple and the World'. *The Journal of Religion* (1984): 275–98.

Levine, Baruch A. *In the Presence of the Lord: A Study of Cult and Some Cultic Terms in Ancient Israel*. Leiden: Brill 1974.

Levine, Baruch A. *Numbers 1–20: A New Translation with Introduction and Commentary.* New York: Doubleday, 1993.

Levine, Baruch A. *Numbers 21–36: A New Translation with Introduction and Commentary.* New York: Doubleday, 2000.

Levine, Baruch A. *The JPS Torah Commentary: Leviticus.* Philadelphia: Jewish Publication Society, 1989.

Locher, Clemens. *Die Ehre einer Frau in Israel: Exegetische und Rechtsvergleichende Studien zu Deuteronomium 22, 13-21.* Vol. 70. Göttingen: Vandenhoeck & Ruprecht, 1986.

Lorerbaum, Jair. *In God's Image: Myth, Theology and Law in Classical Judaism.* Cambridge: Cambridge University Press, 2015.

Lundberg, Marilyn J. 'Cities of Refuge'. In *Eerdmans Dictionary of the Bible*, edited by David Noel Freedman, Allen C. Myers and Astrid B. Beck, 257. Grand Rapids: Eerdmans, 2000.

Mabee, Charles. 'Jacob and Laban: The Structure of Judicial Proceedings (Genesis XXXI 25-42)'. *Vetus Testamentum* 30, no. 2 (1980): 192–207.

Mace, David R. *Hebrew Marriage.* London: Philosophical Library, 1987.

Mangum, D., Derek R. Brown Douglas, Rachel Klippenstein, and Rebekah Hurst. *The Lexham Theological Wordbook: Electronic Edition.* Bellingham: Lexham, 2014.

Mathews, Kenneth A. *The New American Commentary: Genesis 1–11: 26.* Nashville: Broadman & Holman, 1996.

Mathews, Kenneth A. *The New American Commentary: Genesis 11:27–50:26.* Nashville: Broadman & Holman, 2005.

McBride, James. 'Capital Punishment as the Unconstitutional Establishment of Religion: A Girardian Reading of the Death Penalty'. *Journal of Church and State* 37, no. 2 (1995): 263–87.

McClenney-Sadler, Madeline Gay. *Recovering the Daughter's Nakedness: A Formal Analysis of Israelite Kinship Terminology and the Internal Logic of Leviticus 18.* London: T & T Clark, 2007.

McConville, J. Gordon. *Apollos Old Testament Commentary: Deuteronomy.* Downers Grove: IVP, 2002.

McKeating, Henry. 'The Development of the Law on Homicide in Ancient Israel'. *Vetus Testamentum* 25, no. 1 (1975): 46–68.

McNutt, Paula M. 'In the Shadow of Cain'. *Semeia* 87 (1999): 45–64.

Meacham, Tirzah. 'The Missing Daughter: Leviticus 18 and 20'. *Zeitschrift für die Alttestamentliche Wissenschaft* 109, no. 2 (1997): 254.

Melcher, Sarah J. 'The Holiness Code and Human Sexuality'. In *Biblical Ethics and Homosexuality: Listening to Scripture*, edited by Robert L. Brawley, 87–102. Louisville: Westminster John Knox, 1996.

Meltzer, Françoise. 'A Response to René Girard's Reading of Salome'. *New Literary History* 15, no. 2 (1984): 325–32.

Merrill, Eugene H. *Deuteronomy.* New American Commentary. Nashville: Broadman & Holman, 2001.

Merrill, Trevor Cribben. 'Critiques of Girard's Mimetic Theory'. In *The Palgrave Handbook of Mimetic Theory and Religion*, edited by James Alison, Wolfgang Palaver, Trevor Cribben Merrill and Sheelah Treflé Hidden, 455–61. New York: Palgrave Macmillan, 2017.

Middleton, J. Richard. *The Liberating Image: The Imago Dei in Genesis 1.* Grand Rapids: Brazos, 2005.

Milbank, John. 'Stories of Sacrifice: From Wellhausen to Girard'. *Theory, Culture & Society* 12, no. 4 (1995): 15–46.
Milgrom, Jacob. 'Israel's Sanctuary: The Priestly Picture of Dorian Gray"'. *Revue biblique* 83, no. 3 (1976): 390–9.
Milgrom, Jacob. *Leviticus 1–16: A New Translation with Introduction and Commentary*. New York: Doubleday, 1991.
Milgrom, Jacob. *Leviticus 17–22: A New Translation with Introduction and Commentary*. New York: Doubleday, 2000.
Milgrom, Jacob. *Leviticus 23–27: A New Translation with Introduction and Commentary. New York: Doubleday,* 2001.
Milgrom, Jacob. *The JPS Torah Commentary: Numbers*. Philadelphia: Jewish Publication Society, 1990.
Milgrom, Jacob. *Studies in Levitical Terminology*. Berkeley: University of California Press, 1970.
Miller Jr, Patrick D. 'The Place of the Decalogue in the Old Testament and Its Law'. *Union Seminary Review* 43, no. 3 (1989): 229–42.
Moi, Toril. 'The Missing Mother: The Oedipal Rivalries of René Girard'. *Diacritics: A Review of Contemporary Criticism* 12, no. 2 (1982): 21–31.
Moyer, James C. 'Hittite and Israelite Cultic Practices: A Selected Comparison'. In *Scripture in Context II: More Essays on the Comparative Method*, edited by William W Hallo, James C. Moyer and Leo G. Perdue, 19–38. Winona Lake: Eisenbrauns, 1983.
Neusner, Jacob. *The Mishnah*. New Haven: Yale University Press, 1988.
Neusner, Jacob. *A Theological Commentary to the Midrash: Sifré to Numbers and Sifré to Deuteronomy*. Lanham: University Press of America, 2001.
Niditch, Susan. *War in the Hebrew Bible: A Study in the Ethics of Violence*. Oxford: Oxford University Press, 1995.
Nihan, Christophe. 'Forms and Functions of Purity in Leviticus'. In *Purity and the Forming of Religious Traditions in the Ancient Mediterranean World and Ancient Judaism,* edited by Christian Frevel and Christophe Nihan, 311–68. Leiden: Brill, 2013.
Olyan, Saul M. '"And with a Male You Shall Not Lie the Lying Down of a Woman": On the Meaning and Significance of Leviticus 18:22 and 20:13'. *Journal of the History of Sexuality* 5, no. 2 (1994): 179–206.
Olyan, Saul M. *Rites and Rank*. Princeton: Princeton University Press, 2000.
Palaver, Wolfgang. *René Girard's Mimetic Theory*. East Lansing: Michigan State University Press, 2013.
Palaver, Wolfgang, and Richard Schenk. *Mimetic Theory and World Religions*. East Lansing: Michigan State University Press, 2017.
Péter-Contesse, René, and John Ellington. *A Handbook on Leviticus*. New York: United Bible Societies, 1990.
Phillips, Anthony. *Ancient Israel's Criminal Law: A New Approach to the Decalogue*. New York: Schocken, 1970.
Phillips, Anthony. 'Another Example of Family Law'. *Vetus Testamentum* 30, no. 2 (1980): 240–5.
Phillips, Anthony. *Deuteronomy*. Cambridge: Cambridge University Press Archive, 1973.
Phillips, Anthony. *Essays on Biblical Law*. London: T&T Clark, 2004.
Philo. *The Works of Philo*. Translated by Charles D. Yonge. Peabody Hendrickson, 1993.
Pink, Arthur W. *Gleanings in Genesis*. Chicago: Moody, 1922.
Porter, Joshua Roy. *Leviticus*. Cambridge: Cambridge University Press Archive, 1976.

Postell, Seth. *Adam as Israel: Genesis 1–3 and the Introduction to the Torah and Tanakh.* Eugene: Wipf & Stock, 2011.
Pressler, Carolyn. 'Sexual Violence and Deuteronomic Law'. In *A Feminist Companion to Exodus to Deuteronomy*, edited by Athalya Brenner, 102–12. Sheffield: Sheffield Academic, 1994.
Pressler, Carolyn. *The View of Women Found in the Deuteronomic Family Laws*. Berlin: de Gruyter, 1993.
Propp, William. *Exodus 19–40: A New Translation with Introduction and Commentary*. New York: Doubleday, 2006.
Rattray, Susan. *Marriage Rules, Kinship Terms and Family Structure in the Bible.* Atlanta: Scholars Press, 1987.
Reeder, Caryn A. *The Enemy in the Household: Family Violence in Deuteronomy and Beyond.* Grand Rapids: Baker, 2012.
Reyburn, William, and Euan McGregor Fry. *A Handbook on Genesis.* New York: United Bible Societies, 1997.
Reynolds, Bennie H. 'Molek: Dead or Alive?' In *Human Sacrifice in Jewish and Christian Tradition*, edited by Karin Finsterbusch, Armin Lange and Diethard Römheld, 133–50. Leiden: Brill Academic, 2007.
Ridderbos, N. H. 'Cities of Refuge'. In *The New Bible Dictionary, Third Edition*, edited by D. R. W. Wood and Ian Howard Marshall, 205–7. Downers Grove: Inter-Varsity, 2001.
Robinson, Gnana. 'The Prohibition of Strange Fire in Ancient Israel: A New Look at the Case of Gathering Wood and Kindling Fire on the Sabbath'. *Vetus Testamentum* 28, no. 3 (1978): 301–17.
Rodriguez, Angel Manuel. 'Substitution in the Hebrew Cultus and in Cultic-Related Texts'. PhD diss., Andrews University 1979 (available via University Microfilms International, 1986).
Rofé, Alexander. 'Family and Sex Laws in Deuteronomy and the Book of Covenant'. *Henoch* 9, no. 2 (1987): 131–58.
Rooke, Deborah W. 'The Blasphemer (Leviticus 24): Gender, Identity and Boundary Construction'. In *Text, Time, and Temple: Literary, Historical and Ritual Studies in Leviticus*, edited by Francis Landy, Leigh M. Trevaskis and Bryan D. Bibb, 153–69. Sheffield: Sheffield Phoenix, 2015.
Rooker, Mark F. *The New American Commentary: Leviticus.* Nashville: Broadman & Holman, 2000.
Roop, Eugene F. *Believers Church Bible Commentary: Genesis.* Independence: Herald, 1987.
Ryle, Herbert Edward. *The Book of Genesis.* Cambridge: Cambridge University Press, 1921.
Sæbø, M. 'נָבֵל'. In *Theological Lexicon of the Old Testament*, edited by Ernst Jenni and Claus Westermann. Peabody: Hendrickson, 1997.
Sailhamer, John. *The Pentateuch as Narrative: A Biblical-Theological Commentary.* Grand Rapids: Zondervan, 1992.
Salmon, John M. 'Judicial Authority in Early Israel: An Historical Investigation of Old Testament Institutions'. PhD diss., Princeton Theological Seminary, 1969.
Sarna, Nahum M. *The JPS Torah Commentary: Genesis.* Philadelphia: Jewish Publication Society, 1989.
Sarna, Nahum M. *The JPS Torah Commentary: Exodus.* Philadelphia: Jewish Publication Society, 1991.

Saydon, P. P. 'Sin-Offering and Trespass-Offering'. *The Catholic Biblical Quarterly* 8, no. 4 (1946): 393–8.

Schenker, Adrian. *Recht und Kult im Alten Testament*. Göttingen: Vandenhoeck & Ruprecht, 2000.

Schwager, Raymund. *Must There Be Scapegoats? Violence and Redemption in the Bible*. Leominster: Gracewing, 1987.

Schwartz, Baruch J. 'The Bearing of Sin in the Priestly Literature'. In *Pomegranates and Golden Bells: Studies in Biblical, Jewish, and near Eastern Ritual, Law, and Literature in Honor of Jacob Milgrom*, edited by J. Milgrom, D. P. Wright, D. N. Freedman and A. Hurvitz, 3–21. Winona Lake: Eisenbrauns, 1995.

Schwartz, Baruch J. 'The Prohibitions Concerning the "Eating" of Blood in Leviticus 17'. In *Priesthood and Cult in Ancient Israel*, edited by Gary A. Anderson and Saul M. Olyan, 34–66. Sheffield: JSOT, 1991.

Schwienhorst-Schönberger, Ludger. *Das Bundesbuch (Ex 20,22-23,33): Studien zu Seiner Entstehung und Theologie*. Berlin: de Gruyter, 1990.

Scubla, Lucien. 'The Christianity of Réne Girard and the Nature of Religion'. In *Violence and Truth: On the Work of Rene Girard*, edited by Paul Dumochel. Stanford: Stanford University Press, 1988.

Sharp, Dudley. 'Death Penalty Paper'. http://www.prodeathpenalty.com/dp.html#F. Christianity.

Shemesh, Yael. 'Shemesh, Yael: The Story of Dinah and Shechem (Genesis 34)'. *Zeitschrift für die Alttestamentliche Wissenschaft* 119, no. 1 (2007): 2–21.

Simango, Simon. 'The Law and the Image of God'. *Old Testament Exegesis* 26, no. 2 (2013): 445–70.

Skidmore, Simon. 'A Mimetic Reading of Deuteronomy 21:18-21'. *The Heythrop Journal* 61, no. 6 (2020): 913–23.

Skidmore, Simon. 'A Mimetic Reading of Exodus 4:24–26'. *The Heythrop Journal* (2021): 1–12.

Sklar, Jay. *Sin, Impurity, Sacrifice, Atonement: The Priestly Conceptions*. Sheffield: Sheffield Phoenix, 2005.

Smart, Ninian. 'Review of Violence and the Sacred, by Rene Girard'. *Religious Studies Review* 6, no. 3 (1980): 173–82.

Smedt, Johan, and Helen Cruz. 'The Imago Dei as a Work in Progress: A Perspective from Paleoanthropology'. *Zygon* 49, no. 1 (2014): 135–56.

Smith, Brian K. 'Capital Punishment and Human Sacrifice'. *Journal of the American Academy of Religion* 68, no. 1 (2000): 3–25.

Smith, James E. *Old Testament Survey Series: The Pentateuch*. Joplin: College Press, 2006.

Snaith, Norman. 'The Image of God'. *The Expository Times* 86, no. 1 (1974): 24.

Snaith, Norman. *Leviticus and Numbers*. Nashville: Nelson, 1967.

Speiser, Ephraim A. *Genesis: Introduction, Translation, and Notes*. New York: Doubleday, 1965.

Stern, P. 'The Origin and Significance of "the Land Flowing with Milk and Honey"'. *Vetus Testamentum* 42 (1992): 554–7.

Stiebert, Johanna. *The Construction of Shame in the Hebrew Bible: The Prophetic Contribution*. Edinburgh: A. & C. Black, 2002.

Stone, Ken. *Sex, Honor and Power in the Deuteronomistic History: A Narratological and Anthropological Analysis*. Sheffield: JSOT, 1996.

Stuart, Douglas K. *The New American Commentary: Exodus*. Nashville: Broadman & Holman, 2006.
Stulman, Louis. 'Sex and Familial Crimes in the D Code: A Witness to Mores in Transition'. *Journal for the Study of the Old Testament* 17, no. 53 (1992): 47–63.
Styers, Randall. 'Slaughter and Innocence: The Rhetoric of Sacrifice in Contemporary Arguments Supporting the Death Penalty'. In *Human Sacrifice in Jewish and Christian Tradition*, edited by Karin Finsterbusch, Armin Lange and Diethard Römheld, 321–51. Leiden: Brill Academic, 2007.
Sulzberger, Mayer. *The Ancient Hebrew Law of Homicide*. Philadelphia: J. H. Greenstone, 1915.
Sun, Henry. 'An Investigation into the Compositional Integrity of the So-Called Holiness Code (Leviticus 17–26)'. Claremont Graduate School, 1990.
Thurston, Thomas M. 'Leviticus 18:22 and the Prohibition of Homosexual Acts'. In *Homophobia and the Judaeo-Christian Tradition*, edited by M. L. Stemmler and J. M. Clark, 7–23. Dallas: Monument, 1990.
Tigay, Jeffrey H. *The JPS Torah Commentary: Deuteronomy*. Philadelphia: Jewish Publication Society, 1996.
Timmer, Daniel. 'Creation, Tabernacle and Sabbath: The Function of the Sabbath Frame in Exodus 31:12–17; 35:1–3'. PhD diss., Trinity Evangelical Divinity School, 2006.
Traube, Elizabeth. 'Incest and Mythology: Anthropological and Girardian Perspectives'. *Berkshire Review* 14 (1979): 37–54.
Trevaskis, Leigh M. 'Dangerous Liaisons: Sex with the Menstruating Woman in Leviticus'. In *Text, Time, and Temple: Literary, Historical, and Ritual Studies in Leviticus*, edited by Francis Landy, Leigh M. Trevaskis and Bryan D. Bibb, 131–52. Sheffield: Sheffield Phoenix, 2015.
Trevaskis, Leigh M. 'The Purpose of Leviticus 24 within Its Literary Context'. *Vetus Testamentum* 59, no. 2 (2009): 295–312.
Valentine, Carol A. 'Soncino Babylonian Talmud: Translated into English with Notes, Glossary and Indices under the Editorship of Rabbi Dr. I. Epstein'. http://www.come-and-hear.com/yebamoth/yebamoth_61.html#61a_3, accessed 12 October 2018.
Van den Eynde, S. 'Keeping God's Sabbath: אות and ברית (Exod 31,12-17)'. In *Studies in the Book of Exodus: Redaction, Reception, Interpretation*, edited by Marc Vervenne, 501–11. Leuven: Peeters, 1996.
Van der Toorn, Karel. 'Echoes of Judaean Necromancy in Isaiah 28, 7-22'. *Zeitschrift für die alttestamentliche Wissenschaft* 100, no. 2 (1988): 199–217.
Van Huyssteen, J Wentzel. *Alone in the World? Human Uniqueness in Science and Theology*. Grand Rapids: Eerdmans, 2009.
Van Selms, A. *Marriage and Family Life in Ugaritic Literature*. London: Luzac, 1954.
Von Rad, Gerhard. *Deuteronomy: A Commentary*. Louisville: Westminster John Knox, 1966.
Von Rad, Gerhard. *Genesis: A Commentary*, Translated by John H. Marks. Louisville: Westminster John Knox, 1972.
Von Rad, Gerhard. *Old Testament Theology*, volume 1. Translated by D. M. G. Stalker. New York: Harper & Row, 1962.
Vroom, Jonathan. 'An Eye for an Eye in Context: The Meaning and Function of the Lex Talionis in the Torah'. Master of Arts Thesis, McMaster Divinity College, 2009.
Vroom, Jonathan. 'Recasting Mišpāṭîm: Legal Innovation in Leviticus 24:10–23'. *Journal of Biblical Literature* 131, no. 1 (2012): 27–44.
Walton, John H. *Genesis 1 as Ancient Cosmology*. Winona Lake: Eisenbrauns, 2011.

Walzer, Michael, Menachem Lorberbaum, Ari Ackerman, and Noam J. Zohar. *The Jewish Political Tradition: Membership, volume 2*. New Haven: Yale University Press, 2006.
Warren, James. *Compassion or Apocalypse: A Comprehensible Guide to the Thought of René Girard*. Washington: Christian Alternative, 2013.
Watts, James W. *Reading Law: The Rhetorical Shaping of the Pentateuch*. Edinburgh: A. & C. Black, 1999.
Weinfeld, Moshe. *Deuteronomy and the Deuteronomic School*. Winona Lake: Eisenbrauns, 1992.
Weiss, David Halivni. 'A Note on אשר לא ארשה'. *Journal of Biblical Literature* 81, no. 1 (1962): 67–9.
Wellhausen, Julius. *Prolegomena to the History of Israel*. Translated by John Sutherland Black and Allan Menzies. Atlanta: Scholars Press, 1994.
Wenham, Gordon J. *The Book of Leviticus*. Grand Rapids: Eerdmans, 1979.
Wenham, Gordon J. *Word Biblical Commentary: Genesis 1–15*. Waco: Word, 1987.
Wenham, Gordon J., and J. Gordon McConville. 'Drafting Techniques in Some Deuteronomic Laws'. *Vetus Testamentum* 30, no. 2 (1980): 248–52.
Wenham, Gordon J. 'Betûlāh "a Girl of Marriageable Age"'. *Vetus Testamentum* 22, no. 3 (1972): 326–48.
Westbrook, Raymond. 'Adultery in Ancient near Eastern Law'. *Revue Biblique* (1990): 542–80.
Westbrook, Raymond. 'Lex Talionis and Exodus 21, 22-25'. *Revue Biblique* (1986): 52–69.
Westermann, Claus. *Creation*. Philadelphia: Fortress, 1974.
White, Hayden. 'Ethnological "Lie" and Mythical "Truth"'. *Diacritics* 8, no. 1 (1978): 2–9.
White, Lynn. 'The Historical Roots of Our Ecological Crisis'. *Science* (1967): 1203–7.
Whitelam, Keith W. *The Just King: Monarchical Judicial Authority in Ancient Israel*. Sheffield: JSOT, 1979.
Williams, James G. *The Bible, Violence, and the Sacred: Liberation from the Myth of Sanctioned Violence*. Eugene: Wipf & Stock, 2007.
Williams, James G. *The Girard Reader*. New York: Crossroad, 1996.
Willis, Timothy M. *The Elders of the City: A Study of the Elders-Laws in Deuteronomy*. Atlanta: Society of Biblical Literature, 2001.
Wold, Donald J. 'The Kareth Penalty in P: Rationale and Cases'. Paper presented at the Society of Biblical Literature Seminar Papers, 1979.
Wolff, Hans Walter. *Anthropology of the Old Testament*. Translated by Margaret Kohl. Philadelphia: Fortress, 1974.
Wright, Christopher J. H. 'The Israelite Household and the Decalogue: The Social Background and Significance of Some Commandments'. *Tyndale Bulletin* 30 (1979): 101–24.
Wright, David P. 'Deuteronomy 21:1-9 as a Rite of Elimination'. *The Catholic Biblical Quarterly* 49, no. 3 (1987): 387–403.
Wright, David P. 'Holiness in Leviticus and Beyond: Differing Perspectives'. *Interpretation* 53, no. 4 (1999): 351–64.
Wright, David P. 'The Spectrum of Priestly Impurity'. In *Priesthood and Cult in Ancient Israel*, edited by Gary Anderson and Saul Olyan, 150–82: Sheffield: Sheffield Academic, 1991.
Young, Robert L. 'Religious Orientation, Race and Support for the Death Penalty'. *Journal for the Scientific Study of Religion* (1992): 76–87.

Zevit, Ziony. 'The 'Egla Ritual of Deuteronomy 21:1-9'. *Journal of Biblical Literature* 95, no. 3 (1976): 377–90.
Zimmerli, D. W. 'Die Eigenart der Prophetischen Rede des Ezechiel: Ein Beitrag zum Problem an Hand von Ez. 14 1-11'. *Zeitschrift für die Alttestamentliche Wissenschaft* 66, no. 1 (1954): 1–26.
Zimmerli, Walther. '"Heiligkeit" Nach Dem Sogenannten Heiligkeitsgesetz'. *Vetus Testamentum* 30, no. 4 (1980): 493–512.
Ziskind, Jonathan R. 'The Missing Daughter in Leviticus XVIII'. *Vetus Testamentum* 46, no. 1 (1996): 125–30.

Index of References

Hebrew Bible/ Old Testament		3:15	4	7, 24, 27, 28, 34, 66, 128	6:8-9	112
Genesis				101, 112, 165	6:8	11, 33
1	16, 19				6:9–8:19	83
1:1–2:4	93		4:1-24	102, 190	6:9	19
1:1–2:3	20, 41, 81–4, 135, 187		4:1-16	99–101, 112	6:11-12	112
					6:11	33, 99, 102, 146, 190
1:4	135		4:3-5	100	6:13	33
1:7	135		4:6-7	100	6:14	103
1:14	135		4:7	28	7:4-10	82
1:18	135		4:8	100, 164	8:10-12	82
1:26-28	13, 17, 29, 30, 41		4:10	100, 164	9	29
			4:11	100	9:1-7	31, 190
1:26-27	18, 41		4:12	100	9:1	26, 29, 33, 41, 112
1:26	16, 151, 188		4:13	100		
			4:14-15	101, 102	9:2-4	33
1:27	11, 14, 15, 17, 32, 151		4:14	100	9:3-4	33
			4:16	114	9:5-6	32, 33
			4:17-22	28	9:5	32, 152
1:28	15, 16, 20, 112, 151, 188		4:23-24	101, 102	9:6	8, 10, 12, 18, 23, 27–34, 41, 77, 102, 115, 119, 131, 183, 189, 190, 194
			4:25	28		
			5	17		
2–3	29		5:1-32	28		
2	19		5:1-3	17, 18, 22, 41		
2:15	87					
2:16-25	151		5:1	11		
2:17	36		5:3	17		
2:21-22	29		5:24	19	9:7	26
2:25	126		6–9	11, 28, 82, 109, 111, 112, 119, 120, 190	9:12-17	88
3	24, 29, 119				9:18-29	29
					9:20-21	112
3:1	119				9:21-27	26
3:6-24	126		6–8	33, 102	9:21-24	29
3:10	100		6:1-7	111	9:22-25	126, 139
3:13	100		6:5-9	28	9:22	29
3:14-19	100		6:5	111	9:23	30
3:14-15	135		6:7	152	9:24-27	29

Genesis (cont.)		2:11-15	63, 64	21:12-14	99, 102,
9:25	24, 183	2:11-12	64, 77		111, 116,
10	30	2:11	64		118–20,
10:2-6	30	2:12	64		184
10:6-19	30	2:13	64	21:12	23
10:10-32	30	2:14-15	64	21:13	22
12:1-3	135	2:14	64	21:14	118, 119
12:3	66	3:1	25	21:17	135, 176
12:10-20	18	3:2-5	147	21:18–22:15	119
14:22	92	3:8	135	21:20-21	193
17:12	18	4:18	25	21:22-27	77
19:24	147	4:22-23	13, 17, 71	21:23-25	119
20:1-18	18	4:23	19	21:36	76
21:22-34	18	5	93	22:3-8	159
26:1-11	18	5:5-23	94	22:9	74
26:3	100	5:7	93	22:15-16	124
26:17-25	18	5:12	93	28:36	86
26:26-31	18	9:23-24	147	28:43	74
29–35	145	12:1-30	63	29:30	82
29	82	12:1-28	195	29:35-37	82
31	174	12:15	82	29:36-37	108
31:25-32	175	12:43	18	30:10	86
31:29	175	13:6-7	82	30:11-16	105
31:32	175	13:21-22	147	30:37	86, 87
32:20 Eng.	105	14:8	92, 94	31:12-18	92
32:21	105, 106	14:22	41	31:12-17	2–4, 81,
34	72, 160	14:29	41		83, 84,
34:2	160	15–16	113		86–8, 95,
34:7	160	15:19	41		97
34:25-29	160	16	83, 85	31:13-14	87
34:31	160	16:20	83	31:13	86-88
37	145	16:24	83	31:14-15	85
37:18-28	196	16:27	83	31:14	82, 85, 86
38	174	18:1-12	25	31:15-17	86
38:24	175	19:5-6	86, 88	31:15	84-86
40:19	147	19:6	88	31:16-17	87, 187
42–50	25	20–21	189	31:16	87
49:3-4	139	20:10-11	85	31:17	84, 85, 87,
90:20-27	29	20:10	88		88
90:22	29	20:13-16	116	32:11	93
18:22	152	20:13	2, 32	32:25-29	72, 196
		20:16	116	32:25	72
Exodus		21	77	32:26-28	72
1	25	21:8-11	119	32:27-29	71
1:1-7	24	21:12–22:14	77	32:29	72
1:8-14	163	21:12-17	80	32:35	72
1:15-22	63			35:1-30	81

Reference	Page(s)
35:2	95, 97
35:3	85, 93, 94
39:30	86

Leviticus
Reference	Page(s)
4:1–5:19	90
4:17	82
4:26	103, 108
8:11	82
8:33-35	82
9:1–10:3	147
9:1-24	147
10:1-3	71, 147, 196
10:10-11	130
10:17	69, 70, 196
11:44-45	86
13:5	82
13:21	82
13:26	82
13:31	82
13:33	82
13:50	82
13:54	82
14:7	82
14:8	82
14:51	82
15	141
15:19-24	140
15:24	140, 141
16	75, 86, 103
16:2	36
16:13	36
16:14	82
16:19	82
16:20-22	75
16:21-22	73, 74
16:22	69, 75
17:10	37
17:11	54, 104, 105, 108
18	8, 122–30, 137–9, 141, 143, 144, 148, 150, 151, 153, 154, 156, 184, 185
18:1-23	124
18:1-5	123, 135
18:3	125
18:6-16	127
18:6	123, 143
18:9-14	123
18:12-13	140
18:16	129
18:17-18	144, 147, 184
18:17	127, 144–6
18:18	144, 145
18:19	140, 141
18:20	127
18:21	127
18:22-30	126
18:22	127, 148–50, 152
18:23	123, 126, 127, 151, 152, 188
18:24-30	2, 4, 47, 122–4, 129, 133, 134, 139, 141, 149, 152, 188
18:24-28	114, 125, 131
18:24-25	122, 124
18:25-28	126
18:25	8
18:28	8
18:29	126, 127, 140, 141
19:2	86
19:17	68
19:18	136
19:29	145, 146
19:31	127, 133, 134
20	8, 36, 121–9, 131, 132, 134, 136–9, 141, 143, 144, 148, 150, 153, 154, 156, 184, 185, 188
20:1-21	4
20:1-16	11
20:1-5	2, 4, 123, 124, 128, 129, 132
20:1-3	131
20:2-5	127, 130, 131, 163, 184
20:2-4	128–30, 148
20:2-3	131
20:2	36, 131
20:3	37, 130, 131
20:5-21	129
20:5	37, 131, 133
20:6-23	124
20:6-9	123, 133
20:6	37, 133, 134, 136
20:7-8	133, 136
20:7	86, 134
20:8	134
20:9	127, 130, 133, 135, 185
20:10-21	123, 129, 136, 144
20:10-16	39, 52, 132
20:10-14	185
20:10-12	141, 146
20:10	127, 136, 141, 161, 162

Leviticus (cont.)		21:9	36	24:23	61, 64, 66,
20:11-21	136, 137, 141	21:12	130		67, 76, 78, 183
		21:15	88		
20:11-12	127, 138, 140, 142, 144, 187	21:23	88, 130	25:1-55	88
		22:9	36, 88	25:18-22	85
		22:16	88	26:1-13	20
20:11	29, 39, 139, 142	22:32	88	26:14-39	21
		23:3	96	27	74
20:12	126, 139, 142, 151	23:20	86	27:28-32	86
		24:10-23	2–5, 8, 11, 35, 47, 51, 59–65, 67, 68, 74–8, 90, 175, 183, 186, 193–6		
20:13-16	129			*Numbers*	
20:13	127, 137, 148–50, 152, 185			3:7-8	87
				3:11-13	71
				3:12	71, 72
20:14	36, 39, 127, 144–7, 184			3:44-48	71
				6:8	86
		24:10-16	67, 76, 78–80, 90, 94, 97, 120	6:22-27	100
20:15-16	127, 148, 151, 152, 185			8:14-19	71
				9:13	68, 74
				14:4	93
20:15	137	24:10-14	61, 76	14:14	147
20:16	137	24:10-11	62, 65, 75	15	90
20:17-21	39, 91, 132	24:10	64, 66	15:22-31	90, 92
		24:11-16	186	15:22-29	90, 92
20:17-19	141	24:11-12	65	15:30-36	94, 95, 97
20:17-18	140	24:11	64–6, 68	15:30-31	90, 92
20:17	139, 140	24:13-14	62, 65	15:30	93, 94
20:18	137, 140, 141	24:14	67, 75	15:31	95
		24:15-22	76	15:32-36	2, 5, 11, 27, 35, 38, 51, 79, 80, 83, 89, 93–5, 97, 120, 175, 183, 186, 195, 196
20:19	140	24:15-16	60, 67, 68, 70, 74, 75, 77, 78		
20:20-21	140-43				
20:20	68, 74, 135, 142				
		24:15	67, 68, 70, 73–5, 79		
20:21	129, 142	24:16	2, 4, 36, 61, 67, 68, 76		
20:22-26	123, 134, 135			15:32	93
20:22-23	128, 134	24:17-22	75–8	15:33-35	186
20:22	131	24:17-21	76–9	15:33	93
20:24-26	134	24:17	77	15:34	95
20:24	134	24:18	77	15:35	36
20:25	135	24:19-20	77	16	71
20:27	127, 128, 133, 136	24:20	77	16:1-35	107
21	130	24:21	77	16:35	147
21:1-11	86	24:22	61, 76	16:44-50 Eng.	108
21:1-6	130			17:6-10	108
21:8	88				

Index of References 215

17:9-15	105, 108, 109		188, 190, 191, 194		184, 188, 191, 194
17:11-15	108	35:31	36	19:11	117
17:11	108	35:33-34	36, 112–14	19:12	101, 102, 117
17:12-13	108				
17:36-40	71	35:33	73, 113–15	19:13	113, 120
18:1	114, 196			19:15-21	158, 159
18:5-6	87	35:34	113	19:15	162
18:22	68			19:17-18	163
18:23	72	*Deuteronomy*		19:18-21	162
18:32	68	1:26-46	9	19:19	158, 162, 163
21:20	25	1:26-28	179		
21:21–25:18	51	1:35-38	179	19:21	163
21:21	25	5:14	88	20:1-18	11
22–24	135	5:15	88, 94, 187	20:12-18	26
25:1-15	72			20:14	26
25:1-3	51	6:1-3	9, 178, 180	20:16-18	26, 195
25:6-8	51			21:1-23	170
25:7-8	51	6:5-6	178	21:1-9	117, 118, 170, 171
28:9-10	96	6:6-7	178, 180		
30:15 Eng.	74	8:20	180	21:6-8	117
30:16	74	9:7	179	21:10-13	170, 171
31	51	9:23	179	21:14	170, 171
31:3-54	25, 26	12	20	21:15-17	170, 171
31:14-17	25	12:1–24:7	171	21:18-21	9, 11, 168–81, 185–7
31:48-54	105	13	132		
33:3	92, 94	13:5	163		
35	193	13:9-10	66	21:18	171, 180
35:6-15	184	14:1	17	21:19-20	177, 180
35:9-34	110, 114, 116, 127	16:1-8	195	21:20	171, 177
		16:18–18:22	171, 176	21:21	9, 163, 169, 174, 177, 180, 186
35:14-16	26	17:2-7	66		
35:16-21	111, 184	17:3-7	163		
35:16-18	36	17:7	66, 163		
35:21	36, 101, 102	19	193	21:22-23	170, 171
		19:1-13	36, 97, 99, 102, 109, 116–20	22	164, 166
35:22-29	111			22:13-29	153, 154, 166, 168, 185
35:25-26	111				
35:25	114	19:1-10	184		
35:30-34	2-4, 8, 11, 32, 97–9, 102, 103, 106, 109, 110, 112–20, 124, 130, 131, 184,	19:4-10	117	22:13-28	8
		19:4-5	116	22:13-27	154
		19:6	111, 117	22:13-21	50, 154, 156, 158–62, 168, 185, 187
		19:10	113, 116, 117		
		19:11-13	4, 8, 32, 73, 117,	22:13-19	158
				22:13-17	156, 166

Deuteronomy (cont.)

22:14	156
22:16-17	156
22:17	163
22:18-19	157, 158
22:20-27	185
22:20-25	11
22:20-21	74, 158, 177, 185
22:21	159-61, 169
22:22-29	154, 161, 167
22:22-27	161, 167
22:22-24	167
22:22	161, 162, 164
22:23-27	161, 164
22:23-24	161, 165
22:24	159, 162, 165, 166
22:25-27	161, 164–6
22:25	165
22:26	164, 165
22:28-29	124, 161, 166, 167
22:28	166
22:29	166
23:4	135
23:7-8 Eng.	25
23:8-9	25
24:7	163
25:3	157
25:5-10	129, 142
27:7	195
27:20-23	128
28:1-68	169, 172
28:1-14	21
28:15-68	9, 21, 180
34	25

Joshua

7	91
9:4	24
18:1	20

Judges

8:18	18
19	72

1 Samuel

3:6	18
17:44	147
18:17	18
26:21	90

2 Samuel

2:7	18
3:30	111
3:34	18
8:11	20
9:11	18
16:20-22	139
23:5	87

1 Kings

11:26	92
20:35	19

2 Kings

8:9	18
16:7	19

2 Chronicles

28:10	20

Ezra

10:18	19

Nehemiah

3:8	19

Psalms

72:4	18
72:8-11	19
78	171
78:5-8	171
106:34-41	114
106:38-39	113
110:2	19

Proverbs

16:14	105
23:19-21	172
31:5	18

Ecclesiastes

3:20-21	147
12:7	147

Isaiah

5:11-12	172
5:22-23	172
55:3	87
56:10-12	172

Jeremiah

32:40	87
50:5	87

Ezekiel

5:11	113
9:7	113
37:26	87
45:20	90

Hosea

10:9	18

Amos

4:1	172

NEW TESTAMENT

John

8:1-11	189

Acts

15	188
15:19-20	188

MISHNAH

Avot

3:14	21

Makkot

1:10	37

Qiddushin		
3:12	62	

Sanhedrin		
6:2	73	
6:4	67	
7:4	152	
52b	136	

Yoma		
28b	21	

BABYLONIAN TALMUD
Baba Metzi'a
114b   11

Kerithot
6b   11

Yebamot
61a   11

OTHER JEWISH AND RABBINIC WORKS
Genesis Rabbah
26:5   21
95:3   21

Leviticus Rabbah
10:6   114

Pirke de Rabbi Eliezer
21   24

Sifre Numbers
CLXI:III:1   114

Maimonides
Torts
1:1   23
2:10-11   23

Rambam
Guide for the Perplexed
1:1   14

Philo
On the Creation
31   14

CLASSICAL AND ANCIENT CHRISTIAN LITERATURE
Irenaeus
Against Heresies
III:18:1   22

John of Damascus
An Exact Exposition of the Orthodox Faith
II:12   14

INSCRIPTIONS
Babylonian Akitu Festival
line 354   104

Hittite Laws
§187   151
§188   151
§199   151
§200a   151

KTU
1.6 III: 12-13   135

Index of Authors

Alcorn, R. 189
Alexander, D. T. 17–19
Alison, J. 43
Alter, R. 39
Amit, Y. 81
Anderson, A. K. 192

Bailie, G. 72, 102, 192, 193, 196
Bar, S. 145, 147
Barmash, P. 110, 111, 114, 117
Barr, J. 19
Barth, K. 14, 15
Bartor, A. 39, 112, 117, 126, 139, 149, 156, 177
Bassett, F. W. 126
Bechtel, L. M. 126, 157, 160
Bellefontaine, E. 171, 173, 174
Benjamin, D. C. 118
Bernat, D. A. 53, 58
Biale, D. 149
Bibb, B. D. 62, 65, 66, 75
Bigger, S. F. 109, 129, 137, 142, 145, 151, 152
Bird, P. A. 15
Blyth, C. 160
Boecker, H. J. 174
Boswell, J. 148, 149
Brenner, A. 148
Brueggemann, W. 16
Buber, M. 39
Burke, K. 45
Burnside, J. 38, 39, 85, 89, 93, 111, 116, 119, 130–3, 139–41, 146, 155, 156, 159, 165, 170–2, 176, 180

Calasso, R. 53
Cardascia, G. 143
Cassuto, U. 84, 85
Chapman, H. A. 192
Cherry, S. 14, 24

Chilton, B. 47, 55, 58
Clements, R. E. 179, 195
Clines, D. J. A. 16
Coats, G. W. 32, 171
Cohen, S. J. D. 47, 62
Cohn, R. G. 57
Collins, B. 54
Colson, C. W. 189, 193
Cowdell, S. 6, 192
Craigie, P. C. 176
Crouch, C. L. 13, 17
Crüsemann, F. 91
Cruz, H. 13
Currid, J. D. 158, 165, 166

Daube, D. 117, 156, 157
Day, J. 132
De Heusch, L. 54, 57
Delitzsch, F. 73
Dion, P. E. 177
Dorff, E. N. 37
Douglas, M. 103
Driver, S. R. 114, 118, 175
Durham, J. I. 147

Eckman, J. P. 2, 193
Edenburg, C. 17, 40, 41
Ehrlich, A. B. 69
Eilberg-Schwartz, H. 149
Eissfeldt, O. 132
Ellens, D. L. 129, 150, 155, 161, 162, 164–7
Elliger, K. 143
Ellington, J. 36, 95, 128, 148
Erickson, M. J. 13

Falk, Z. W. 175
Feinberg, J. S. 2
Feinberg, P. D. 2

Feinstein, E. L. 113, 123–7, 136, 140, 143, 144, 148, 149, 151, 152
Finkelstein, J. J. 5, 27, 66, 93
Fiske, S. T. 192
Fleishman, J. 156, 159, 173, 176
Flemming, C. 58
Foucault, M. 191
Fox, M. V. 88, 147
Fry, E. McG. 100
Frymer-Kensky, T. 4, 143, 149, 182

Gane, R. 69, 70, 75, 90–2, 103, 104, 106
Garr, W. R. 16, 20
Gerstenberger, E. S. 146
Gilders, W. K. 54, 103–6
Girard, R. 2, 3, 43–50, 52–6, 58, 63, 65, 67, 72, 98, 107, 130, 138, 139, 145, 150, 157, 167, 191, 192
Goldberg, L. 160
Golsan, R. 57
Good, R. M. 36
Goodhart, S. 145
Gorman, F. H. 81, 82
Greenberg, M. 36, 110
Greifenhagen, F. V. 25, 65
Grenz, S. 14
Guillaume, P. 81

Hagedorn, A. C. 37, 173, 177
Hamilton, V. P. 81
Harding, R. M. 6, 59
Harland, P. J. 1, 3, 10, 12, 17, 28, 82, 112, 182, 189, 190
Harris, L. T. 192
Hartley, J. E. 146, 147
Hartung, J. 117
Hasel, G. F. 36, 85, 86, 88
Haven, C. L. 55
Hayes, R. B. 17, 40
Heider, G. C. 132, 133
Hendrix, R. E. 85
Hens-Piazza, G. 20
Hertz, S. S. 189
Hieke, T. 37, 95, 128
Hoffmann, D. 103, 146
Hoffner, H. A. 151
Hooke, S. H. 118
Houston, W. 28
Hutton, R. R. 62, 66, 76

Jackson, B. S. 39
Janowski, B. 69, 103, 105, 118
Janzen, W. 77, 88, 147
Jenson, P. P. 88
Joosten, J. 134
Joseph, A. L. 160

Kaminsky, J. L. 25–7
Kaminsky, J. S. 29
Kaufman, S. A. 171
Kazen, T. 27, 126, 149
Keil, C. F. 73
Kim, Y. S. 76, 194
Kiuchi, N. 69, 104, 105
Klawans, J. 4, 53, 58, 133, 182
Kline, M. G. 81
Knohl, I. 95, 96
Koch, K. 73, 114
Köhler, L. 14
Kraemer, D. 73

LaCocque, A. 24, 29
Labuschagne, C. J. 92
Landy, J. 55
Lefort, G. 44–6, 49, 53, 63, 65, 107, 150
Lemos, T. M. 96, 148
Levenson, J. D. 20, 58, 81, 82
Levine, B. A. 3, 65, 68, 86, 90, 93, 103, 105, 108, 143, 147, 148, 152, 190
Locher, C. 155
Lorerbaum, J. 22
Lundberg, M. J. 110

Mabee, C. 175
Mace, D. R. 156
Mangum, D. 103
Mathews, K. A. 1, 2, 10, 12, 24, 28, 29, 31, 33, 82, 100, 112, 139, 193
McBride, J. 6
McClenney-Sadler, M. G. 127
McConville, J. G. 159, 170, 177
McKeating, H. 118
McNutt, P. M. 101
Meacham, T. 145
Melcher, S. J. 129, 136, 137
Meltzer, F. 57
Merrill, E. H. 117, 151, 157, 158, 179
Merrill, T. C. 57
Middleton, J. R. 16
Milbank, J. 53

Miles, J. C. 114, 175
Milgrom, J. 3, 36, 54, 61, 68, 69, 86, 90–2, 95, 103–6, 113, 114, 122, 124, 129, 131–7, 139, 140, 147–50, 152
Miller, P. D., Jr. 176
Moi, T. 56
Moyer, J. C. 151

Neusner, J. 114, 152
Niditch, S. 195
Nihan, C. 124, 125, 131, 134

Olyan, S. M. 52, 148–50
Oughourlian, J.-M. 44–6, 49, 53, 63, 65, 107, 150

Palaver, W. 44, 45, 54, 101, 107, 130
Péter-Contesse, R. 36, 95, 128, 148
Phillips, A. 85, 91, 110, 111, 118, 160, 175, 176
Pink, A. W. 29, 112
Porter, J. R. 137
Postell, S. 20, 24
Pressler, C. 155, 157, 160, 164, 166, 167, 174
Propp, W. 82, 84, 87

Rattray, S. 143
Reeder, C. A. 156, 159, 172, 174, 176, 177
Reyburn, W. 100
Reynolds, B. H. 132
Ridderbos, N. H. 110
Robinson, G. 85
Rodriguez, A. M. 69, 90, 91, 105
Rofé, A. 166
Rooke, D. W. 65
Rooker, M. F. 68, 86, 90, 91, 189
Roop, E. F. 2, 10, 12, 33, 175
Ryle, H. E. 100

Sæbo, M. 160
Sailhamer, J. 29, 112
Salmon, J. M. 174
Sarna, N. M. 10, 12, 77, 83, 86, 87, 100, 147, 151, 195
Saydon, P. P. 90
Schenk, R. 54
Schenker, A. 92
Schwager, R. 5, 44, 55, 56, 130, 132, 187

Schwartz, B. J. 54, 69, 75, 105
Schwienhorst-Schönberger, L. 77, 194
Scubla, L. 58
Sharp, D. 999
Shemesh, Y. 160
Simango, S. 17
Skidmore, S. 63, 169
Sklar, J. 69, 70, 86, 104, 106
Smart, N. 58
Smedt, J. 13
Smith, B. K. 6, 59, 192
Smith, J. E. 24
Snaith, N. 16, 149
Speiser, E. A. 29
Stern, P. 135
Stiebert, J. 157
Stone, K. 138, 150, 151, 156
Stuart, D. K. 77, 86, 87, 147, 195
Stulman, L. 37, 176, 177
Styers, R. 189
Sulzberger, M. 111
Sun, H. 143

Thurston, T. M. 149
Tigay, J. H. 111, 116, 118, 129, 151, 166
Timmer, D. 88
Toorn, K. van der 133
Traube, E. 57
Trevaskis, L. M. 61, 62, 140, 141

Valentine, C. A. 11
Van Huyssteen, J. W. 13, 14
Von Rad, G. 7, 16, 20, 32, 166
Van Selms, A. 151
Van den Eynde, S. 87
Vroom, J. 61, 62, 76, 77

Walton, J. H. 81, 84
Walzer, M. 23
Warren, J. 57, 99, 102, 107, 108, 112
Watts, J. W. 174
Weinfeld, M. 166
Weiss, D. H. 166
Wellhausen, J. 36
Wenham, G. J. 1, 10, 12, 86, 155, 170
Westbrook, R. 77, 142, 175, 194
Westermann, C. 15
White, H. 54
White, L. 19
Whitelam, K. W. 174, 175

Williams, J. G. 24, 52, 55, 71, 101, 145, 196
Willis, T. M. 114, 118, 156, 159, 173, 174, 176, 177, 180
Wold, D. J. 134
Wolff, H. W. 19
Wright, C. J. H. 176, 177
Wright, D. P. 5, 86, 118, 124, 134, 140

Young, R. L. 188

Zevit, Z. 118
Zimmerli, D. W. 69
Zimmerli, W. 135
Ziskind, J. R. 129, 137, 139–41, 143

www.ingramcontent.com/pod-product-compliance
Lightning Source LLC
Chambersburg PA
CBHW062221300426
44115CB00012BA/2164